The Offshore Game: Today's Ocean Racing

Also by the Author

THE INTERNATIONAL BOOK OF CATAMARANS AND TRIMARANS
MULTIHULL SAILBOATS
SAILING AND RACING CATAMARANS

The Offshore Game: Today's Ocean Racing

by EDWARD F. COTTER

CROWN PUBLISHERS, INC., NEW YORK

Dedicated to William Theodore Snaith, 1908–1974

Bill Snaith at the helm of *Figaro* in the 1968 Block Island Race

Editorial Assistant: Florence E. Conley
Drawings by Mark Smith
Photographs by the Author unless otherwise credited
Designed by Laurie Zuckerman

Inquiries should be addressed to Crown Publishers, Inc.,
One Park Avenue, New York, N.Y. 10016
Printed in the United States of America
Published simultaneously in Canada by
General Publishing Company Limited

Library of Congress Cataloging in Publication Data

Cotter, Edward F
    The offshore game: today's ocean racing

    Includes index.
    1. Yacht racing. I. Title.
GV826.5.C6 1977   797.1'4   77-2317
ISBN 0-517-52884-3

CONTENTS

PROLOGUE

I am often asked, "How does a person get a berth aboard a top offshore racing yacht?" There are many routes into the sport. This is how it happened to me.

As a youth growing up on Long Island Sound I found it natural to be interested in boats—sailboats in particular. My first was a nine-footer which I built to my own design as a young teenager. Through sailing her in New Rochelle Harbor one day, I met William F. "Bill" Crosby, then the editor of *Rudder* magazine and the designer of a number of small day-sailers including the highly successful 15½-foot *Snipe*. He taught me a great deal about yacht racing while I served as his crew aboard his actively raced *Snipe*. Later I graduated to skippering one of my own.

After a year of successfully skippering a 34-foot cruising cutter in handicap racing around-the-buoys on Long Island Sound, joining the U.S. Coast Guard seemed a logical choice when World War II broke out. There I learned the professional aspects of seamanship and ocean navigation and put them into practice on North Atlantic convoy duty in three progressively more responsible escort vessel commands. After the war, I accepted an offer to stay in the Coast Guard as a regular officer.

In my spare time, I continued to skipper a wide variety of day-sailing one-designs in areas where my postwar Coast Guard assignments took me. The responsibilities of a Coast Guard officer are demanding and time-consuming and the opportunity to take off for long periods of racing is not often present due to the press of other duties. Except for a couple of less than demanding offshore races as navigator, it was not until I retired from the Coast Guard as a captain in 1966 that I began to consider seriously an extensive participation in the sport. But how to begin?

I had followed the doings of the offshore set in the yachting press and I was familiar with their names and places. I had, in fact, been patrol commander for an ocean race along the Pacific Coast and saw the sport from that angle. One incident impressed me deeply. My ship had to go to the assistance of a contestant's yacht. The skipper gave me his supposed position and during the voice radio conversation we took a direction finder bearing on his transmission and asked him for a sounding of the depth at his yacht's position. These did not check with his reported position. We ran down the radio bearing at top speed, located him quickly and provided the necessary assistance. His actual position was 22 miles from where he figured he was! Not very close to the mark for a racing yacht, I thought. If position finding is extremely important for a rescue vessel, shouldn't it also be important to win races? Thus, when I was asked by a friend to navigate

La Forza and *Gusto* reach across the
Gulf Stream off Miami.

aboard a 37-foot yawl in the 1967 Annapolis–Newport Race (I had since retired, taken civilian employment near Philadelphia), I was ready to give it a try.

This was a boat that had finished poorly in the previous race two years before, and whose owner had come into a little unexpected money to spend on it. He was interested in doing better in his races and called upon some experienced sailors to select, organize, and train the rest of the crew and to outfit and tune the boat. Comparing the rudimentary navigational equipment, the informal organization and manning of his 37-footer with the cutter I had commanded a few years before, I could see why racing was a less precise business than Coast Guard work. But I could also see how years of experience as a one-design skipper and as a professional ocean mariner could be productively applied to the sport.

We did well in that race. Participants will remember that of 99 starters only about half of them finished due to an unexpected gale midway through the race. We were the smallest boat to finish, but not the last one, and narrowly missed a win in our class by about three minutes on corrected time. A rough but pleasurable introduction. As Cleody Snaith was in that crew, this led to an assignment a year later on his father Bill's *Figaro IV* in the famed Bermuda Race where we finished 11th in fleet on corrected time, sailing almost an identical track to that of the overall winner, Ted Hood's *Robin.* Hood's boat was brand-new and Snaith's was several years old, particularly from the design standpoint. We consoled ourselves with thinking that this may have had something to do with the difference in final positions.

Preparing for that 1968 Bermuda Race I had had trouble finding available sources for background data on the race. So I wrote an article for *Yacht Racing* magazine on the next Bermuda Race which was designed to be helpful for those looking for the same information. It turned out to be more helpful for me than the others participating, because the boat I was aboard in that race was Dick Nye's *Carina,* the overall winner. I was supposed to have sailed aboard Bill Snaith's new *Figaro V.* But Larry Huntington, who was slated to sail aboard *Carina* as navigator, had to withdraw for business reasons about the time *Figaro V* was scratched because of technical problems. Two weeks before the race, over a luncheon table in New York, Snaith solved Nye's problem of a vacant navigator's slot.

The combination of the prerace article and the win was the catalyst which made possible the opportunity for me to participate in racing as a navigator on a variety of top boats and in a variety of ocean racing classics to the extent that my spare time, energy and financial resources allowed (navigators on ocean racers are required to be amateurs). It also led to a few more wins, some great sailing and to the production and publication again in *Yacht Racing* of an unbroken string of 50 monthly columns and articles on the subject of offshore racing, with emphasis on the navigational aspects. This work, of necessity, caused me to explore and think deeply about many of the facets of the sport which have seldom been documented in depth or organized under one cover. I realized that many writers took for granted that participants were as familiar as they were with some of the details and the personalities, but soon found that a great many of those who liked to read about the races had never participated and were not familiar with them. Even with this realization, it is not possible in a single magazine article to give the in-depth coverage needed.

This book attempts to do that. It is designed to have the broadest reader appeal and is intentionally written so that a nonparticipant will gain through this background material an understanding of what this complex, anachronistic, yet highly technical sport is all about, why those who experience it get hooked on it, why some yachts always lose and others win more often than the law of averages would indicate. An important point is that we are not rehashing information that has long been available in other books on the subject.

There are many countercurrents at work on the sport today which have changed and will continue to change it radically. The decade 1967–77, where the entry lists rose, peaked and then declined (for a variety of reasons) may have been its golden years.

I last sailed with Bill Snaith in England in the 1973 Admiral's Cup series aboard *Salty Goose*. Bill passed away that winter during open heart surgery. I am greatly indebted to him for opening the door for me to this world and to all the other skippers who have made possible my continuing participation. You will read more about some of them and their boats later on.

Ted Hood's 1968 *Robin*

Prologue

Dick Nye

Cleody Snaith

What Is Offshore Racing?

PART I

The long-range objectives of the Bermuda Race are to encourage the designing, building and sailing of seaworthy yachts, and the development in the amateur sailor of the art of seamanship and proficiency in the science of navigation.

—Bermuda Race Committee

Starting flag hoist of the Royal Yacht Squadron, Cowes, England

The start of a race is usually quite dramatic. Regardless of the length of the course, everyone wants to get the best start possible without being over the line early. The line is set between the Committee Boat and a buoy and may or may not be at right angles to the wind of the moment. In fact, in the longer races it usually is oriented at right angles to the direction of the first mark. Therefore, although the line may be long enough to accommodate all the boats in the class that are starting, usually there is a preferred spot on the line which makes the start a bit more hectic as everyone tries to be in that favored position.

There is a preparatory signal 10 minutes from the start, a warning signal five minutes from the start and the starting signal itself. The actual indication is a signal on the Committee Boat. A gun is fired or a horn is blown at the moment the signal is hoisted. Hopefully, these are simultaneous, but the signal governs. Engines may be used up to the five-minute gun.

There are many aspects to consider in preparing for the start—the wind direction and velocity, the speed of the boat, the length of the line, the sea conditions, the direction and velocity of current, the number and sizes of the boats actually starting and their maneuvering in relation to your boat. What is really important is where you are five minutes after the gun and not necessarily where you are at the gun.

Once started, the crew remains keyed up because the excitement generated by the start wears off slowly. The momentum generated by a good start can keep the crew buoyed up for the rest of the race.

Here's a transcript of a tape recording of an actual race start which illustrates in its dialogue many aspects of starting maneuvers and considerations. No attempt is made to identify the voices as to their crew assignments. The breeze was light and fluctuated in direction.

OK—10-minute gun.
Wind is light from the SE.
Committee Boat is favored.
Our first heading is 185 degrees. Slightly cracked off.
Looks like a light reacher set.
The breeze is coming and going.
OK, you got everybody assigned, Jeff?
Yes.
OK.
That looks pretty good, sail selection looks good.
What is the current?
It's just starting to change; it's changing against us.
It's a little bit late from the tables.
Mark, let's stay above the Committee Boat.
Coming about.
Six and a half minutes.
Give the engine a good shot. You want to get her moving now.
A minute to go on the engine . . . give it hell.

All right—stand by to kill it.

Watch *Sorcery.*

Come up now. Go underneath her.

There's the drop. Stop the engine.

OK, that's good, come off a bit.

Five-minute gun coming up.

There's the five-minute gun.

This is the short end right here.

Can't make a whole lot of difference which way you go.

Listen, Mark, put her down on a reach, go that way and keep her headway up, and then we can reach back.

Keep your headway.

That line is biased 25 degrees and there's going to be room for only one boat and one boat in it.

Watch out for *Goose.*

THREE MINUTES.

Hold your course.

Go right, go right, QUICK.

Cut her stern very close—keep your headway.

Tack.

TWO AND A HALF MINUTES.

Watch *Siren,* cut his stern.

TWO MINUTES.

ONE AND A HALF.

Good position—keep your headway up.

ONE MINUTE TEN SECONDS.

Everybody to leeward.

Just get her moving, trim for speed.

FORTY-FIVE SECONDS.

How about your main. Can your main come out a little?

THIRTY-FIVE SECONDS.

Trim that main.

There's the drop.

TWENTY SECONDS.

FIFTEEN SECONDS.

TEN, 9, 8, 7, 6, 5, 4, 3, 2, 1—GUN.

Good start.

Clear air, nobody near us.

Get the weight out of the bow.

OK—*Running Tide* is well to leeward.

Red Breast dead in the water.

Pirana ahead and to leeward.

OK, OK—settle down and make her move.

Committee Boat on Long Island Sound with special mast for starting signals

A good lookout is needed during prestart maneuvers.

Starting line collision at Cowes

One-Ton Class start off Newport, R.I.

Spinnaker start in Tampa Bay

1   THE SPORT

The sport of offshore racing in sailing yachts has its origins in the indomitable spirit of the great explorers: in the zest of Grand Banks fishermen competing to be first to market with their catch; in the contests between the magnificent clippers racing homeward in the trade winds with their cargos from the Orient. Mastering the oceans under sail has for centuries been man's determination. When the advent of steam made ocean sailing noncompetitive for business purposes, it was still possible for amateurs to pursue pleasure and pain under canvas by racing across trackless miles of open sea to compete for a cup worth only a small fraction of the cost of participation.

As powered vessels increased in capability, size and efficiency, much of the challenge of outwitting wind and sea, the unpredictability, the dependence upon human brawn and brain and the potential for human error have been minimized, if not eliminated. Picture today's commercial and naval vessels—superbly designed monsters with automated engine rooms and bridges, thousands of horsepower available at the push of a button; positions derived by weatherproof radio-satellite navigation, automatically fixed every two hours or less with an accuracy close to one-tenth of a mile and an automatic pilot to guide the vessel along the constantly updated computer-derived track.

While all this has been happening, the sport of offshore racing still requires propulsion by sails alone. By race committee design in most major races, the allowable navigational instruments are severely restricted. Some are basic from past decades. Thus has been preserved an anachronistic art form, a test of the man more than the machine, but refined year by year by technology applicable within these narrow confines to an extent not thought possible only a few years back.

Offshore racing has been defined by some as the dreary interval between cocktail parties before the start and after the finish. Offshore racing crews, as an occupational group, are certainly not noted for their abstinence, but the sport is more than that.

Offshore racing is a testing ground not found in plant or office, a microcosm of life in all its facets. A con man or a bumbler cannot survive in its environment and the fainthearted soon tire of it.

It is definitely hard work, intellectually satisfying and physically demanding. It can also be boring when the wind dies; scary, grueling and sheer drudgery in a full gale, and always expensive. It is heartbreaking for most, for there can be only one winner in each race. But for those aboard the winning boat it is exhilarating and supremely satisfying to best both the ocean and all the competition.

It is also habit-forming. The winner wants to win again and for those who didn't, the next race is another opportunity to try.

Relationship to Other Sports

How does offshore racing relate to other sports? An interesting study of the differences between sports has been made by the Institute of Sports Medicine and Athletic Trauma of New York City under the direction of Dr. James A. Nicholas. Thirty sports have been classified by 22 identifiable factors relating to the demands placed upon the participant.

Sailing, as a sport, rates overall 14th in the list which leads off with football and ends with hiking.

Neuromuscular (physical) factors applied to sailing, with the exception of its top-rated factors "reaction time" and "accuracy," do not score highly in the study, compared with other listed sports. In fact, body type, flexibility and speed all rate zero (on a scale of three). However, the mental and psychometric factors and the environmental factors necessary for sailing, according to the study, are highly scored, placing sailing at the top in these factors, tied only with auto racing.

The study does not attempt to define types of variations or different competitive levels within a sport. As Dr. Nicholas says, "We have used the sailing figure primarily as a guide to encompass the entire sport generally, and to get people to think of the sport in terms of all the performance factors and in comparison to other sports.

"The chart relates to the demand factors in a sport," he further explains. "Therefore, the lower the demand, the greater opportunity for any individual to participate in the sport; in football, which is ranked #1, with 56 demand points, it has one of the lowest participation rates in this country according to a recent Nielsen survey. The differences (in a given sport) are what we will be studying intensively for decades to come. The problem now is that of awareness. We would be interested in your rating of ocean racing as compared to sailing."

I have accepted the Doctor's invitation and have constructed ratings for ocean racing, a rigorous part of offshore racing. These are inserted in the Doctor's chart below the Institute's rating for the sport of sailing. I have rated ocean racing higher than sailing in the neuromuscular and physical factors of strength, endurance, flexibility and speed, giving ocean racing seven more total points than sailing.

Ratings and Handicaps

Any athletic contest requires some sort of a sponsor and some type of organization to run it, as well as an agreed-upon set of rules for the contestants to follow. Offshore racing is no exception. Because of its international nature, it is only logical that the hierarchy of organization begins with the International Yacht Racing Union. This is not a union in the sense of the United Mine Workers or the Teamsters, but a union in terms of bringing together worldwide those who are interested in the sport. The IYRU has, therefore, promulgated an interna-

NEUROMUSCULAR (PHYSICAL) FACTORS

Sports	Strength	Endurance	Body type	Flexibility	Balance	Agility	Speed	Coordination	Timing	Reaction time	Rhythm	Steadiness	Accuracy	Subtotal A
Football	3	2	3	2	3	3	3	2	3	3	3	3	3	36
Hockey	3	3	2	2	3	3	3	3	3	3	3	3	3	37
Boxing	3	3	2	2	3	3	3	3	3	3	3	3	3	37
Gymnastics	3	2	2	3	3	3	2	3	3	3	3	3	3	36
Basketball	2	3	3	2	3	3	3	3	3	3	2	2	3	35
Karate	2	2	2	3	3	3	2	3	3	2	2	3	3	33
Surfing	2	3	2	0	3	3	0	3	3	3	2	3	3	30
Ocean Racing	2	3	0	3	1	2	1	2	2	3	2	3	3	27
Mountain climbing	3	3	1	2	2	2	1	2	3	3	2	3	2	29
Auto racing	2	2	1	0	1	0	0	3	3	3	1	3	3	22
Diving	1	1	2	3	3	3	1	3	3	2	2	3	3	30
Soccer	2	3	1	2	3	3	3	3	3	3	2	2	2	32
Baseball	2	1	1	2	2	2	2	3	3	3	2	1	3	27
Volleyball	2	2	2	2	3	3	2	3	3	3	2	1	3	31
Sailing	1	2	0	0	1	2	0	2	2	3	2	2	3	20
Tennis	1	2	1	2	2	3	2	3	2	2	2	2	2	26
Skiing	1	2	1	2	3	3	1	3	1	2	2	2	1	24
Badminton	1	2	1	2	2	2	2	3	2	3	2	2	2	26
Golf	1	1	1	2	2	0	0	3	3	1	3	3	3	23
Swimming	2	2	2	2	2	1	2	2	2	2	3	2	3	27
Bobsledding	2	2	1	1	3	1	2	2	3	3	2	2	3	27
Scuba	1	2	0	1	2	1	0	2	2	3	3	2	2	21
Motorcycling	1	1	0	0	2	0	0	3	3	3	2	2	3	20
Handball	2	2	1	2	2	2	2	2	2	3	2	2	2	26
Bicycling	2	2	2	1	2	1	1	1	1	2	3	2	2	22
Field hockey	2	2	1	1	2	2	2	2	2	2	2	1	1	22
Table tennis	1	1	1	1	1	2	2	2	3	3	2	1	3	23
Calisthenics	1	1	2	2	2	1	2	2	2	1	3	2	1	22
Bowling	1	1	0	1	1	0	0	1	2	1	3	2	3	16
Bridge	0	1	0	0	0	0	0	0	3	1	2	2	3	12
Hiking	1	2	1	1	1	0	0	1	1	1	1	1	0	11

	MENTAL AND PSYCHOMETRIC FACTORS						ENVIRONMENTAL FACTORS					
	Intelligence	Creativity	Alertness	Motivation	Discipline	Subtotal B	Total A + B	Playing conditions	Equipment	Practice	Subtotal C	FINAL TOTAL A + B + C
Football	2	1	3	3	3	12	48	2	3	3	8	56
Hockey	0	0	3	3	3	9	46	2	3	3	8	54
Boxing	1	0	3	3	3	10	47	0	1	3	4	51
Gymnastics	0	0	3	3	3	9	45	1	1	3	5	50
Basketball	1	1	3	3	2	10	45	1	1	3	5	50
Karate	2	3	3	2	3	13	46	0	1	3	4	50
Surfing	1	3	3	3	3	13	43	3	1	3	7	50
Ocean Racing	2	3	3	3	3	14	41	3	3	3	9	50
Mountain climbing	2	0	3	3	3	11	40	2	2	3	7	47
Auto racing	2	3	3	3	3	14	36	3	3	3	9	45
Diving	1	2	2	3	2	10	40	1	1	3	5	45
Soccer	0	0	3	3	2	8	40	1	1	2	4	44
Baseball	1	1	3	2	2	9	36	3	2	3	8	44
Volleyball	0	1	3	1	2	7	38	2	2	2	6	44
Sailing	2	3	3	3	3	14	34	3	3	3	9	43
Tennis	1	2	2	2	2	9	35	2	2	3	7	42
Skiing	1	1	2	2	2	8	32	3	3	3	9	41
Badminton	0	1	2	1	2	6	32	3	3	2	8	40
Golf	1	2	1	2	3	9	32	2	2	3	7	39
Swimming	1	0	3	2	2	8	35	1	0	3	4	39
Bobsledding	1	1	3	2	2	9	36	0	0	3	3	39
Scuba	1	1	3	2	2	9	30	2	3	2	7	37
Motorcycling	1	2	3	2	2	10	30	2	3	2	7	37
Handball	0	1	2	2	2	7	33	1	1	2	4	37
Bicycling	1	2	2	1	2	8	30	2	2	2	6	36
Field hockey	1	1	2	2	2	8	30	2	2	2	6	36
Table tennis	0	2	2	2	2	8	31	0	1	2	3	34
Calisthenics	1	2	2	2	2	9	31	0	0	2	2	33
Bowling	0	2	2	2	2	8	24	1	2	2	5	29
Bridge	2	2	3	2	2	11	23	0	0	3	3	26
Hiking	0	2	1	1	2	6	17	1	0	0	1	18

tional formula for handicapping yachts of different sizes and of dissimilar characteristics called the International Offshore Rule.

As this has generally been adopted by most national yacht racing organizations, taking the cue from the IYRU, and since most of the newer boats, regardless of country of origin, have been built in compliance with and to take advantage of this rule, it is quite simple for a yacht, say of American design and construction, to race in England or France or South America or Australia with very little red tape involved provided it has an IOR (International Offshore Rule) rating. This rating is now in its third modification (IOR Mark III) since its inception in 1970. The United States Yacht Racing Union (USYRU) is the national body administering the rule for United States sailors.

While the concept of an internationally accepted rating rule has made a lot of sense and had to have enough support to be accepted, this did not come about without objections. It is fair to say that all the boats previously designed to a national or local rating rule were at one fell swoop made obsolete in top international competition, even though they had many years of use remaining when the new IOR was promulgated. Naturally, the owners of these boats were not all willing to sell them and get new ones built to the new rule. As a result, various national and even local rules have been continued or originated so that these boats could continue to race with each other, mostly in local competition. Boats designed to the IOR can be raced under local rating rules but most owners of them prefer the elite status of racing with the IOR group when possible.

A rating is derived from a complex formula which uses as inputs measurements such as hull dimensions, height and location of mast, boom length and sail limits. The result, when all required dimensions are cranked into the formula, is expressed in feet to the nearest tenth of a foot. The complexity is evident when one examines the rating certificate form and the measurements used for just the sails and spars for a sloop rig as shown on pages 13 and 15.

This rating can then be used for handicapping a yacht with a larger rating against one with a smaller rating. The handicap is expressed in time. There are various ways this is figured.

- *Time on Time:* The theoretical time it should have taken a rated yacht to complete the race vs. the actual time. Here the smaller rated yachts are favored if it is a slow race, and the larger yachts if it is a fast race.
- *Time on Arbitrary Distance:* The actual time difference between two yachts of different ratings for an arbitrary distance different from the actual distance. This is sometimes used to correct for a constant such as in the St. Petersburg–Fort Lauderdale Race where the Gulf Stream flows *with* the fleet from the Florida Keys to the finish line. The official distance in this race is less than the actual straight-line distance.
- *Time on Actual Distance:* The actual time difference between two yachts of different ratings for the straight-line race distance.

The method most often used is time on actual distance. A standard set of allowance tables is entered with a yacht's rating and the tables will show the yacht's time allowance per nautical mile. When compared with the time allowance of a yacht with a different rating, the difference in time allowance can be determined. This difference is then multiplied by the number of miles in the race.

While this will handicap the yachts, it is not always a true difference. The allowance tables assume an arbitrary mix of sailing conditions, that is, a certain proportion of beating, reaching and running. This seldom works out in a particular race. For example: the 1976 Bermuda Race was mostly beating, thus favoring the large, close-winded yachts. The Miami–Nassau Race is often a downwind slide, thus favoring light-displacement smaller yachts when this happens. Or, fleet leaders may be becalmed in a race and overtaken by yachts formerly behind. Thus begins a new race with fewer miles to go.

Nevertheless, some system, no matter how imperfect, needs to be used to race dissimilar yachts together.

Here's how an actual example would work: Your yacht rates 35.0. The USYRU tables indicate that the time allowance per nautical mile for that rating is 149.11 seconds. Now suppose that my yacht rates 36.0. Her time allowance is 144 seconds from the tables. To find the difference in time allowance between the two yachts for one nautical mile we subtract the lower time allowance from the higher. This gives 5.11 seconds. To arrive at the time allowance between the two boats for a specified race it is now necessary to multiply the time allowance difference by the official length of the race. In the case of the Bermuda Race, this would be 635 miles times 5.11 seconds which results in a time difference for that race for these yachts of 3244.85 seconds. To convert to minutes and seconds, we divide by 60 and get 54 minutes and five seconds. My higher-rated yacht would have to finish at least 54 minutes and six seconds before yours to beat her on corrected time.

With the increased use of computers by race committees, time differences are more often expressed in decimal time to four decimal places. One hour, 15 minutes, 30 seconds would be 1.2583 decimal hours.

The numerical rating of a yacht is also useful in dividing large fleets into classes of similar size. A typical race might have 180 boats divided into six classes, with each class containing boats close together in rating and having a separate start. The difference in starting times is applied to finish times to figure actual elapsed time in the race for each class. Ratings are often used as well to determine the length of a course with boats of smaller ratings sailing a shorter course during the same time interval than larger boats. These, of course, would be separate races.

Other Rules and Committee Duties

IYRU also functions as the promulgator of the sailing rules which range from the right-of-way rules through the governing rules of a particular class to suggested methods of conducting a particular race.

Acting within these international rules, and often within the rules of a particu-

1	INTERNATIONAL OFFSHORE RULE	RATING CERTIFICATE NO.
2	MARK III AMEND. TO NOV. 74	MEASUREMENTS IN METRES AND KGS
3		
4		
5	CLASS	YACHT
6	DESIGNER	SAIL NO.
7	BUILDER ....YEAR	
8		OWNER
9		
10	RIG	
11	KEEL	
12		
13		LOCATIONS FROM STEM/WEIGHT
14	PROPELLER	ANCHORS BALLAST RAFTS
15	TYPE	1 ..../ 1 ..../ 1
16	INSTALLED	2 ..../ 2 ..../ 2
17		3 ..../ 3 ..../ 3

	HULL				
18					
19	LOA	BMAX	FF	AW	APD
20	FGO	B	FFI	BW	BPD
21	AGO	BWL	FFD	CW	CPD
22	LBG	BF	FMD	DW	DPD
23	GSDA	BFI	FAI	AWD	PL
24	GSDF	BAI	FA	BWD	SBMAX
25	FD	BA	VHAI	CWD	SPD
26	CMD	GD	VHA	DWD	SDM
27	MD	Y	BHAI	MAW1	MAW2
28	OMD	DM	BHA	MACG1	MACG2
28.5	GDFI				
29	EW	EWD	PD	PRD	PBW
30	ESL	ESC	ST1	ST2	ST3
31	CD	WCBA	WCBB	CBDA	CBDB
32				CBLDA	CBLDB

	FORETRIANGLE		MAINSAIL		
33					
34	I	SPL	P	HB	PC
35	J	SPH	E	BL1	IC
36	LPG	SL	BAD	BL2	JC
37	LPIS	SMW	BAL	BL3	EC
38	FSP	SMG	BD	BL4	MX SL
39	FS	SF		BL5	MXSMW
40	FBI	HBS		BLP	MX LP
41					

	MIZZEN				
42					
43	IY	PY	BY1	HBY	PYC
44	EB	EY	BY2	BLPY	EYC
45	YSD	BADY	BY3	S1	
46	YSF	BALY	BY4	S2	
47	YSMG	BDY	BY5	S3	
48					
49					
50					

51	L	S	
52	B	DC	RATING............FEET
53	D	FC	
54	CGF	MR	RATING............METRES
55	EPF	R	
56	MAF		
57	MEASURER		I CERTIFY THAT I UNDERSTAND MY
58	MEASURED EXPIRES		RESPONSIBILITIES AS COVERED IN THE IOR
59			RULE:
60	NATL' AUTHORITY		OWNER

Rating certificate form

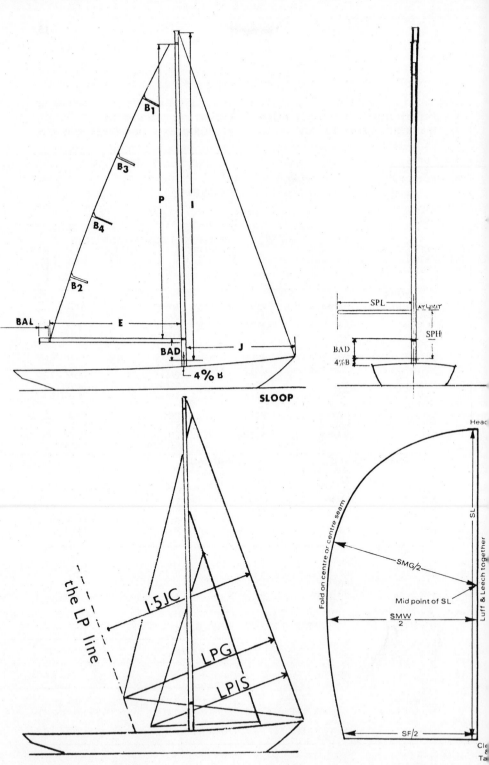

Measurements for sails and spars

lar country as well, the sponsor of an offshore race must furnish a committee or committees to handle the entries, to determine skipper and yacht qualifications, to advise the accepted entries as to the particular rules for that race, including specified course, to conduct the start and, at the other end, to record the finish. Other important details are race patrols, monitoring and controlling spectator fleets, tracking down missing boats, aiding those in trouble, facilitating governmental and customs clearances, recording and publicizing results, providing trophies and awards and promoting fellowship and conviviality at related social events. As Ted Tolson of the St. Petersburg (Florida) Yacht Club, "Mr. Race Committee" to hundreds of North American sailors, says, "The prime purpose and function of a race committee is to render a good service to the contestants."

Since most of the classic races have been run for a number of years, established patterns and past practice serve to provide continuity for committee efforts. The "old boy network" has provided recruits who "move up the chairs" to take care of this myriad of detail, most of which has to be done before the race starts. On the other hand, this continuity sometimes can be a handicap since committees often become inflexible and slow to change in response to changes in the sport.

The marvel of any rating system on which handicaps are based allows a mixed bag of boats, ranging from 35 feet to 80 feet, to race over the same course and distance and still provide a creditable winner. That no one usually knows for sure who the winner is until after all the boats have finished or the time allowances in hours, minutes and seconds have expired seems not to bother the contestants for they sometimes know the results between individual boats well before the committee's computer has digested, analyzed and spewed them forth. If you finish close to a boat that rates a foot lower than you, you know without calculations that he has beaten you on corrected time. You also know who your top competition is, and once you have their finish times and apply them to yours, you can figure out who did what to whom.

Here are some of the other organizations, not yacht clubs per se, which help the sport in various ways. The Cruising Club of America for many years administered the CCA rule, predecessor of the IOR in the U.S., and participates in the planning and committee work for the Bermuda Race. The Storm Trysail Club is active in rule-making councils and runs the Block Island Race and Block Island Week, a U.S. counterpart of Cowes Week in England. The (British) Royal Ocean Racing Club is influential in rule-making and in the running of the Fastnet Race. The Corinthians are a group based in the northeastern U.S. who assist owners in obtaining crews for their racing yachts. A new organization called The Ocean Racing Club of America, many of whose members are also in other such clubs, has pressed for new ideas and faster solutions to evident problems in offshore racing.

A fine point on definitions. The term "offshore," as used here, encompasses a wide variety of races in cruising-type boats whether in a bay, sound, estuary or open sea. It includes day races round-the-buoys or long voyages of days or weeks. But it is always done in "boats with lids." The term "ocean racing" applies in a more narrow sense to racing in the larger cruising-type boats across the open sea for long distances and off soundings.

Thus, a yacht may be classified as an offshore boat but not as an ocean racer.

This, then, is a thumbnail sketch of the sport of offshore racing, a sport with many elements and combining many disciplines. Many participants feel that it is one of the few frontiers left in this modern, overorganized world.

Windancer on Lake Huron

Caught in the tide rips at the Gut, Long Island Sound

Oyster in the Solent

Carina heads for Bermuda

Salty Goose off Eddystone Light in the English Channel

Sorcery surfing at 14 knots off the Atlantic coast

2 THE PLAYERS

Who are the players in the offshore game? At first glance one might think it would be only the people crewing the yachts, but if one accepts the fact that most offshore races are won before they start, the definition of "player" is expanded considerably. We will get back to the crews. Let's look first at some of the others who don't sail the boat but are no less important.

The Designer

One of the most significant is the designer. If the boat is not right for her time, the best crew in the world can't save her. But put a "hot" crew on a "hot" design and even Jimmy the Greek might not bet against her. But which designer? It is a difficult choice. The designer who came up with last year's winner may not be able to do it again, and the designer of next year's winner may be an unknown today. An established designer seldom will depart in major ways from last year's success, but rather will make incremental improvements. A new designer with no track record and little to lose is more inclined to go for the "breakthrough" boat, but is also more likely to design a failure.

Other considerations are the prospective owner's requirements and the sailing waters. Some owners like to have cruising amenities in the boat, others are content with uncomfortable, stripped-out racing machines. It is not unknown in these days of conspicuous consumption to have the "throw-away" boat, that is, one designed for a particular race or a particular sailing area and with little useful life otherwise. This is the exception, of course, as most owners cannot afford such luxury. Some designs are commissioned to be first-to-finish on elapsed time, others to have a good chance on corrected time; some to go well in light weather, others to go well in heavy weather, still others to go upwind better than downwind or vice versa.

It is obvious that a lot of thinking needs to be done both by the prospective owner and the designer, but not until the boat is built, launched and raced do they really know how well they have succeeded. Boat designing is still a rather imprecise science in spite of the tank testing of models of proposed designs and computer analysis of the results, as witness the spectacular failure of *Mariner* in the 1974 America's Cup contest.

The Builder

The design problem also includes the materials from which the boat will be made and a choice of a builder who is expert at working with the selected

Design conference. *Left to right:* Steve Crane, builder; Brit Chance, designer; Scott Allan, sailmaker; Randy Scarborough, owner

materials. A lot of the foregoing is taken care of automatically by selecting what is known as a "stock" design, that is, one already designed and being built in quantity, and already successful in races, but this theoretically reduces the potential for design advantage. I say "theoretically" because even a stock boat can be customized to some extent in terms of weight, rig, sail area, deck layout, keel and rudder.

A compromise between the two approaches is sometimes used—that is, taking a successful custom design and scaling it up or down to suit the needs of an individual customer. However, this is more often unsuccessful than not as weight, sail area, wetted surface and other factors don't always react the same to changes in scale.

Another element not often thought about, but a related one, is how the personalities of the prospective owner, designer and builder blend. This can be an exacerbating factor when the goals of the parties involved are different or incompatible.

Before one gets too far, deck layout and equipment need to be considered. These have to be harmonized with the rig, the number in the crew and length and width of the boat at deck level. Where the string pullers and winch grinders are located will affect the trim of the boat as well as their working efficiency.

The Parts People

Here a few new players enter the scene—the custom rigging and mast maker, the equipment supplier and the sailmaker. Before a custom design can be finalized there needs to be heavy involvement by all these key people. Envision further that all being tops in their field or "heavies," as they are known in the game, they are possessed of strong opinions and sometimes massive egos. Some owners who have been through this before have found it a good idea to have a project manager assigned full time as a buffer to look out for their interests and resolve the inevitable conflicts, or refine them to a point-of-decision by the owner. An owner has to be a remarkable person just to survive this experience successfully, let alone race the boat after it is designed, built and outfitted. But if all of this comes off well, and the yacht crosses the starting line with a little edge of speed over the competition, she has already beaten a good percentage of the contestants.

Some of the less visible players include the person who holds the mortgage on the boat, the people who keep the owner's business going while he is out sailing and his wife who lets him go because she enjoys the parties before and after the races.

The Crew

It is recorded that the first yacht races in the United States took place in 1835 between the schooner yachts *Wave* owned by Commodore John C. Stevens of New York and *Sylph* owned by Commodore Robert B. Forbes of Boston. The races were sailed in Vineyard and Nantucket Sound off Cape Cod.

In those days crews were mostly professional with the owners along more for the ride than as participants. This gradually gave way to mostly amateurs, friends of the owner, with a couple of professionals to do the dirty work, but not actively participating in race strategy or boat handling. The amateur requirement was written into race rules, thus preserving this concept to the present day, and is particularly applicable to skippers and navigators.

Is there a typical crew? There probably was in the early days (1880–1910). The sons of independently wealthy members of the proper clubs learned to sail as a matter of course during idle summers at the fabled resorts of the very rich. The opportunity to ship on as a crew in their father's or uncle's boat provided the experience to move up to skipper at the appropriate time, and the right club memberships brought the invitation to compete. In addition, the process by which this type of offshore sailor was developed also ensured that the competition would be gentlemanly and not too cutthroat. Nature's elements were deemed demanding enough. Interlopers whose boats were patently faster were dealt with summarily. Their designs were just declared ineligible, or their rating was increased.

After World War I, with relatively smaller but more numerous yachts, a higher level of ability by amateurs, an increasing number of yacht clubs, a tightening of the rules, and a burgeoning interest in deep sea voyaging, modern ocean racing was born. United States skippers of the day like Bob Bavier, Sr., John Alden, and John Parkinson were not the ultrarich mentioned above and they picked their crews very carefully from the top local "round–the–buoys" amateur skippers. They and others like them can be considered founders of the sport as we know it.

Now, there is no stereotype. Today, money, time, ability and the will–to–win are all that is needed. And as inflation continues, the cost of participation is forcing more and more veteran owners into smaller boats or out of the sport and bringing in a newer breed, not always as cultured or suave as those who went before.

No longer can the owner afford to crew a boat with friends or relatives unless they are fully qualified. This now has resulted in talent more than connections being the prime requirement for a crew member. In fact, there has developed a group who are classed by some as "professionals" even though they are not paid to race the boat in the strict sense. As the sport has grown, and as the related industry has become bigger and more competitive, it has meant a great deal for the designers, builders and suppliers of sails and equipment to be associated with a winner. It is in their best interest to see that their boats or products are sailed as well as possible. Many of the best crew members and skippers work for these people both in making and selling the products and in sailing them to victory. Thus the "factory team" concept has grown and more and more the amateur concept has suffered accordingly.

Visualize a boat which has in its crew an "account executive" for the sailmaker, a designer's representative, a builder's representative, a hardware representative and *their* friends who are all top-notch sailors. You can see the problem of an owner who can't attract this array of talent. We will discuss the crew's duties and interrelationships later on in more detail.

Others

To support a racing yacht during a heavy racing schedule we must add the boatyards that make between-race repairs and alterations, the many technicians who keep the gear in operating condition and the logicians who maintain a full racing crew complement, boat supplies and provisioning, as well as the ferry crews who move the boat to the next race starting point.

Finally, we must include in the cast of players those known as "boat birds." These are the girls who are attracted by the glamor surrounding the yachts and their crews and take part in the pre- and post-race festivities. Where they come from and how they get there is often mysterious; but they are present, nevertheless, wherever the fleet gathers, like the groupies who follow the rock bands from place to place. They also have a purpose, however hazily defined.

3 THE YACHTS

It was only a short time ago that offshore yachts were designed and built to last for 15 to 20 years and were rugged enough to withstand most of the conditions to be encountered in any ocean anywhere in the world. There was every expectation at that time that they would have a long and useful life as competitive racers. They were also designed to be comfortable to live aboard and to have an easy motion in a sea. The quest for greater speed in the last few years has changed all that.

Today the fastest yachts are more likely to be uncomfortable to ride in, to be light, stripped-out racing machines with few amenities, more subject to gear failures while racing and to have a very short useful life. It is almost the age of the "disposable" yacht. Take the yacht designed and built for a particular race or series after consideration of the weather and sea conditions expected at that time and in that area. This means that a boat of that type will not necessarily do as well in another area and in another race, and by the time the race or series for which it was designed comes around again, a better one may have been designed and built to beat her under those conditions.

The major factor that has brought all this about is the rapidly developing technology now applied to boat design and construction. Spin-offs from space technology, particularly in the area of metallurgy, and participation in the expensive and highly concentrated competition for the America's Cup, have made this much more feasible and in a greatly compressed time frame. For example, aluminum, until very recently considered impracticable for hull construction, has become the most commonly used material for custom boats due to strength, lightness and ease of fabrication (while fiberglass is also a very commonly used material for modern-day hulls, it is more suitable for production boats due to the high initial cost of the molds involved). Another great advantage of welded aluminum as a hull material is that alterations in the hull shape after the boat is built and sailed can easily be made by cutting out the areas that need change, fabricating the new section in the new shape and welding it into place. This would have been almost impossible to do in a satisfactory manner with the old wooden hulls. It is also a lot cheaper than getting a whole new boat. Fiberglass hulls can be altered in a less satisfactory way by the use of microballoons added to the original hull shape.

New metals and new techniques have also revolutionized spars and rigging as well as sail handling equipment. Synthetic fibers and new wire rope materials have also updated halyards and sheets. New technology has also been responsible for exotic sailmaking materials which have resulted in sails which are less porous, more faithful to design shape and more flexible in adjustability to changing wind velocities and points of sailing.

Sails

A successful yacht will have a large inventory of sails. While only one mainsail is allowed, there are no limits on the number and type of headsails, staysails and spinnakers, though there is now agitation to limit and define the number and type carried in a race. At present a large yacht's sail inventory sometimes runs as high as 40 sails. This can be one of the most expensive aspects of the sport as these sails must be constantly recut for greater efficiency or repaired after race damage and replaced when no longer usable.

To illustrate the variety of types and uses, I have included on the following pages information on headsails and staysails from Hood Sailmakers, Inc., and on spinnakers from North Sails, reproduced with their permission.

Headsail Types   (Courtesy Hood Sailmakers, Inc.)

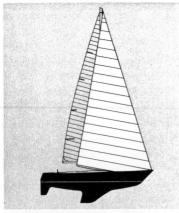 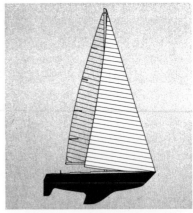

Light #1 Genoa: A full cut genoa, designed to provide maximum power in light air, but cut with a fine entry to ensure optimum pointing ability. Amazingly effective in both choppy and smooth water, this genoa is a necessity on any racing boat. Range: 4-15 knots of apparent wind; cloth 2.9 oz., 3.5 oz., 4.1 oz.

#2 Genoa: In most cases this is a full-hoist sail with an overlap of between 130% and 145%. Shaped much as the heavy #1, flat for pointing, but with adequate shape to provide power in disturbed water. Hood has been very successful in building "hybrid" #2 (and #3) genoas, constructed with heavier cloth in the foot and head panels to give added strength at the points of maximum stress. Range: 20-30 knots; cloth 6.3 oz., 8.2 oz.

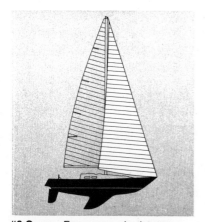

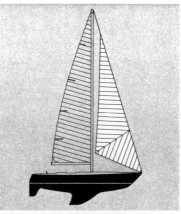

#3 Genoa: For many racing boats a high aspect #3 (95% hoist, 110-120% LP) has proven superior to the classic low aspect #3. The increased luff length creates a more efficient windward sail which, in conjunction with reefs in the main, has a broader wind range than a lower aspect design. Racing boats prone to lee helm and full keeled cruising boats continue to perform best with a low aspect design, whose center of effort is lower and further aft. Range: 26-36 knots, Cloth: 6.3 oz., 8.2, 10.0.

#4 Genoa, Jibs: Heavy weather headsails are designed in accordance with a boat's tenderness and rig and deck layouts. A #4 genoa is generally 90% on the luff and 85% on the LP; smaller jibs are designed correspondingly. For fear of cloth distortion, such sails have often been so flat that they provide little forward power. Hood jibs are shaped to provide power to drive the boat in extreme conditions, with the draft well forward to ensure that the sail lifts the boat over a wave, rather than push it to leeward. Wind range: 35 knots +, Cloth: 8.2 oz., 10.0.

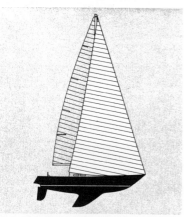

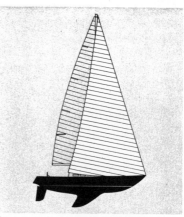

Regular #1: Cut flatter than the light #1 with a maximum draft placed further forward. For use in moderate air, this sail has a very fine entry for superior pointing, and yet remains extremely effective for footing through slop or ocean swells. The precise adjustability of Hood sailcloth allows the regular #1 a great versatility over a wide range of wind. Range: 10-22 knots; cloth 4.1 oz., 5.5 oz., 6.3 oz., 8.2 oz.

Heavy #1: Cut with more leech hollow to reduce heel, and slightly flatter than the regular #1, the heavy #1 is a devastating weapon for upwind work. Recommended for large racing boats whose stiffness allows three full LP genoas. Range: 15-22 knots; cloth 6.3 oz., 8.2 oz.

Working Jib ("Mule", "Lapper"): Intended for use on cruising boats. 90% on the hoist with an overlap of 90% to 105%, and cut with a high clew to keep the foot out of the water and to aid visibility. Designed fairly full for power, this is the ideal moderate to heavy air cruising sail for beating and reaching. Range: 22-36 knots; cloth 6.3 oz., 8.2 oz., 10.0 oz.

Reacher (#1 Jib Top): A powerful sail for close reaching, cut full with a round leading edge for maximum drive. The reacher sheets to the transom to achieve maximum effective overlap for a given LP, and to create maximum slot width to allow the staysail to be flown inside. A reacher/staysail double head rig is the most powerful headsail combination available, giving optimum drive through a variety of sea conditions. Wind angle: 40° to 85°. Wind strength: 6-22 knots; cloth 3.5 oz., 4.1 oz., 5.5 oz., 6.3 oz.

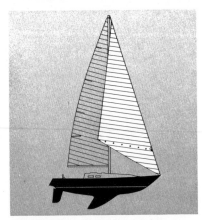

Blast Reacher: A smaller reacher designed with full hoist and short overlap (100-120%), this is a racing sail to be used close reaching when a full reacher would overpower the boat. The large overlap that is needed for power when reaching in light air creates drag and heeling force in heavy air — thus, the blast reacher has a short overlap. The blast reacher sheets forward of the transom to allow a lower clew point, which produces a lower center of effort and less heeling force. The blast reacher is an excellent sail to be equipped with reef points. Wind angle: 45°-95°; wind strength: 25-35 knots; cloth: 6.3 oz., 8.2, 10.0.

Windward Reacher: Flatter than a true reacher and shaped with a finer entry to enhance close windward performance. An excellent sail for light air windward work, and in conjunction with a staysail, when real power is needed to fight through a slop. In more than 12 knots of breeze a genoa is a more efficient windward sail; thus, the windward reacher is a light air sail available only in lighter cloth weights: 2.9 oz., 3.5, 4.1. Wind range: 5 to 14 knots.

Staysail Types

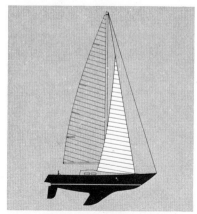

Reacher/Drifter: Similar to the windward reacher to allow its use as a windward sail, but built only in lightest cloth to accommodate its drifter qualities. Intended for use in very light air to get the boat moving and develop apparent wind speed. A drifter can also be designed as a high clewed genoa for use on larger boats. Range: 0 to 5 knots; cloth .75 oz. Marnac, 1.5 oz. Marnac, 2.2 oz. Nylon, 2.0 oz. Dacron.

Genoa Staysail: Most often used for footing to windward and close reaching, set inside a reacher (jib top) or high-clewed genoa. The GENOA STAYSAIL is a free-standing, wire-luffed sail which sets on a masthead halyard and sheets either inside or outside the shrouds, depending on the wind angle. The GENOA STAYSAIL has a luff length of 70% of full hoist and an LP, 75% of J, tacks on centerline at a point 50%-60% of J forward of the mast, and thus overlaps the mainsail by approximately 15%. For use in heavy air, Hood designed a lower hoist, shorter LP GENOA STAYSAIL, which provides slot effect and drive, but little heeling force. Cloth: 2.9 oz., 3.5, 4.1, 5.5, 6.3, 8.2.

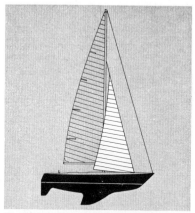

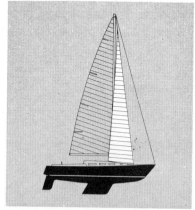

Forestaysail: Similar to the GENOA STAYSAIL, but set off an inner forestay rather than free-luffed, and hoisted with a special staysail halyard. The FORESTAYSAIL is usually 65% of full hoist, depending on the location of the forestay on the mast, and has an LP of 70% of J. Like the GENOA STAYSAIL, the FORESTAYSAIL is used inside high clewed genoas or reachers, and can be designed to maximum dimensions for use in moderate air, and as a smaller STORM FORESTAYSAIL for use in heavy air. Cloth: 3.5 oz., 4.1, 5.5, 6.3, 8.2.

Tallboy: The original free-luffed tall narrow staysail for use inside a genoa when sailing too close to the wind to use a larger genoa staysail. Upwind, the TALLBOY functions as a forward extension of the mainsail, creating a greater slot effect with the primary headsail. Dead downwind, the TALLBOY can be tacked to the weather rail and sheeted flat across the boat, catching lower level wind that is missed by a spinnaker or spinnaker/shooter combination. Cloth: 2.9 oz., 3.5, 4.1.

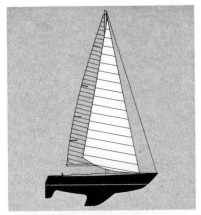

Big Boy Spinnaker Staysail: For use inside a spinnaker when beam or broad reaching (80°-145° apparent). The BIG BOY is full hoist, free-luffed, with an LP of 110% and a high clew to achieve maximum effective overlap of the main-sail. The BIG BOY tacks on centerline at 70% of J forward of the mast when the wind is on the beam and tacks pro-gressively outboard and aft as the spin-naker pole is squared. Cloth: 2.9 oz., 3.5, 4.1.

Mizzen Staysail: For all split rig vessels, a light to moderate air staysail which is hoisted free-luffed from the mizzen mast and sheets to the mizzen boom. Like a BIG BOY, the MIZZEN STAYSAIL has a range of 80°-145° ap-parent, and tacks on centerline or the weather rail in accordance with the wind angle. Cloth: 1.5 Marnac, 2.0 Dacron, 2.9, 3.5. Certain racing rigs can carry smaller, heavy air MIZZEN STAYSAILS, which are most beneficial, provided they do not create too much weather helm. Cloth: 5.5 oz., 6.3, 8.2.

SPINNAKER SELECTION CHART FOR SINGLE SPINNAKER BOATS.

TYPE	CLOTH WT.	RANGE	CONDITIONS	CHARACTERISTICS
All-purpose Tri-Radial	.75 oz. (also 1.5 oz. for larger boats)	65°-180°	Light and moderate reaching; light, mod-erate and fresh run-ning.	Stable; easily flown; pole slightly further aft on reach than con-ventional spinnaker; on a close reach, pole can be kept as low as clew without making sail over-full.

Note: Smaller, lighter boats with limited reaching capability may require a modified Radial Head.

ADDITIONAL SPINNAKER SELECTION CHART FOR THE SPINNAKER ENTHUSIAST.

TYPE	CLOTH WT.	RANGE	CONDITIONS	CHARACTERISTICS
Light Air Radial Head (Tri-Radial on boats about 44′ and larger)	.50 oz.	70°-180°	Very light air reaching; light air running.	Cut for maximum stability; good reaching speed tacking downwind in shifting conditions; flies well with pole low in dead light air.
Running Radial Head	.75 oz.	120°-180°	Running in light, moderate and fresh breezes; especially valuable in sloppy conditions.	Cut full with extra wide head angle; broad projected area; especially stable; pole carried quite high.
Reaching Tri-radial	1.5 oz.	60°-180°	Reaching in medium and heavy air; running in fresh breezes.	95% to 100% of maximum at mid girth; narrow shoulders; very flat, very open leaches.
Star Cut	1.5 oz.	50°-70° 70°-180°	Very close reaching. Heavy weather running.	Smaller and less powerful than the tri-radial reacher; 75% to 90% of maximum at mid-girth; very small shoulders; very flat; not very stable; low heeling force.

Courtesy North Sails

Yacht Life Cycle

The increase in the number of knowledgeable people applying themselves to advancing the art of yacht racing is another factor causing rapid innovation and rapid obsolescence.

The result is that an owner can no longer expect a winning boat to stay that way very long. The typical cycle today is to have a new boat delivered in time to compete in the Southern Ocean Racing Conference in Florida and the Bahamas early in the calendar year where it can be debugged and tuned for the summer season. Further refined the second year, and assuming no major changes are necessary in hull and rig, the owner can enjoy a full year of sailing with a competitive boat. But it is during this period that he should be seriously considering his next design so that it will come on-stream the third year to repeat the cycle. Well-considered major alterations can sometimes stave this off for one more year, but by then a complete new outfit of sails and running rigging is usually required.

One-year-old *Charisma* sports new stern section in 1976 which decreased overall length one foot and helped to decrease her rating to 40.0.

Level-Rating Yachts

A recent development is the popularity of what is known as level-rating yachts (yachts of dissimilar design but with identical ratings). First introduced in the One-Ton Class, a designation of no significance weight-wise, where boats all sailed with an IOR of 27.5, it has spread to Two-Tonners rating 32, Three-Quarter-Tonners rating 24.5, Half-Tonners at 21.7 and One-Quarter-Tonners at 18. This concept allows boats of a particular "Ton" class to race boat-for-boat without handicap. It has been more successful at the lower end of the rating scale where the number of boats in a particular class is greater and the boats are less likely to be raced in mixed fleets on a handicap basis.

These yachts, in the classes below Two-Ton, because of their size, are less classifiable as ocean racers, even though they do have crew accommodations of a sort and are more akin to round-the-buoys day-sailers. Unfortunately, the level-raters are no less immune to obsolescence than the others, and the spirit of competition engendered by this group because of their comparatively lower cost makes possible a more rapid application of new concepts tending to increase further the rate of change.

The Midget Ocean Racing classification should also be mentioned. This encompasses yachts of 30 feet or less rated according to the MORC rule. Thus, a Half-Tonner could also race as MORC when not "level" racing against other Half-Tonners.

Two-Tonner hull prior to planking

Half-Tonner hull prior to decking

One-Tonners

Lightnin' was on U.S. Admiral's Cup Team in 1973.

America Jane III, new in 1975 and redesigned twice by late 1976

Vamp, in 1975, earlier in the year as *Stinger* won the SORC

One-Tonners race downwind with spinnaker and blooper.

One-Tonners on the wind. Foreground: *America Jane III left, Pied Piper,* 1975 class World Champion, *right.*

Cockpit arrangement on *Dynamite,* 1974

Tyche (ex-"Marauder"), a Cassian & Cuthbertson
42-footer built in 1975

Golden Dazy, a Holland 41-footer, 1975 Canada's Cup
Winner

Fire-One, 1976. *(Jeff Cotter photo)*

Impetus, member of 1976 Canadian Onion Patch Team. *(Jeff Cotter photo)*

Williwaw, a new aluminum Two-Tonner launched in 1976 is typical of the latest racing machines. She was designed by Doug Peterson for Seymore Sinett.

Williwaw's chart table instrumentation includes Tracor Omega Nav 2, Modar VHF, Kenyon installed dial-type sea temperature thermometer, a Data Marine Pacifica depth sounder 10 to 100 fathoms, two to 199 feet, plus depth alarm, a Bimini 550 radio telephone, Signet log and wind instruments.

On deck there are port and starboard duplicate clusters of instruments well positioned for use by the helmsman. Each include a Ritchie compass, deck mounted, and Signet DAD knot meter, wind speed, close hauled and wind point.

Inside, the boat is completely open with the forward part bare to the skin of the hull and used for sail stowage. Amidships, starboard side, is a conventional head with curtain enclosure and aft of that the compact navigator's station. On the port side is a small galley area. There are eight piperail bunks installed aft of the midlength, four to a side. The off watch shifts to the windward side after each tack. Hydraulic controls are used to adjust both forestay and backstay.

Sheet lead positions and halyard and boom outhaul tensions are clearly indicated for quick and ready reference in waterproof Magic Marker on mast, boom and deck, for various wind strengths and sail combinations.

Williwaw's inventory of sails included an 8-oz. main with a flattening reef and three quick reefs, two No. 1 genoas at 160 percent, a No. 2 at 130 percent, No. 3 at 110 percent, and a No. 4 with three reefs at 90 percent—the reefs could be used to make the No. 4 into a No. 5 or a very heavy air blast reacher. There were five spinnakers: a half-oz. radial head, ¾-oz. all-purpose triradial, 1½-oz. running radial head, 1½-oz. minimum triradial, and a 1½-oz. starcut. *Williwaw* also had a blooper, 140 percent drifter with a wire that could be tacked 3 ½ feet behind the headstay and used as a light air large spinnaker staysail, and two other spinnaker staysails—an ounce and a half 90 percent for light air broad reaching, and a 4-oz. 110 percent standard spinnaker staysail for windier reaching. The entire inventory was by North sails.

Williwaw's deck layout.

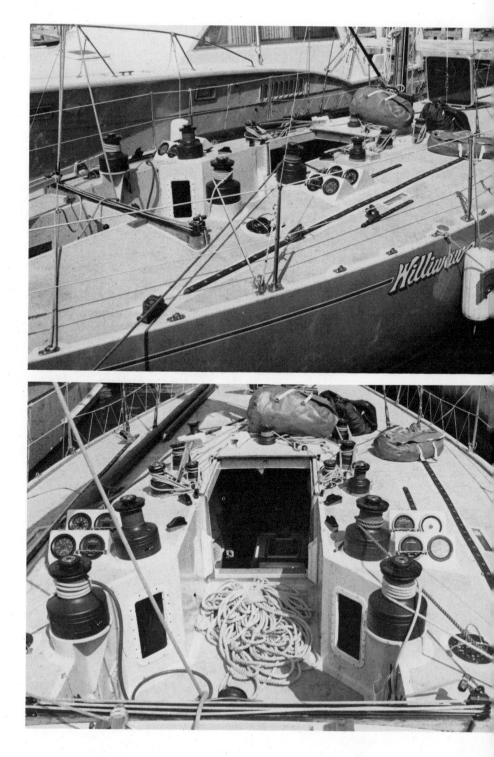

The Yachts

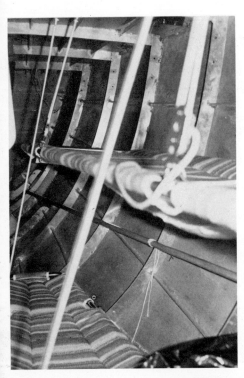

Williwaw's Spartan interior.

Figaro IV

Doric

Typical offshore yachts of the 1960s were beamy, with heavy displacement and long overhangs. Yawl rigs were popular. These yachts were designed to the CCA rule.

Barlovento

Palawan

Jubilee III (foreground)

Yachts launched in 1970 and 1971 were lighter and faster, but the influence of the CCA rule rather than the IOR was still evident.

Crusade

Carina

Sorcery

Improbable

Charisma

Yachts appearing in 1972 and later reflected rapid design and rating changes as designers became more familiar with the IOR.

La Forza del Destino, 1972, a Mull 51-footer

Dora IV, 1972, a Sparkman & Stephens 61-footer

→

Phantom, 1972, a Cassian & Cuthbertson 66-footer

Saudade, 1973, a Sparkman & Stephens 47-footer

Siren Song, 1974, a Sparkman & Stephens 58-footer

Scaramouche, 1974, a Frers 54-footer

The new *Charisma,* a Sparkman & Stephens 55-footer, 1975, rated 4.2 feet lower than the earlier *Charisma,* vintage 1970, though about the same length overall.

Ginkgo, 1973, a Miller 46-footer

Saga, 1972, a Sparkman & Stephens 57-footer

Equation, 1972, a Chance 68-footer

Rattler, 1976, a Frers 46-footer

Whistle Wing V, 1976, a Peterson 53-footer

Bumblebee 3, 1976, a Frers 43-footer

Maxi yachts are designed to be first-to-finish.

73-footer *Windward Passage*

73-footer *Blackfin*

75-footer *Southern Star.* Coast Guard cutter *Vigilant,* in background, starting line Committee Boat for 1972 Bermuda Race

Ondine (III), 98 feet from bow to tip of stern-mounted trampoline (used for trimming mizzen sail)

79-footer *Kialoa (III)*

Deck view of *Kialoa,* a small fortune in deck gear

Former America's Cup yachts—originally designed to the 12-meter rule and later converted to offshore yachts.

Northern Light

American Eagle

American Eagle's cockpit area

67-footer ex-12-meter *Weatherly, left,* alongside 68-footer *Equation* shows differences in design concepts and volume.

Phoenix

Exceptions to the rule

Pen Duick III, shown in 1972, was designed more for long ocean passages than to take advantage of the IOR.

Cascade, shown in 1973, was designed to take full advantage of the IOR. The result, a rating of 22.8 for a 38-footer. With this rating, she created havoc in the 1973 SORC. Later, *Cascade*'s rating was arbitrarily increased under a clause in the rule prohibiting radical departures from current designs.

The making of *Salty Goose,* a 54-foot custom aluminum yacht, designed and built in late 1972 by Bob Derecktor

Test models used to refine hull shape

Goose's massive centerboard

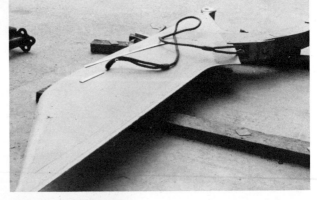

Cockpit area takes shape.

Distinctive stern section and rudder position

Interior is solidly ribbed.

Awaiting finishing touches after launching at Derecktor's Mamaroneck yard

4 THE AFTERGUARD

"Afterguard" is an ancient nautical slang word with two basic meanings: "The owner of a yacht and his guests" and "The officers quartered in the stern of a ship." In the context of offshore racing it means those responsible for the policy decisions that determine the success or failure of a yacht in a particular race.

These include the owner, the skipper, the navigator and the watch captains, who are generally older and more experienced hands, and exclude the remainder of the crew who are no less important, but carry out policy rather than participating in making it.

Though individual yacht organizations will vary, the typical structure will look like the diagram below which indicates the relationship between afterguard and crew:

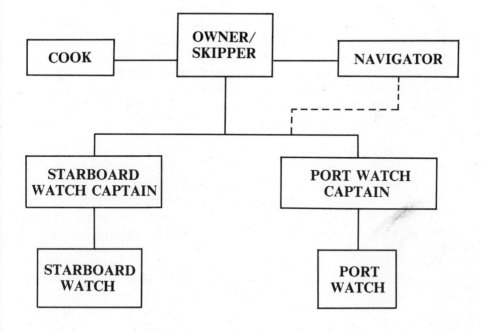

On a functional basis the duties are usually divided like this:

Owner/Skipper: Provides yacht, pays bills, formulates overall policy, makes final strategic decisions.

Navigator: Advises skipper and watch captains on strategy and tactics, maintains navigational plot. Serves as yacht information center.

Watch Captains: Carry out overall policy, supervise watches to produce maximum speed through water by choice of proper sail combinations, efficient sail changes and helming.

Cook: Supervises procurement and stowage of food, plans menus and provides meals.

Deck Watch: Carries out orders of watch captains.

Owner/Skipper may be one person or two.

In the event there are two, the person running the yacht may be called sailing master in cases where the owner is aboard, and skipper when he is not. Yes, yachts are sometimes raced without the owner. Most often the owner is the skipper and in some cases may also be the navigator. The relative importance of the various roles in a particular instance will depend greatly on the skills and experience of the individuals involved and may even change as a race progresses. The variations are endless and depend a great deal on how the key people relate to each other.

What are these sailors like? Obviously, they must be the participating type, inured to the privations of life aboard a small craft in mid-ocean, spartan accommodations, lack of privacy and creature comforts, constant and often violent motion, limited menus and malfunctioning equipment. They must be congenial and able to adapt. They suffer the boredom and discomfort of long, cold and wet watches on deck with hearty disdain. They need to be clear-thinking in emergencies, and able to work as part of a well-trained team. Each one brings to the effort his or her own unique combination of skills and experience.

Yet they are all different, and are recruited from virtually all walks of life. Some are young, making their first trip and supplying only eagerness and muscle. Others are middle-aged and older, veterans of 10 to 15 passages, offering wisdom and experience as their ticket.

The owner of the yacht is a special breed. He needs interest and capability, plus money and free time in large quantities. He may spend years preparing for the big race; building, outfitting, redesigning, tuning, retuning, campaigning in lesser events to prove or disprove ideas for faster sailing, organizing and reorganizing his crew. Beginning early in the racing season, he must finalize his plans. His yacht, crew and gear must arrive at the starting line at the peak of perfection.

On the following pages, with photos and captions, let's look at some of the real-life persons playing these roles. The choice is random but representative.

Chuck Kirsch

At the Royal Bermuda Yacht Club after the 1974 Bermuda Race, I talked with Chuck Kirsch and asked him what was the secret of his boat's big win. He is an astute businessman whose well-run Kirsch Company of Sturgis, Michigan, has captured 40% of the drapery fixtures market. This has provided him the means and the know-how to put a winning boat together. He made these points.

"I started with a fine design by German Frers, then I tried to put together the best crew I could find. Once I assembled them I had confidence in them. They do many things better than I do and I allow them to do them. If there are any questions, I make the final decision after hearing the facts, but they functioned so well that 98% of the time there were no disputes to arbitrate. The crew in this race really came through for me. Peter Bowker, my navigator, showed us the way to go and my watch captains, Dave Irish and Ed 'Schuff' Willman, kept the boat moving at top speed. The rest of the crew members gave them full support. In my business we have a motto, 'Give it all you can, and then some.' The *Scaramouche* crew lived up to that motto."

Ted Turner

Ted Turner grew up in Georgia and was educated in southern prep schools prior to attending Brown University where he was on the sailing team. His college life was first interrupted by a tour in the United States Coast Guard and upon his return to school some homecoming high jinks brought it to a close.

As a young man learning the family business, he was unexpectedly forced to take it over on the death of his father when Ted was twenty-four. He has since built it up into a communications conglomerate based in Atlanta, Georgia, which has supplied him the funds to pursue a busy sailing avocation as well as acquisition of the Atlanta Braves baseball team in early 1976, and later in the year a controlling interest in the Atlanta Hawks basketball team.

Turner was World Ocean Racing Champion in 1970 and is one of the most visible skippers in the sport. Alternately introspective and garrulous, his style as skipper is loud and unrestrained, leading to his soubriquet as "the mouth from the south." He is a founder of the nonestablishment Ocean Racing Club of America (ORCA).

Britton Chance

Born into an old Philadelphia family in 1940 and descended from a long line of engineers, scientists and inventors as well as sailors, he grew up in dinghies and later crewed for his father, Britton, Sr., in the 5.5 meter class.

Dropping out of the University of Rochester in his junior year, he became an apprentice yacht designer until 1962 when he was commissioned to design and build a 12-meter for Baron Bich, a French sportsman and ballpoint pen millionaire. He later designed many production boats and such custom yachts as the successful *Equation* and *Ondine* as well as the ill-fated *Mariner*.

In 1976 Brit came back with a big win in the World One-Ton Championship, skippering *Resolute Salmon,* a new and highly original Chance design.

Lowell North

A former Star boat Olympic champion and head of North Sails, Inc., one of the two most successful producers of racing sails (along with Hood Sailmakers, Inc.), Lowell North sort of backed into ocean racing. But in the last few years he has shown the old-timers a thing or two. He crewed for Dennis Connor in *Stinger,* overall winner of the 1975 SORC, then went on to skipper *Pied Piper,* to the World One-Ton Championship.

In 1976 he was back in the SORC as skipper of the Two-Tonner *Williwaw,* which swept the first three races of the six-race series and finished first overall in the "hot" boat division.

North is known as an "innovator and tinkerer" and makes no secret of his goal. Winning is everything. North has developed the factory team concept into an art form.

James French Baldwin

"Jimbo," one of the more colorful skippers in the sport, in 1976 owned the 68-foot *Sorcery III* which formerly was Jack Potter's *Equation.* Prior to that he campaigned the 61-foot *Sorcery* in a number of races here and abroad, winning line honors in the Fastnet and Miami–Nassau and overall wins in the Venice and Lucaya races and in the Annapolis–Newport Race. A former racer of speedboats and airplanes, he has also been a big game hunter and a deep-sea fisherman. Baldwin was one skipper who never worried about cost. He is now retired from the sport.

Bob Derecktor

Although Bob Derecktor is one of the top custom boat builders in the country, he is more at home at sea at the helm of a fast ocean racer. From his yard in Mamaroneck, New York, have come many of the top yachts since its opening in 1947. Derecktor also has a yard in Dania, Florida, which is used extensively by the fleet racing in the SORC.

Derecktor began building boats when he was fourteen, became a yard foreman at the age of twenty and after a World War II hitch in the Navy, came home to start his own business.

As skipper of *Salty Goose,* which he also designed and built, he touches all the bases.

A near genius in technical matters and as strong as a Sumo wrestler, no job on a boat is beyond his grasp.

Norm Raben

Real-estate investor, land developer and entre-
preneur par excellence until the credit crunch of
the mid-70s, Norm Raben now works for *Sail
Magazine* and sails a stock 38-footer. But in his
heyday, his 50-foot custom yacht, *La Forza del
Destino,* was the scourge of the offshore circuit. In
her he was twice winner of both the Vineyard Race
and the Marblehead–Halifax Race. Norm is less
active in his latest yacht. In 1976 Norm campaigned her to see if the well-crewed stock 38-
footer with excellent sails and gear could compete
with the custom machines . . . she couldn't. *La Pic-
cola Forza* was the last yacht to finish in the 1976
Bermuda Race.

He worked with Ted Turner in founding ORCA,
and in 1977 was elected its Commodore.

Donald Lazarz

Dr. Donald Lazarz of Houston, Texas, is typical
of the new breed of amateur skipper, and he came
into his own in the 1976 SORC as owner and skipper of *Barbarian,* a new and highly successful 41-
foot Two-Ton sloop. Dr. Lazarz, an orthopedic
surgeon, fleeted up from local racing in one-designs
and small cruising boats, his previous boat being an
Erickson 39. He learned how to do his own navigating because, as he put it, "There is not much
place for an owner who can't do anything, on a
Two-Tonner." When he had the money and the
know-how to head for the big time, he went with
who, in his opinion, were the best designer (Peterson) and the best sailmaker (North). Building on
a nucleus of local crew members and a few top-
quality additions, he sails the boat with eight or
nine persons, meanwhile having a stand-by group
of about four or five. In preparation for the SORC,
the boat was delivered in October of 1975, raced
locally in the Galveston Bay area, for tuning and
debugging as well as crew training. The approach
paid off—*Barbarian* was well sailed, was highly
competitive in the 1976 SORC and finished fourth
in class. The doctor estimates the boat cost him
$175,000 "all up" and he has spent about $10,000
to $15,000 to campaign for and in the SORC.

Commenting on his yacht's performance, Lazarz said: "My watch captains are constantly on
the alert for slight changes in wind direction and

velocity and ready to capitalize on any advantage.
The crew is just as competitive. If the off watch is
needed for sail changes, they are up without com-
plaint day or night. The watch on deck is positioned at all times for maximum weight
advantage."

Bob McCullough

Jim Kilroy

John Marshall

Bob Bavier and Wally Frank

Al Van Metre and Franz Schneider, Jr.

Don McNamara

Norm Raben and Archie Cox

Bill Ficker

Bill Ficker and Peter Nicholson

Professor Jerry Milgram

Huey Long and George Moffatt

Peter Grimm and Peter O'Neill

Dick Grossmiller, Bobby Symonette and E. Lloyd Ecclestone, Jr.

Dennis Connor, *left*—Ted Turner and Ted Hood, *right*

Bob Connell and Ken Bechell

Dick Jayson

Vitie Thomas, Jeff Cotter and Mark Usiskin

Buddy Friedrichs

Bill Snaith, Bob Bavier and Bob Derecktor

5   THE DECK WATCH

To keep the yacht moving at top speed at all times, day or night, a skilled, energetic and highly motivated deck watch is needed to assist the watch captain in carrying out his responsibilities. While one watch is on deck the other is below eating, resting or sleeping. A typical watch sequence popular in many yachts is as follows:

0700–1300	Port Watch
1300–1900	Stbd Watch
1900–2300	Port Watch
2300–0300	Stbd Watch
0300–0700	Port Watch
0700–1300	Stbd Watch

This provides an automatic rotation of the schedule each 24-hour period, shorter watches during the night and accommodates well to the meal schedule, with the off watch being fed before going on duty and the on watch eating after being relieved. When not much is going on a certain amount of flexibility can be introduced into the schedule and at other times all hands may be needed on deck for major sail changing evolutions.

On a small yacht the watch may consist of the watch captain and two other persons. On a "maxi" yacht the watch may consist of eight or nine persons. The members of the watch on a given yacht are recruited from many sources. Some are veterans of many passages, others are brand-new to the game. The muscle to perform some of the more athletic jobs such as grinding a winch to trim a large headsail may be all that is required of a beginner. But when to trim and how much, requires experience. Regardless of muscle or experience, the watch must work as a team to be successful, particularly in a blow because of the powerful forces which are generated in the sails and the rigging. The will to win must be equally present in the deck watch as in the afterguard.

In addition to the watch captain, who has worked up to that position through experience at all positions and demonstrated leadership ability, the deck watch includes helmsmen who rotate in that position at regular intervals of about a half hour, sail trimmers, sail changers, gear adjusters, and repairmen. Some are chosen for strength, others for skills, others for a combination of both. On a large yacht, a foredeck boss will supervise major sail changes and adjustments. This requires knowing what sails, lines and gear to use, where they are stored, how they are best rigged and the best sequence of tasks for each evolution to minimize confusion and loss of speed when changing from one sail combination to another.

A crew member may be a brawny eighteen-year-old six-footer, or a thin, medium-height grizzled veteran. But all share common traits—a liking for the sea, compatibility and the willingness to cooperate and produce, particularly under extreme and often dangerous conditions that can lead to dismastings, blown sails and gear failure.

Three crew members were lost overboard in raging storms in the 1974 Round-the-World Race and several yachts never finished and were presumed lost in the 1976 Single-Handed Race from England to the United States. The yacht *Wimoweh* grounded on the coral off Great Isaac Light in the 1974 Miami–Nassau Race and was a total loss; and in the 1976 Miami–Nassau Race, during a rough weather Gulf Stream crossing, the yacht *Mary E. II* cracked her hull and sank. In the latter instances all crew members were saved by nearby competing yachts. However, it is a tribute to the skill and experience of the crews and the safety requirements of the committees that these incidents are rare.

Rough . . .

or calm . . .

The work of the crew is never-ending.

Dick Nye and Steve Lirakas

Adam Ostenfeld *(Jeff Cotter photo)*   Rick Hadley

Chris Wells, John Eggars and Bud Delaney
(Jeff Cotter photo)

Bert Sachse

Maury DeClercq and the Smith brothers

Bill Shay

Bruce Raben

Eddie Kajak

Norm Raben and Jeff Smith

Bodie Rhodes and Brewster Righter

John Potter, Jr., and Steve Kasnet

Charlie Simpson

Hoisting and lowering sails

Checking sail trim

Winch grinding

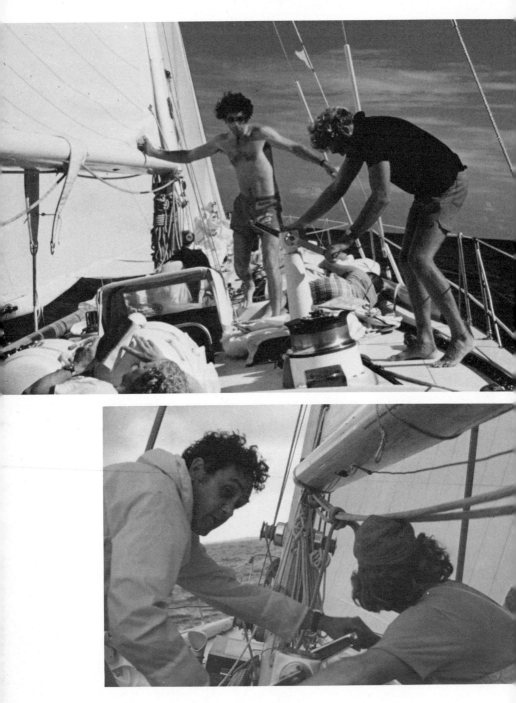

Adjusting halyards

Making emergency repairs

Keeping an eye on the competition

Spinnakers need constant trimming.

And when there's nothing else to do, get the weight on the windward rail.

6   THE PRIZES AND THE PARTIES

The Prizes

Each committee sponsoring a race decides what type and how many prizes to award. Usually there are first, second and third prizes for the owners of the fleet winners on corrected time. Then there may be a like number for the top boats in each class within the fleet.

There may also be special awards within fleet and class for best performing boats over a certain age or of a certain type or from a particular organization, locale or country.

There is usually an award for the first boat to finish on elapsed time in recognition of the fact that this boat actually was the fastest, but this is less significant than the corrected time award because boat size is a function of speed potential and the largest boat may actually be the fastest, but still may not be sailed up to her rating and will plummet in the corrected time standings. These prizes go to the owner or charterer of the yacht.

Crew members aboard an ocean racing yacht are mostly fated to toil in anonymity. On rare occasions a particular event will be rewarded with unaccustomed notoriety—such as falling overboard, being hoisted aloft in the bight of a spinnaker sheet, or being the cook aboard the last boat to finish. But for most, other than the gratitude for a job well done expressed by the skipper after the finish line is crossed, their vauable labors remain unsung and without visible recognition. They know that these are the breaks of the game, and the thrill of offshore competition is reward enough.

But on occasion, there are prizes for the navigator of the winning boat. As an example, the Newport to Bermuda Race provides two real opportunities for which a crew member may personally compete. The navigator of the first yacht to finish is awarded the Schooner Mistress Trophy, and the navigator of the overall winner, the yacht having the best corrected time, is awarded the George W. Mixter Memorial Trophy.

The Mixter Trophy was donated to The Cruising Club of America by Felicie Mixter in memory of her late husband, an avid offshore yachtsman. First awarded to William H. Powers II, navigator of *Baruna,* the winning yacht in 1948, it has been a highly prized Bermuda Race Trophy ever since.

George W. Mixter, for whom the cup was named, was born in Rock Island, Illinois, in 1876. A Yale graduate, he worked as an industrial and consulting engineer—but his consuming hobby up until his death in 1947 was the study and practice of navigation. Mixter's classic book, *Primer of Navigation,* published in

1940, was well timed. With its emphasis on practicality, it became a best-selling textbook with students in the naval services during World War II. It was one of the texts I studied as a Cadet at New London in 1942 and put into practice aboard the schooner *Teragram,* donated by Mixter to the Coast Guard Academy as a training vessel in 1941. The *Primer*'s Fifth Edition, published in 1967, is still going strong.

Mixter's *Teragram* was a regular entrant in the Bermuda Race in the thirties. Due to the eccentricities of the Gulf Stream, the Bermuda Race places unusual importance on navigation, compared to other deep-water contests. During the Race, George Mixter would train young crew members eager to master the challenging navigational aspects. One of his students in the 1932 Race was Charles "Chick" Larkin II. When Mixter put up a special trophy for the winning Bermuda navigator in 1946, Chick, not surprisingly, was the winner. Chick is also the only repeat winner of the Mixter Memorial Trophy to date, taking it in 1958 and 1960 in *Finisterre* and again in 1966 in *Thunderbird.*

Early winners were William H. Powers in *Baruna,* 1948, and Edward R. Greeff in *Argyll,* 1950. Then came John Barney in Dick Nye's previous *Carina* in 1952, Daniel D. Strohmeier, skipper and navigator of *Malay* in 1954, and Corwith Cramer, Jr., navigator in *Finisterre*'s first of three Bermuda victories in 1956. Daniel Bickford charted the venerable schooner *Nina*'s victory in 1962, Dr. Ernest H. McVay won it in *Burgoo* in 1964 and Robert N. Bavier, Jr., followed his America's Cup win with a winning navigator's passage in *Robin* in 1968.

To complete the record, the author won it in 1970 aboard *Carina,* Ted Hicks claimed it in 1972 in *Noryema,* Peter Bowker won it in 1974 in *Scaramouche* and Dick Stimson in 1976 in *Running Tide.*

Last but not least, in some races there is awarded a prize for the cook aboard the last boat over the line on elapsed time, in recognition that the longer the boat is racing the more meals must be served.

The author accepts Mixter Trophy, 1970 Bermuda Race. *(Bermuda News Bureau Photo)*

Prize-giving at Bermuda

Navy Kennedy Cup for collegiate crews racing in 44-foot yawls

Bermuda Trophy is modeled after . . .

Mount Hill Light on St. David's Head

Admiral's Cup and Fastnet Trophies

Lipton Cup (Florida) Trophies

SORC Series Trophies

First-to-Finish and Class A First Trophies for Miami–Nassau Race, won by *Equation,* 1974

Ted Hood and crew, 1974 SORC Series winners

West Germany's team wins the 1973 Admiral's Cup.

Shorty Trimingham accepts the Trophy for Best Finishing Bermuda Yacht from Governor
Leather, 1976 Bermuda Race.

German Frers takes the Snaith Memorial Trophy for the designer of the winning Bermuda Race
yacht, 1974.

Jim Baldwin accepts First-to-Finish Trophy for the 1973
Fastnet.

Johnny Potter proudly displays the First-to-Finish
Trophy for the inaugural Ocean Triangle Race, 1974.

Monica Theslof wins the cook's Trophy, 1974 Bermuda
Race.

The Parties

Before and after the big races there are usually a variety of parties for the committees, contestants and their friends. These take the form of welcoming get-togethers before the race and of gatherings to celebrate the successful conclusion of a race or to award the trophies to the victors.

In past years these have mostly been somewhat formal events requiring rather strict dress codes and impeccable behavior. But some had deteriorated to the extent that a clause was inserted in some race instructions to make the skipper of each boat responsible for the behavior of his crew at such events under penalty of disqualification for gross violation of etiquette. This has served to check the trend.

There are still race parties where the old-time ambience has been preserved, as can be seen in the accompanying photographs.

The Guild Hall, Plymouth, England

Coral Reef Yacht Club, Florida

On the dock. Newport, R.I.

Steel band performs at Royal Bermuda Yacht Club.

Chicago Yacht Club

Max Aiken's waterfront home at Cowes, Isle of Wight

Cruising Club of America Raft Up, Hamilton, Bermuda

Entering Government House, Hamilton, Bermuda

Government House

Government House

Australian Admiral's Cup Team relaxes at poolside, Plymouth, England.

Lunch at Paradise Island, Nassau

Pilot House, Nassau

Storm Trysail Club party, Miami Beach, Florida

Hotel Bermudiana, Hamilton, Bermuda

Crew party, Paget, Bermuda

Dockside champagne, Fort Lauderdale, Florida

Beach picnic, Paradise Island, Nassau

Bull session, Chicago Yacht Club

Organizing for Performance

PART II

There's no alibi needed after giving your all and losing to good solid competition. Some say that if you don't win, all that effort was for nothing. Well, winning is a big part of it, but I can tell you this—you lose more than you win.

—Norm Raben
Successful offshore skipper of
La Forza del Destino

The *X* factor in offshore racing is organization. A well-designed yacht with a poorly organized crew won't win races.

How well the crew is selected, assigned, trained and led will determine how well it will perform as a unit when stacked against equal competition.

No one has all the answers, but an examination of the many variables and interrelated factors can lead to an approach that will eliminate the more obvious disaster areas.

Here are a few tips on how to put it all together and make it work.

7 THE OVERALL VIEW

It's the day of the big race. The offshore boats are milling around the starting line waiting for the gun for the first class, one of five into which the fleet of 150 is divided. The planning, preparation and cocktail parties are behind them. On each boat the hope for a big win is at its highest; but for some, victory is already beyond their grasp. They have not taken advantage of all the opportunities available for improved performance.

An area of opportunity that is becoming more and more obvious, as yachts become closer in performance potential, is in the management and organization of the boat. This is a neglected area and it is somewhat of a paradox as a large proportion of today's offshore skippers are hard-nosed successful businessmen who run their businesses very well. Otherwise, they couldn't afford to stay in the game. But do they run their boats like their businesses? Sometimes.

You may wonder why a businesslike approach would be applicable to this field, particularly if you hold the view that offshore yacht racing is mostly fun and relaxation in the fresh air and is a release from the business world. But it really isn't, unless you just want to take it easy, go cruising and not worry about where you finish. To enter a race implies that you have more than a passing interest in winning it, and that you are willing to exert a lot of effort to do so. Top boats appearing consistently in the winner's circle are run in a very businesslike way indeed. The days of friendly competition, where the skipper with a few close friends and relatives enjoys a leisurely couple of days offshore, and once in a while, by being in the right place at the right time, takes a cup, are pretty much over, to the lament of those who can't stand the competition.

People complain about "factory teams," but complaining about them is not going to beat them. A competitive skipper will leave the likes of Cousin Charlie at home and sign on the best crew he can get, provided he has the boat and the potential to attract them. He can still take Cousin Charlie on the club cruise where the living is easy.

The bigger the boat, the larger the crew, the more the skipper has to depend on others to get things done. Functions have to be defined, crew members have to be selected who can perform them well and assignments have to be definitely made so that there is little overlapping of responsibilities and a minimum of confusion over who does what—particularly when the going gets rough. The objective should be to free the skipper for major decision-making, seeing the big picture and welding the crew into an effective team.

A recent quote in a business journal seems quite applicable. Dr. George S. Odiorne, Dean of the University of Utah College of Business, said, in discussing

115

leadership style, ". . . organizations in which the boss presumes to know every-thing, do everything, make every decision, solve every problem and have every new idea are limited in scope, have a poor track record for long-run survival, and are terrible places to work." Boats run that way are no fun to sail aboard, either.

Following the same reasoning, on boats where the skipper has to do everything because his crew does not have the experience to help him, a similar situation would result.

A good example of the other way is *Noryema,* 1972 Bermuda Race winner. When Ron Amey, her owner, had to leave for England just before race time, he had selected, trained and organized his crew so well that even though he was not aboard they functioned smoothly. Ted Hicks, her navigator, being close to the strategic picture, was able to take over as acting skipper and the results are in the record books.

There is an old seagoing expression, "different ships, different long splices," meaning there are many ways to achieve the same seagoing objective.

One problem that is apparent in assembling a "hot-shot" crew is the ability to manage them and make them a cooperative unit rather than a bunch of independent virtuosos. The sharper and more experienced the individual crew members are, the more leadership is required to keep control. But, in business, would you want to have a sales manager who is a hard-driving, aggressive, independent thinker with whom you not always agree, but who brings in the business; or a placid "yes man" whom everybody enjoys having lunch with but who can't sell anything? The same thing is true on a boat. If you have gotten the best sail trimmer in the business, you should listen to his ideas and let him do his thing; but he should still realize that you are the skipper.

This does not mean that you need "all-stars" in your crew. In fact, boats have sometimes suffered by having too many individual and divergent opinions on almost every subject; and if a leadership vacuum exists, someone is going to fill it. You can take a different approach and train your own group from scratch, but this takes a lot of practice before you're ready for the big race. In short, there needs to be a nice balance between capability and availability. Emotionalism, though hard to eliminate, has no place in crew selection, either. Compatibility is important and usually comes naturally with an experienced crew member, or he or she wouldn't have gotten the experience in the first place.

The "will to win" is most important. As Ted Turner has said in talking about a good crew, "I want veterans who can go the limit, who can stick it out in tough going even if we have a slower boat."

If you think you have the right hull and rig, are satisfied that your rating is as low as possible, know the strengths and weaknesses of your boat's performance and have your sail inventory well tested, it will pay to spend a little time getting your crew organized.

First—set your goal. Do you want to win or do you just want the fresh air and sunshine? If the former, do you want to win locally or in regional, national or international competition? Whatever your goal, identify all the tasks that need doing on your boat in the race to achieve the goal and write them down. Under headings such as the following, place each of the identifiable functions such as:

1) Navigation 3) Logistics
2) Boat Speed 4) Maintenance

For example—under navigation would come equipment, charts, publications. Under the boat speed department would come helming and choice of sails, sail trim and bottom condition. Under logistics would come menu planning, buying and stowing of groceries. Spare parts and having everything working would come under maintenance. Once you get this list organized, and the above ideas are by no means complete, the next step is to decide who is going to do what. And this, of course, depends upon the size of the crew and their individual capabilities. No two boats are organized alike and different approaches can be equally successful, provided there are no loose ends. Leave as little as possible undone.

You do not need to be a Captain Bligh to run a taut ship. Rather, the implication of a taut ship should be that you have organized and selected your crew so that all the functions are covered and assigned to people who know how to do them. Then, once you're organized, let them perform. Some of the best skippers do very little aboard the boat themselves during a race other than monitoring and peaking the team performance and making crucial policy decisions. Most of their work was done, and done well, before the start. As Norm Raben, the swashbuckling skipper of *La Forza del Destino,* puts it, "I am the glue that holds it all together." Many crewmen will agree that the worst place for a skipper is at the helm when something more important needs his attention. An outstanding helmsman, who is concentrating on only that job, is no more a threat to the skipper's ego than is an outstanding, highly skilled machinist to the owner of a machine shop. The commanding officer of a Navy destroyer would never think of taking the wheel during an intricate maneuver, but he would make sure that an excellent helmsman was in that position.

Just as you would plan a new product line or a sales campaign, you should also plan your approach to a particular race—and as the race progresses and conditions change, amend the plan accordingly, as you do in your own business. Decisions on an offshore race do not have to be "hip shots." There is usually enough time for discussion and evaluation of whatever facts happen to be available before acting. I can recall a race where a disastrous decision was made without deliberation. We were nearing the mark in a dense fog. We thought we were close, but the skipper disagreed and sailed six miles farther before we could confirm our position. We had actually passed less than a mile from the mark. We could have taken all the sails down, thus stopping the boat from going the wrong way while we discussed the pros and cons of what to do. A better decision could have been the result, a mistake could have been avoided, and we could have saved at least an hour in time. This may seem like a ridiculous example, but it should prove the point.

Not only will better organization win you more races, but it will also be self-perpetuating. Good crew members like well-organized boats. A satisfied crew will stick with you and you will have a ready supply of replacements on the off chance that you might have a vacancy. On the other hand, there are poorly organized offshore boats that run through as many as 50 people in the course of a racing season. Just the recruiting process has to take time away from other necessary activities.

Another related aspect is loyalty. As the old seagoing expression points out, "Loyalty down begets loyalty up." The skipper who treats his crew right will be repaid many times over in performance. A crewman's one mistake need not mean banishment. Everyone is human. Give him another chance and perhaps he will surprise you. Also the good skipper doesn't ditch the crew that helped him qualify for the big race.

One of the best recent examples of the application of management principles in offshore yacht racing was that of *Charisma* campaigned by manufacturer Jesse Phillips of Dayton, Ohio, a city far removed from the ocean. Jesse's expertise, perfected as head of Phillips Industries, a leading producer of mobile homes, is in logistics, planning and organization. When *Charisma* was launched she was just another boat. In the ensuing three years she was heavily campaigned and her skipper was well in evidence at award ceremonies at home and abroad. Jesse recognized early in the game that the right people in the right slots working as a team were what made the difference—and that his best role was as "Chairman of the Board."

There are many types of leadership styles and many different ways to make an organization successful. Each skipper should apply his own talents in the best possible way.

Crew of *Charisma* takes a beer break after the race.

8 THE ESSENTIAL TRIUMVIRATE

A triumvirate is defined as a coalition of three men in office or authority; government by three.

We have talked about how an ocean racing yacht should be organized. And we all know how a well-functioning organization aboard a boat will help to win races. Let's talk about the necessarily close interrelationship among the skipper, the watch captain on duty and the navigator. The old Latin word *triumviratus* well expresses the relationship among these three persons who must function as one in order for them to be as effective as possible in their respective roles.

The ideal skipper is one who has been a watch captain and a navigator under other skippers. It helps if the navigator is one who has also at other times been a skipper or a watch captain; and a watch captain, best to relate to his role, should have had experience as a skipper and should be able to perform the duties of a navigator. Only in this way can each of them fully understand and appreciate the demands and the requirements of one another's role. This is not to say that a boat cannot be well sailed if each of the three has only experience in a single function. However, to do so and be completely successful requires an uncommon sensitivity and rapport.

It might be well first to break down the responsibilities of each slot to see where they differ before we show why the team concept is so important. The skipper provides the environment that makes it all possible (which includes leadership ability, competitive drive to excel and the money and time to put everything together) and accepts the full responsibility for the results. This latter can't be delegated as all final decisions are up to him. The navigator provides technical, tactical and strategic know-how, maintains the plot, keeps track of the overall picture and synthesizes the boat's information system. In this he serves in an advisory capacity to both the skipper and the watch captain. The watch captain, as the skipper's direct representative, is responsible for keeping the boat moving at top speed during his watch under all conditions, and for getting the most out of the watch on duty through efficient and correct sail changes, proper helmsmanship assignments and calm and comprehensive instructions to his watchmates. All of these must be consistent with the overall strategy as laid down by the skipper in conjunction with the technical recommendations of the navigator unless changes are required due to changed conditions.

It should be evident that communication among these three persons must be constant and effective. When it is not, victory can be jeopardized.

Some Real Life Examples

Here are a few recent, real life examples from a representative sampling of boats. The accounts have been edited to preserve anonymity.

• The skipper and navigator agreed upon a heading to steer for the next mark which was 25 miles away. The sea was smooth and the breeze was light. The apparent wind direction on the heading chosen resulted in a close reach with appropriate sails set accordingly. Under the conditions, no leeway was figured into the heading to be steered, but the expected course made good was high of the mark. Both the skipper and the navigator turned in for a much needed nap, requesting a call when five miles from the mark. While they were asleep the wind velocity increased, but neither was called until the time previously indicated. In the meantime the boat had made significant leeway to the extent that she fell short of the mark even though she had to be sailed close-hauled in the last few miles. The course could easily have been corrected earlier to lay the mark if the watch captain had been told that no correction had been made for leeway or if he had called either the skipper or the navigator earlier than requested for additional suggestions. Could there also have been the element here of the watch captain feeling that he was in command of the situation and felt it unnecessary to disturb his fellow triumvirs?

• When nearing landfall, the navigator indicated the present position of the boat to the skipper. He did not point out that the position was "suspect" because of inadequate inputs. The skipper relied upon it as a solid position and formulated his final strategy accordingly. Upon making landfall, it was found that the track was off by 12 miles, causing an unnecessary addition of nearly one-and-a-half hours to the elapsed time for the race. Had the navigator explained the degree of reliability of the position, the skipper could have devised a different strategy which would have reduced the additional distance traveled.

• During a long offshore leg in poor visibility, the navigator turned in and left a call to be awakened in three hours. The watch on deck became preoccupied with other matters relating to tactics and sail changes. The navigator was not called as requested and slept for six hours until he awakened without a call. During the period he was asleep, the hourly deck log was not properly maintained by the watch and the inputs to the DR (dead reckoning) plot were lost. The plot could not accurately be restarted because lines-of-position were unavailable.

• In the crucial 50 miles before landfall, the skipper directed the watch captain to ease off from an on-wind course which would have maintained the rhumb line to the finish; the reason being to take the strain off the rig in the heavy weather conditions. He instructed the watch captain not to bother the navigator who assumed the proper heading was being steered. The result was that landfall was made six miles to leeward of where expected. This added two hours to the elapsed time. Had the navigator checked the heading actually steered, a discussion with the watch captain and the skipper would have been in order.

• The boat was broad-reaching at hull speed under spinnaker in a rainstorm with zero visibility. The navigator, realizing after several closely spaced electronic fixes that the boat was not making the required course good due to a leeward set, recognized that a radical heading change to windward was indicated, but was reluctant to make such a significant recommendation without further checks. He did not alert the watch captain to this eventuality until after additional calculations were made. The result was that by the time additional off-watch crewmen were awakened to make the necessary sail changes, the heading change was made too late and the boat wound up to leeward of the finish line.

• The navigator advised the skipper that the boat was standing into shallow water. The watch captain agreed. The skipper called them "overly cautious" because other boats were in the immediate area on the same heading, and proceeded on course. The boat went aground.

A replay of the above incidents, but with things done right, is not hard to imagine. In fact, in the race where the fifth incident took place, another boat did make the sail changes and heading change in time and beat the 98-boat fleet, but with a corrected time only two-and-a-half minutes ahead of the second boat. In the grounding incident, other boats in the area also grounded. Still others changed course in time and did not.

Does this convince you that the members of your triumvirate should be on the same wavelength at all times? Could the right way make the difference between winning and not winning? There will always be some competitors who are doing things right! You can't afford to forget this in the heat of battle.

9 THE NAVIGATOR'S ROLE

The relationships among navigator, owner and skipper of a sailing yacht are delicate and complex. When all of these roles are filled by the same individual, there is no problem defining where one starts and the other ends. But there are instances where owner, skipper and navigator are three different individuals, and other combinations are also possible. This can lead to problems if all tasks are not clearly understood, definitely assigned and agreed upon.

We have heard of instances where an indecisive skipper's prerogatives have been usurped by a navigator, as well as occasions where a navigator's input has been thoughtlessly ignored in the decision-making process. On at least one occasion a navigator was actually "fired" by a dissatisfied owner during an ocean race with two days remaining before the finish. These extremes only serve to point up how the situation can go adrift when the proper elements are ignored.

It is no happenstance that these relationships are well defined in the case of a naval vessel at sea. Many years of trials and tribulations have brought it to its present highly regulated state wherein all parties have a clear understanding of who does what. This rigid but effective set-up is not always practical or even possible on a pleasure boat.

On a windjammer, be it ocean racer or leisurely cruiser, there is often a loosely structured arrangement and a wide variation in the approach used. The sharing of tasks depends on a multitude of factors, but mostly upon a forthright relationship between navigator and skipper.

Frequently, the navigator will have additional duties assigned, quite unrelated to navigation. This is all right on a cruise or an overnight race where navigation is not a full-time job. But in a highly competitive, lengthy and navigationally demanding race, where constant accurate positioning is essential, proper attention to the task rates a full-time effort.

An owner, if only by virtue of his investment, must have his wishes respected. What these are will first depend upon his interest in and understanding of the navigator's role. He may want to be his own navigator. If not, the navigator he selects must establish his credibility through experience and past performance and be able to articulate this role to be effective.

Navigational Duties

In the general sense, what does the navigator's function entail, whoever performs it? Primarily it is the safe and efficient guiding of the yacht to its intended destination. The preparation phase should include:

- Recommendations as to navigational equipment, charts and publications to be carried, and location and layout of the navigator's station and storage areas.
- Supervision of equipment checks and preparation of calibration curves and tables sufficiently ahead of departure to allow time for remedial action.
- Supervision of obtaining, updating and maintaining relevant charts and navigational publications including the addition of supplementary information specifically applicable to the intended voyage.

The operational phase should include:

- Being able to operate all navigational equipment on board and keep it in working condition.
- Daily checks of compasses and timekeeping devices.
- Maintaining an accurate, continuous plot of the boat's position using all available means.
- Compiling and analyzing available weather information.
- Making navigational reports as scheduled and furnishing requested navigational information in a timely and accurate manner, indicating the degree of reliability in each case.

The detailed application of the above will depend upon the particular yacht. For example, the skipper may want a neat and clean master plot maintained on a separate chart with fixes or DR positions added every four hours. The assignment of tasks will depend upon the mix of skills of the people involved. In any case, establishing who does what, when and how is necessary. Finally, all should recognize that the ultimate decision-making authority remains with the owner.

An illustration of the ideal: when Carleton Mitchell was putting together the highly successful ocean-racing yacht *Finisterre* (three times Bermuda Race winner), Corwith Cramer, Jr., his prospective navigator, was consulted on navigational aspects of construction and equipage. When the boat was in commission the navigator had what he needed to perform, was expected to do so, and knew without question what his duties were.

Adaptability and Compatibility

Adaptability is another important quality. This is helped if the navigator is also a sailor. Although the skills of navigation are similar whether on an ocean liner, an airliner, or a 40-foot sloop, their application is different. It's not easy for a big ship navigator or an airline captain to step directly aboard a sloop and adapt to the relatively cramped and unstable platform, the lack of creature comforts and the rudimentary equipment dictated by space and power supply available, without some prior experience with that environment.

The navigator should strive to develop and maintain a good working relationship with the watch captains. They can be of great assistance in many ways, and particularly in furnishing inputs for the DR plot.

The navigator should also be tolerant of the foibles of his fellow crew members.

Critiquing the "naviguesser's" performance is a favorite pastime, as is the constant query, "How many miles to go?" A satisfactory answer should be available for the latter and a good-humored reaction to the former will keep it in perspective.

Endurance

An ocean race produces many different kinds of weariness. Ideally, you should give your all, and make it last until the finish line is crossed. A winch-grinder's weariness is mostly physical; the navigator's is both physical and mental.

A watch-stander is relieved, hits the sack and can often forget it all until his next watch. The navigator is really never off duty. He has found the mark this time, but there is always another one ahead. As a top navigator recently told me, "I'd gladly trade my kind of fatigue after a gruelling race for that of a watch-stander anytime." Only when the finish line has been crossed and the boat is safely in port is the navigator able to relax.

This means that he must be very aware of his own endurance capability and pace himself. He needs to be just as sharp at the finish as he was at the start. An experienced navigator knows this is not as easy as it sounds. The only one who can really gauge it is the navigator himself. In the race planning, he should devise some sort of rough schedule that will indicate the points in the race where full-time attention is needed and points where there is opportunity for a nap without losing race continuity or looking like a goof-off.

He should get a good night's sleep before the race starts. In the weeks before the race he should do as much work as possible so that the work load during the race is cut down to only those things that cannot be done previously. During the race, instead of staying up and telling sea stories with the off-watch when the going is easy, he should turn in and rest and save the casual conversation for the post-race cocktail parties.

But the navigator should be up when each watch changes so the on-coming watch captain can be briefed. This would include a rundown on the progress during the previous watch, explaining the present position and outlining what may be expected in the forthcoming watch.

Shared Duties

If there are tough situations ahead requiring his full-time efforts, these should be planned and full use made of available and qualified members of the watch to assist. The navigator should not hesitate to ask for this type of assistance as it helps him to perform more efficiently and minimizes physical wear and tear. Climbing the ladder from the chart table to the deck to take frequent visual or RDF bearings, then going down to the chart table to plot them can use up a lot of energy, particularly on a boat with a 10-foot ladder. With a crew member on deck who is qualified to take the bearings and relay them below, the navigator can stay at the chart table, conserve energy, get more fixes in the same period of time and actually be more efficient.

As an example, in the 1973 Vineyard Race aboard *Equation,* we were entering Long Island Sound through Plum Gut at about 10:30 P.M. It was dark, but visibility was good. We were tacking into the narrow entrance with a 4.5 knot current pushing us to windward. Frequent fixes were vital to minimize the number of tacks and to avoid grounding or being swept to the wrong side of Orient Point Light. Don McNamara was on deck taking visual bearings on three selected lights in sequence. I was maintaining a continuous plot at the chart table using those bearings plus soundings. With information from this plot, Watch Captain Bob McCullough was able to make a safe, speedy and effective passage through the Gut.

The hourly log is normally maintained by the watch under the direction of the watch captain. This, to be faithfully followed, needs a complete understanding between the watch captains and the navigator. An extension of this function could be for the watch also to advance the DR position on the chart, again assuming the capability is available, but with the responsibility still the navigator's, for double-checking the plot.

Other tasks lend themselves to this approach, such as tuning in and recording scheduled weather broadcasts or reading and recording sea temperatures when needed at more frequent intervals than each hour. A lot depends upon the demands of the racecourse and the organization and skills aboard the boat. All this requires a good knowledge of the capabilities of the various crew members and establishment of effective working relationships.

Short races in pilot waters, such as the Block Island Race, can be a nonstop marathon for the conscientious navigator. Others, like the Bermuda Race, allow a daily routine to be established when offshore, with time for rest and rejuvenation. But there is still a steady drain on effectiveness. A difficult finish situation should always be expected in any race, and a reserve of energy to meet and surmount what develops should be available.

The Boat's Information Center

More and more the navigator is becoming the boat's strategic and tactical information center rather than just a position finder. Therefore, all the sources of inputs should be operative so that evaluated summaries can be presented to the skipper and the watch captains for decision making as the race progresses. Sharpness, alertness and completeness in the navigator's presentations can often mean the margin of victory.

There is another aspect. When a crew is fresh, compatibility is at its height and people are agreeable. But unexpected seasickness can take its toll; injuries can put crew members out of action; equipment can fail when you need it the most. When fatigue sets in and the going gets rough, personalities can change, tempers can flare and even the best of working arrangements can go awry. So whatever plans you have set up may need amending as you go along. Keep it flexible.

But no matter how the navigator feels, he should, for the benefit of the crew, always try to display a spirit of quiet confidence and optimism. There are a great many questions asked of a navigator during a race by crew members, often at times when it is inconvenient to stop his calculations to answer them. This can be an energy drain but it can be minimized by anticipating some of them and posting the answers in a readily accessible space away from the navigator's station. Items to include would be weather reports, known positions of other boats, handicap differences of the key rivals converted to time for this race, boats known to have finished, and times of finish. It's also a good idea to display a simplified chart of the racecourse (on long races) with updated positions posted thereon to eliminate the frequent, "How many miles to go?"

None of this is intended to imply that other positions on a competitively sailed ocean racer are easy berths. Rather, it is to show how the approach taken by a navigator to *his* task, different from all the others, can significantly help him to perform as well as humanly possible.

Al Dahms

Al is a Coast Guard Commander, age forty. He learned his navigational skill in the Class of 1958 at the U.S. Coast Guard Academy in New London, Connecticut, and further added to it with a concentrated course in air navigation while pursuing flight training at the Naval Air Station in Corpus Christi, Texas, in 1960.

He was on the sailing team at the Coast Guard Academy both in dinghys and in offshore racing in Academy yachts in Long Island Sound.

In the early '60s he mastered Sunfish racing while stationed in Bermuda and made his debut in the offshore game in the 1966 SORC in Don McNamara's *Tara*. He continued with *Tara* in the Bermuda Race, additional SORCs and a Halifax Race, meanwhile fitting in stints aboard Peter Grimm's *Escapade* and Ralph Ryder's *Poirette*. In the late '60s, Al was stationed in Alaska and was pretty much unavailable. In 1970 he came back aboard Ralph Ryder's 50-foot *Phantom* and kept that berth through 1974 aboard the new 66-foot *Phantom*.

"My favorite race of all is the Newport–Bermuda and I hope they keep it pure without electronics," Al says.

Peter Bowker

Peter was born in Manchester, England, and got his sea legs in the Royal Navy. He was soon interested in sailing and learned cruising navigation on his own to get from "point A to point B." The list of boats he has navigated is legendary beginning with the Montego Bay Race in 1963 in *Bolero*. He has sailed aboard *Windward Passage, Escapade, Audacious, Figaro IV, Lightnin'* in both the 1973 SORC and the Admiral's Cup in England, and, of course, *Scaramouche* when she won the Bermuda Race in 1974.

Peter did not start out as a navigator but served in other positions early in his career and helped out the navigator or pinch-hit when necessary. He feels that this is a good way to start —"get exposed." He says, "The outstanding quality of a good navigator is assurance, based on a broad background of experience and the ability to withstand seasickness."

His favorite race is the Fastnet, second only to the Montego Bay Race which he feels has an ideal course but which is not as competitive due to the smaller-sized fleet. Listening to top skippers trying to convince him to go with them in the next race is proof of his own "assurance."

Pat Reynolds

Larry Huntington

Pat is the Dean of our representative navigators. He was born in Newport, R.I., and went to sea for 15 years on merchant ships, mostly as a deck officer with U.S. Lines where he learned his basic navigational skills. In 1941 he went aboard Pan American flying clippers as a navigator and is still with Pan Am in a navigator's capacity. His first Bermuda Race was in 1954 in the ketch *Hallie* and he has since completed eight more Bermudas.

Pat sailed the first of his five Fastnet's in 1955, his first SORC years back in Bill Snaith's *Figaro III* and in 1969 he navigated *Kialoa II* when she won the Transatlantic Race. He has been aboard *Kahili* since before the 1974 Bermuda Race.

Because he has raced in a variety of boats and under a variety of organizational concepts, he has a fine appreciation of the need for the navigator, watch captains and the skipper to be well attuned to be successful.

Bob Berglund

Bob hails from St. Cloud, Minnesota, one of the unlikeliest spots for a seafarer. At thirty-one he is the youngest of our examples. Bob had no formal navigational schooling and although he spent four years in the U.S. Coast Guard, it was all ashore. In 1962 at seventeen he started sailing aboard offshore boats. In 1964 he was in the Chicago–Mackinac Race and in the following year he sailed in *Beau Geste* in the Annapolis–Newport Race as watch captain, continuing on that boat through the 1969 SORC. Later he sailed aboard *Sonny* picking up some navigational experience along the way.

Bob added to his navigational experience by ferrying a variety of boats back from Bermuda and in 1974, his first time as navigator, he helped guide *Recluta* to a third place overall in the Bermuda Race.

Larry grew up in the Long Island Sound area, so sailing was a natural interest. He sailed in the 1952 Bermuda Race as cabin boy aboard *Jane Dore III* and drifted into offshore types rather than one-designs. In 1957, at age twenty-one and just out of college, he spent the summer aboard Blunt White's *White Mist,* participating in the Transatlantic and Fastnet races. With Chick Larkin on board as navigator, Larry was able to learn from the master of them all.

That fall, at Coast Guard OCS he added further to his navigational background. After serving his three-year stint he was back in offshore racing aboard Arthur Hughes's *Lady Linden,* where in his first time as navigator, he helped to win Class C in the 1962 Bermuda Race.

Since 1963 he has mostly sailed aboard Dick Nye's several *Carina*s in Bermudas, Transatlantics and Fastnets but has found time for some races in *Equation* and the 1973 SORC in the celebrated *Cascade.*

His advice to all navigators, "Be humble and have an honest and open relationship with the skipper."

10 THE GALLEY AND THE COOK

One of the most important slots in an offshore crew is the job of cook—yet it is often one of the least appreciated unless the skipper is a gourmet. Even then, the differences in tastes and dietary preferences still make it difficult. The working conditions, particularly in bad weather, and the limited facilities contribute to the cook's problems. Susceptibility to seasickness is a key disqualifying factor. Good planning and preparation are essential. Since very little instructional material is extant covering this vital task, I asked two experienced sailing cooks to help me with the details. Both sail as cooks in their husbands' yachts and perform the planning and logistics for races when other cooks take their place aboard.

Ann Lampman's husband, Ed, skippers *Ginger,* a Ranger 37, and Celia Jayson's husband, Dick, skippers *Pride,* a Swan 44. *Ginger* is campaigned along the New Jersey coast and in Chesapeake Bay with an occasional Annapolis–Newport Race added. *Pride* is extensively raced in Long Island Sound, the Chesapeake, the New England area and in the Bermuda Race. *Ginger* does not have a freezer, *Pride* does. Both have a stove and an oven. Here is what they had to say:

ED: How do you look at the cook's job?

ANN: The galley on a racing machine leaves a lot to be desired. It helps to possess the agility of a circus performer and the cast-iron stomach of a parachute jumper to perform the task. Rough or smooth, hot or cold, dry or wet, energy must be kept at a high level, and that's the job of the cook, regardless of conditions. Those enthusiastic, hardworking crew members deserve the best possible rations—hot, hearty and tasty.

CELIA: You must decide where to start and know how to plan. Whether you are cooking on an overnight race or cooking for a transatlantic race, it won't be an impossible task if you take it step by step.

ED: Let's do that. Where do we start?

CELIA: First, know your galley's facilities. Preparing your meals while on board depends on the galley's equipment and the amount of stowage space available to store your food. Does the galley's stove have one, two or three burners? Is there an oven? Is there a refrigerator, or is there an ice chest? Is there a freezer? How much stowage? Is it dry stowage? These are the questions to ask and these factors will limit the type of meals you will serve.

ED: What about menu planning?

CELIA: Always keep in mind that the meals should be easy to prepare, easy to serve and eat and easy to clean up. To determine what amounts to buy, you need to know the number of crew aboard and the approximate length of the race. You should take into consideration food likes and dislikes of your crew members. If

Ann Lampman
(Ed Lampman photo)

Celia Jayson

Roz Curtis illustrates a cook's frustration
in heavy weather.

Archie Cox, a tall cook in a galley with a
low overhead

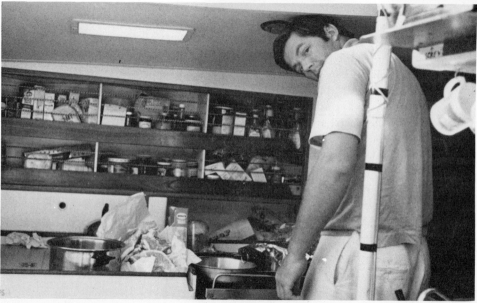

you don't know, ask them. Some can't tolerate onions, fish, etc. You don't want to make a person ill accidentally if he is allergic to shellfish but didn't know it was in the casserole.

Also, take into consideration the temperature during the race. An oven going for two hours could be very pleasant in Nova Scotia, but might prove uncomfortable in the Gulf Stream where hot-weather meals are more apropos. Plan on some rough weather meals and emergency meals in case the race is longer than anticipated.

In designing the actual menu, list all breakfasts, lunches and dinners for each day. Decide what the main dishes for dinner will be. This will help to determine the most compatible vegetables, salads and starches for each main dish. Strive for variety.

ANN: Planning the food supply for a three- to five-day race begins a month or more ahead. At race practices or at crew member meetings, individual likes and dislikes can be discussed. Since cooking facilities are limited and space is at a minimum for both storage and preparation, it is advisable to keep the meals simple, using one-pot meals when possible. That will make the cleanup crew happy too.

Listed among the supplies for a long race must be a sizable quantity of canned goods to assure enough food after the perishables are gone. Canned vegetables can also augment the dinner menu. I do not recommend frozen vegetables on a boat without a freezer. They're perishable and take longer to prepare.

Planning for an overnight race is comparatively simple compared to a three- to five-day race. You don't have to worry about spoilage or extended refrigeration. One large block of ice is sufficient. The main meal can be precooked and frozen and is usually a one-pot dinner—stew or chili, or something that can be heated easily on top of the stove. Include hot rolls and a fresh green salad with either fresh or canned fruit or canned pudding and cookies or brownies or loaf cake for dessert with coffee. Creamed dried beef on canned fried potatoes, or hash and eggs; or if conditions are bad, maybe just coffee and sweet rolls are sufficient for breakfast.

Variety in meal planning is not as important when the crew is aboard for only overnight. Most of the crews I know prefer a nice thick meat and cheese sandwich. On overnights, as well as day races, I make up the sandwiches and pack them in plastic bags, ready to grab and serve as soon as we have a downwind leg. My great favorite on a short race is cold oven-fried chicken, with lots of salt and pepper. It always makes me feel better if the weather is rough.

For either race I always include lots of fresh fruit and washed and cut up fresh vegetables, raisins, crackers and cheese for nibbling and, of course, beer and soft drinks. On hot summer days, iced tea and nice juicy, cold navel oranges are in demand as a change from soft drinks, beer and canned juices. If the weather is damp and cold, hot instant soup in a mug is welcome. Water for coffee or tea or cocoa can be kept hot on a gimbaled bracket Sterno stove throughout the race and makes serving a hot beverage simple.

One cannot ignore sweets. Homemade cookies are great, if they are stored in

Dina Chance takes a break from galley chores.

a plastic freezer container. Sweet cakes and bread are also welcome, but they must not be the crumbly kind. Banana nut bread, brownies, apple cinnamon cake and carrot cake can be wrapped well in silver foil and a plastic bag and served sliced with breakfast, lunch or dinner. Bags of candies (hard or soft) are a nifty sweet treat. The six-pack cans of individual puddings are also great for snacking as well as dessert.

CELIA: Here's a sample three-day menu. The asterisk * indicates dishes made in advance:

	Breakfast	Lunch	Dinner

Monday	Berries and cream
	*Scrambled eggs
	*Bacon
	Coffee cake
	Dry cereal
	Coffee, tea, milk
		Roast beef sandwich
		  on hard roll
		Grapes/apples
		Cookies
		Soda or other
		  beverage
			*Casserole of chicken
			  breasts with gravy
			  on wild and
			  white rice
			*Tossed salad
			Dinner rolls
			Blueberry tarts
			Beverage

Tuesday	Orange juice
	French toast
	Brown and serve
	  sausage
	Beverage
	Dry cereal
		*Egg salad on
		  pumpernickel
		Carrot and celery
		  sticks
		Cookies
		Beverage
			*Pot roast with
			  carrots, onions
			  and potatoes
			*Molded fruit salad
			*Pound cake w/coffee
			  icing
			Beverage

Wednesday	*Fresh orange slices
	  in juice
	Egg and hash pie
	Bacon
	Beverage
	Dry cereal
		Ham and Swiss
		  cheese on rye
		*Potato salad
		Cookies
		Beverage
			*Meat loaf with
			  savory sauce
			Browned potatoes
			  with parsley
			  butter (can)
			*Cole slaw
			Brownies
			Beverage

Note: Sandwiches are made after breakfast cleanup and stored in plastic container in refrigerator.

ANN: My six-day menu might look like this. If it's a slow race, there should be enough food left to improvise after that. I also indicate the stowage location of the ingredients right on the menu itself.

	Breakfast	Lunch	Dinner

Saturday		Potato salad
		Cold chicken and/or
		    cold-cut sandwich
		Celery and carrots
		Pickles
		Iced tea, beer
			Roast beef/gravy
			    (can)
			Bread
			Carrots (can)
			Lettuce and tomato
			    dressing (bottle)
			Fruit salad (can)
			Banana nut bread

Sunday	Frozen orange juice
	Sausage
	Scrambled eggs or
	    pancakes
	Coffee cake
	Tea, coffee, cocoa
		Cold roast beef or
		    cold cuts and
		    cheese sandwiches
		Lettuce and tomato
		Iced tea, beer, soft
		    drinks
			Stew
			Hearts of lettuce
			Sliced tomato ›
			Pears and cookies
			    or sweet bread

Monday	Frozen orange juice
	Bacon (can)
	Eggs
	Coffee ring
	Coffee, tea, cocoa
		Cold cuts and cheese
		    sandwiches
		Fruit—dried or
		    fresh
		Iced tea
			Ham (can)
			Pineapple (can)
			Baked beans (can)
			Bread and butter
			Pudding and cookies

Tuesday	Canned juice
	Corned beef hash
	    (can)
	Eggs
	Bread or sweet loaf
	Beverage
		Ham and cheese
		    sandwiches
		Cold cuts (if left)
		Tuna salad (must
		    be mixed)
		Fruit
		Beverage
			Beefaroni (can)
			Peas (can)
			Three-bean salad
			    (can)
			Peaches (can)
			Cookies
			Beverage

Wednesday	Canned juice
	Cereal—hot or cold
	Eggs (if left)
	Beverages
		Corned beef spread
		    (can)
		Corned beef (can)
		    sandwiches
		Fruit—fresh or dried
		Iced tea
			Beef Stew (can)
			Bread and butter
			Pudding (can)
			Cookies
			Beverage

Thursday	Tang
	Cereal—hot or cold
	Beverages
		Peanut butter/jelly
		    sandwiches
		Cheese sandwiches
		Beverages
			Spaghetti and meat
			    balls (can)
			Pudding
			Cookies
			Beverage

CELIA: After the menu comes the shopping list. With the menu as your guide, write down every ingredient that needs to be purchased. Don't forget things like syrup (for the pancakes or French toast), salad dressing, spices, etc. Write down the amounts to be purchased. How many slices of bread will the sandwiches take? How many sodas per person? How many ounces of breakfast juice per person? How many eggs for breakfast and the egg salad? Does your skipper allow wine at dinner, or beer or a tot of rum? There are skippers who do not allow any alcohol on board. So you'd better check. However, don't forget the bottle of rum to celebrate with after the race.

Include in your list snacks for the crew, all paper and cleaning products. Check the race circular for required emergency rations.

ED: What about the actual shopping?

ANN: Shopping for supplies for a long race can be done over a month's time. Casseroles, roasts, baked goods, canned and dried goods can be bought way ahead of time, labeled and packed, or stored in the freezer. The last-minute supplies include bread and rolls, eggs, fresh fruit and vegetables, delicatessen cold meats and the ice, dry and regular. We buy both delicatessen and supermarket prepackaged cold cuts because the latter lasts longer.

CELIA: If your race is a long one requiring many supplies, you can buy in bulk from a food wholesaler, or if there isn't one around, your local market will probably reduce prices if you buy by the case. Food stores such as S.S. Pierce Company, Boston, Massachusetts, have lists of nonperishable staple foods that could be very useful.

Two or three weeks before the race buy the ingredients for the dishes you are planning to make in advance and freeze. Later you can market for the canned goods, cleaning supplies and paper products. A day or two before the race, purchase the perishables such as fruits, vegetables, butter, eggs and bakery products.

ED: Let's talk about costs (1976 prices).

ANN: The cost for food and associated supplies for a six-day race is about $30 per person. The cost of food for an overnight race would be about $35 for a crew of eight with three meals—lunch, dinner and breakfast.

CELIA: I talked with cooks of several other yachts, large and small, and the rule of thumb cost seems to be about $5 per day minimum per crew member.

Planning meals ahead means economy. If we were as careful in planning our menus at home as we are on the boat, the amount saved would be significant. By planning ahead and buying only the items included in the menu, you resist the temptation of impulse buying. It's the little nonessentials that add up and destroy the budget.

Costs vary according to the boat's location. Island prices are much higher than at home, so when stocking up for the return trip, plan on more money being spent.

The cost of feeding the crew on the boat is not the prime concern of a yacht owner. The food brought on board is limited by the stowage space and weight is of great concern. Food cost in relation to the many other expenses of maintaining a racing yacht is really insignificant. If you lost one winch handle overboard accidentally during a race, the cost of that handle would feed one crew member for 15 days.

ED: You both mentioned cooking in advance.

CELIA: Those "easy" meals aboard mentioned earlier can best be accomplished by cooking the main dishes at home and freezing them for the race. Your kitchen has the distinct advantage of remaining level and motionless. It also contains nontilting counters and an array of appliances not to be found in the boat's galley.

If, at sea, you have forgotten to bring aboard the main ingredient of your casserole, it would be a disaster; at home it's an easy matter to buy it, thereby saving your casserole and your reputation as a cook.

Freeze your dinners in disposable containers that you have clearly labeled. These can be aluminum foil pans that can be put into the oven to be heated; or you can freeze food in boilable, sealed bags that can be heated in a pot of water on top of the stove. When purchasing your containers it is important that you know the size of your oven, your freezer, your refrigerator or ice chest so that the containers will fit in the required space.

When preparing the food in advance, a pressure cooker is an immense help. It saves time and money. For instance, the cooking time for a pot roast made in a pressure cooker is only 30 minutes, while cooking it in the oven would take about an hour and 45 minutes. This is three times faster and when you have a lot of cooking to do for a long race, the time saved is very important. The cheaper but tougher cuts of meat come out tender with a delicious, ready-made gravy. Even tough vegetables like carrots and potatoes cook in just a few minutes, retaining their vitamins and color.

Since racing crews eat in two shifts, I make two casseroles for each dinner. This way, while the on-going watch is eating the first casserole, the second casserole is heating for the off-going watch. This keeps the dinners from overcooking or drying out.

If you don't have a freezer on board, it is still possible to cook your meals in advance. Frozen casseroles will keep in an insulated plastic bag for two days without refrigeration or ice. If you have room for a plastic foam chest with ice in it, the food will keep days longer. Frozen, one-dish meals made at home, that can be carried aboard and reheated later, result in a happy, well-fed crew and a happy cook.

One other hint about casseroles—make sure they contain "recognizable" pieces of meat, chicken or whatever else you may use and undercook at home. This way, when it's reheated aboard, the meal will not have turned to mush.

ANN: Because of conditions when racing, there is no doubt in my mind that everything that can be, should be prepared ahead of time and served as simply as possible. Unless the wind is light or from behind, it is usually a difficult task to work and prepare a meal aboard a racing boat. Many dishes can be prepared and frozen a couple of weeks in advance. Even a roast of beef can be cooked and frozen at home along with its own gravy in a separate container. For variety and convenience, casserole meals can be prepared the same way but these dishes are bulky, difficult to store and usually require an oven for reheating. Glass casserole dishes break and plastic casserole containers melt. Stews and one-pot dinners are best stored in plastic freezer containers and heated on top of the stove in a metal pot.

CELIA: Here are other "ahead-of-time" items. Premixed and seasoned scrambled eggs—just shake, pour and cook. Partially cook bacon to eliminate messy grease, salads in plastic containers, prebuttered and seasoned French bread, wrapped and ready for warming.

ED: Now let's talk about where to put everything so it can best be preserved and easily retrieved.

CELIA: Before taking the provisions to the boat, separate them into categories for easier stowing. Label your boxes and shopping bags as to contents. Potatoes and onions can be put in drawstring bags to be stowed in a dark, ventilated locker; emergency dinners separated and put into individual bags; bakery and bread products stowed in galley lockers. The crews' snacks should be put in an accessible locker or drawer. Separate staples like flour, sugar, coffee, tea, paper products and cleaning supplies. Put frozen and refrigerator items into insulated bags or ice chest.

ANN: There should be several crew members familiar with the menu and the location of all the food. They can learn this by helping with the stowing. Charts should be prepared to indicate the location of all food and supplies.

CELIA: When you stow on the boat do it systematically by arranging the food in order of use. Each day's supply can be color coded with tape or indelible marker.

ANN: In our boat, ice chests are used in addition to the icebox. Each chest is cooled with a half block of dry ice, wrapped in brown paper to prevent the burning of food. The main icebox is kept cold with block ice and contains beer, soft drinks, cans of juice, fresh fruit and fresh vegetables such as lettuce, which keeps better if it remains in its original plastic wrapping from the store, and tomatoes which bruise less if packed in a plastic container.

The meat products and precooked meals are stored in the ice chests and put aboard frozen, but keep in mind that the refrigeration will last only three to four days, depending on the weather. Cold cuts and cheese are also stored in these chests after first being packed into a large plastic box to keep them from getting soggy. Store these chests so as to be readily available to the cook, yet out of the way. Label the contents on the outside.

CELIA: When stowing unrefrigerated foods, make sure the breakables (salad dressing, jelly, mayonnaise) are wedged between boxes of sugar, spaghetti, etc. These items will absorb the shocks and prevent breakage.

ANN: Necessities, such as paper towels, toilet tissue and Kleenex should be wrapped in large plastic bags and tied tightly. I cannot stress enough the importance of keeping dry foodstuffs and the ordinary necessities of life *dry*. This includes anything packaged in paper or cardboard.

Contrary to popular belief, eggs do not have to be refrigerated. The eggs for a race of six days' duration or more can be preserved by greasing with shortening and replacing in their cartons.

CELIA: I agree. If eggs are stored in a cool place, they will keep for several weeks. Turning them over once a week will keep them fresh even longer.

Canned goods can be a problem as they are usually stored in the bilge. Wrap the cans in plastic bags or remove the labels and mark the contents on the can with a waterproof marker. Varnishing the cans will prevent rust. Loose labels can mess up the bilge pump—not to mention how missing labels can mess up the cook.

ED: What do we need to cook and serve the food we now have aboard?

ANN: The galley equipment for a long or overnight race should include one large six-quart pot with a lid. This enables the cook to heat up a dinner for eight all at once. We also need a one-and-a-half-quart pan for heating vegetables and two Teflon-lined frying pans with lids for breakfast cooking. The teakettle stays on the gimbaled bracket Sterno stove and can be kept hot for the duration of a meal. Add two large ladles for serving and the rest of the utensils can be throwaways emptied into large plastic garbage bags after use.

Plates and bowls should be the hard plastic version, not paper. We use a product called "china foam" which has a hard shiny surface and is stiff enough to support mounds of hot food. Use plates with portion separations, small and large bowls, plastic glasses and mugs for hot or cold beverages. If mugs are not throwaways, make each crew member responsible for care and treatment of his own mug. Each can be identified with name or initial in waterproof ink.

Plastic liquid containers with lids are handy for mixing powdered milk, iced tea or frozen juice, beating eggs or tossing lettuce. They also are useful for storage of leftovers.

CELIA: I prefer stainless steel flatware, pots and pans. It resists the pitting and rusting caused by salt and doesn't dent when bumped around. It is the most resistant metal and, therefore, the best investment. If you can find Teflon-lined steel pots and pans, dishwashing will be much easier.

To Ann's list of utensils I would add a coffeepot, a double boiler (the insert can be used as a mixing bowl), two saucepots with lids, an oven roasting pan and an aluminum grill spanning two burners.

In the knick-knack drawer we need a can and beer can opener, ice pick, corkscrew, measuring cup, knife sharpener (Aladdin is a good one), paring knife, carving knife and fork, pancake turner, potato peeler, large wooden spoon, wire whisk, mixing bowl, chopping board to fit over sink, strainer, tray to fit on top of stove for a level counter when stove isn't in use, sufficient sets of stainless steel flatware (if you don't like disposables), heavy-duty plastic Melmac dishes, bowls, mugs and glasses.

Last, but not least, don't forget matches in a waterproof container, "spark" gun to light stove, hot pads, paper towel holder, dustpan and short-handled broom, heavy-duty foil, scouring pads, sponge, pail, wastebasket (to be wedged somewhere where it won't tip), garbage bags, liquid cleaner and powdered cleanser.

ED: Now a few subjects we haven't talked about yet. Let's begin with rough-weather cooking.

CELIA: In rough weather choose simply prepared meals that can be served in

Cooks buying ice before the St. Pete–Lauderdale Race

Figaro crew celebrates Fourth of July at sea.

a bowl and eaten with a spoon, but without too much liquid in the recipe. Keep it bland and easy to digest, like chicken and rice, potatoes and hash or stew.

ANN: When it's rough, the appetites disappear fast and there's not as much cooking to do.

CELIA: Also, anticipate that meals may be interrupted by emergencies on deck, requiring all hands.

ED: That brings up safety precautions when it's rough.

CELIA: Avoid soup. It can scald the cook or crew if spilled. Avoid frying pans and use a large pot instead so the meal won't end up on the bulkhead or overhead in case of a knockdown.

ANN: Wear a safety belt so that you can use both hands.

CELIA: Be careful with large knives.

ANN: Don't cook spaghetti. If it spills, it can wind up in the bilge pump strainers.

CELIA: Don't ever deep-fry anything on a boat. A spill can result in burns to the cook or a fire.

ED: Is it the cook's responsibility to check on the cooking fuel?

ANN: Absolutely. This should be on the shopping list.

CELIA: The cook should check out the stove's condition, too, and remember to bring extra water in plastic jugs.

ED: How about surprise menus on a long race?

CELIA: If there's a birthday, celebrate it. One boat keeps a "party" drawer. This same boat served green mashed potatoes on St. Patrick's Day. This might be extreme, but surprises are morale boosters.

ED: One cook or two, one to a watch?

CELIA: Use one cook.

ANN: If it's one cook per watch he or she should be familiar with the facilities, the location of needed items and stores for a given meal—and how to operate the stove and oven. Cleanup duties can be rotated with the watches.

ED: Anything else?

ANN and CELIA: Yes, after the race, take the cook out to dinner!

11 COMMUNICATION

When we experience a successful race it is easy to lose sight of the fact that many details had been satisfactorily handled to make that success possible. When we live through a race that has turned out to be a horror show, there are usually so many loose ends that it is difficult to catalog them all.

One of the often neglected areas in offshore racing, and essential for good results, is communication. But this is one of the greatest problems of humanity in general and not just peculiar to sailors.

Let's begin with race committee–contestant communication. Have the race instructions been well thought out and clearly explained? We have all heard the facetious admonition, "When all else fails, read the instructions!" But stop and think—how often are we guilty of this last resort? And when we do read the race circular, is the "fog index" higher by far than the much maligned income tax instructions? Is the race circular incomplete, unnecessarily complex in concept or a departure from conventional practice?

The committee must bear some responsibility when contestants are led astray by poorly conceived or poorly written instructions. Competition is tough enough in the fleet without having to compete as well with semanticists or trail blazers on the race committee. And we all know the fate of a contestant who would presume to protest a committee for unclear race instructions, even though committees themselves have been known to misinterpret or not follow their own directions.

Experienced navigators know that it is usually their lot to obtain, digest, understand, interpret and apply the race instructions so that the boat on which they are sailing flawlessly executes all requirements. In this task they are representing an owner who has many other things on his mind and they also have a deep responsibility to the rest of the crew who are working so hard to keep the boat moving at top speed. Everything comes to naught if you don't follow the prescribed course around the marks.

Skippers' meetings are a very useful device to improve communication between committees and contestants; but unless the contestants have instructions available on time they are not able to ask pertinent questions or raise points on subjects which may be troubling them. Skippers' meetings filled with unimportant announcements and irrelevancies do not leave time for clarifying answers to these pertinent questions. Race committees love a captive audience. Where it is not possible to have a skippers' meeting, the instructions should be crystal clear and available well ahead of the start of the race.

Once we have established good communication between the race sponsor and

Skipper's meeting

the contestants, communication must be established within the organization aboard the boat. For example, say a particular chart is necessary for a given race. The navigator thinks the owner is getting it and the owner thinks the navigator is getting it, and while they are maneuvering with four minutes to go to the start, it is discovered that the chart is not on board because no one got it. Poor communication.

Or, the watch on deck thinks the navigator is making the hourly log entries, and the navigator, who has just hit the sack, thinks the watch on deck is making them. The fact is that nobody is making them. Poor communication.

Lest you think that this is restricted to just the navigator's department, how many times have you heard the skipper order a particular sail to be set, only to have the embarrassed rejoinder, "We left it ashore"? Or the instance just before the 1972 Bermuda Race when one boat discovered close to starting time, while at the starting line, that the necessary groceries were left on the dock back at Newport. (Fortunately they were able to get them aboard before the start by radioing in and obtaining delivery services by high-speed motorboat.) In both of these instances, someone wasn't communicating.

In the hustle and bustle aboard an ocean-racer where multitudes of tasks are to be done and there is the requirement for top performance in all of them, it is difficult to keep track of everything that is going on under even the best of conditions. This makes it imperative that communication be at the highest degree of effectiveness using all applicable methods.

Why is it that beforehand there never seems to be enough time to talk calmly and deliberately about preparations for a big race? Yet, after the race there seems to be all the time in the world to rehash what went right or wrong during that race. Is it possible that many of the snafus could have been eliminated by good communication before and during the race? The more I think about it, the more it makes sense to me that the skipper, navigator, watch captains and foredeck bosses should be in constant and frank communication; first by having a meeting before the race and setting the ground rules, and then keeping each other fully informed at all times during the race. Many incipient problems can be eliminated by discussion, by the avoidance of assumptions and by communicating directly and effectively. Can you think of any problems in your last race that good communication could have alleviated?

Some skippers promote communication by issuing informative bulletins or newsletters to the crew between races. These discuss such subjects as racing schedules, crew lists, where and when to join the boat for the next race or details of the last one, and who is in charge of what. On other boats, it is a practice of the skipper to confer with the crew and go over race details before departing for the starting line. Still others will critique a race after it is over while the details are fresh in everyone's mind with the aim of making the next race even better. All of these surely help get the word from one head to another. The climate for communication aboard a boat must be set by the skipper. If the channels are closed off, "Murphy's Law" takes over. (Everything that can go wrong, will go wrong.)

Finally, the "word" must have the same meaning for the originator as the recipient.

12 RECRUITING THE TEAM

The question is often asked, "How is a crew put together for an offshore racer?" The process takes place in a complex and constantly changing marketplace. Some hot boats are easily manned from long lists of persons wanting to get aboard, and some crew members have several berths from which to choose. Designers, builders and sailmakers are very influential in the recruiting process. Navigators and watch captains are probably more interchangeable than some of the other specialists, because their skills are less related to a particular boat. Though the skipper has the final say, it is not always the skipper who makes the selection.

There was a time when recruiting was easy. Each department of an offshore racer was a hit-or-miss proposition. Most crews included at least one recently mustered-out Naval veteran who had picked up a smattering of the art sufficient to be entrusted to keep the boat off the rocks and somehow find the intended destination with an allowable amount of lost motion. This relaxed standard was comparable in other departments. An outfit of sails was usually good for several years; boat designs were not outdated as soon as they were launched and the entire environment aboard an ocean racer had a "clubby" aura. Someone inevitably won the race, but few could say how he actually did it. The essence of the sport was "men against the elements," and finishing was more important than winning. Sagas performed by casual amateurs, such as sailing the last half of the race without a rudder, sewing replacement sails with rudimentary equipment, mending sick crewmen with the aid of only a first-aid manual, abound in the literature of those times. Today it is a bit different.

What the Crew Member Looks For

Now, on a competitive boat, winning is all. The elements are considered tameable and everyone in the crew is expected to be an expert in his field. Owners spend agonizing hours recruiting and holding a top-notch crew, just as good crewmen spend a comparable amount of time deciding which boat they prefer from among their several offers.

Of the different crew positions, the navigator's choice of a boat is perhaps more difficult. A helmsman knows that most of his potential boats will have an adequate wheel with which to steer, and sail trimmers can be assured that there will be a suitable sail inventory and an acceptable array of winches and sheets with which to perform their duties. The navigator's decision is based not only on equipment but also psychological factors and, because his slot has a high measure of visibility, he must be mindful not only of his working conditions, but also the very apparent results of his work.

When the foredeck crew hoists a spinnaker sideways, or when taking one down dumps it in the water under the bow, the usual reaction, after the spontaneous profanity, is, "Oh, well, that could happen to anyone." When the navigator misses a buoy or a landfall, it is a disaster for which only he is accountable and his name may live forever in infamy. Few others aboard consider that this could be the result of inadequate equipment, an outdated chart portfolio or even disregard of the navigator's previous recommendations.

Obviously, a new crew member has to start somewhere and must choose from what boats are available to him, accepting whatever risk is entailed. An experienced proven sailor has better options.

What are some of the things you should look for? First of all, if you want to win you should get aboard a boat that is capable of winning. A navigator should arrange to have some say in the outfitting of the navigator's station. Any navigator who has experienced a race in which he has been reduced to Stone Age methods for position finding will not knowingly subject himself to another such experience. He should make every endeavor to be a full participant in the selection of charts and publications, being sure they give full coverage and are the latest available for a particular race. On occasion, owners have been known to use outdated charts from year to year.

You should avoid, whenever possible, putting yourself in a position of sailing aboard a boat where the crew includes a plethora of others with navigational skills who feel that *they* should have been the navigator. This can lead to endless tugs-of-war and interminable second-guessing. By the same token you should look for a skipper who understands a navigator's problems. This is one who knows that he cannot be both skipper and navigator at the same time and will allow the navigator to be the navigator.

Watch captains should be familiar with the yacht's deck layout, the sail inventory and stowage, and know something about the members of their watch. If possible, they should have a hand in their selection.

There are times when this approach cannot be used, such as when a person is substituting for another at the last moment (making a pier-head jump, they call it) and must live with the choice as well as the other's preparation. Normally there is an opportunity to "case" a boat in a few afternoon "around-the-buoy" races to check out and evaluate that boat's environment. This still will not tell what the effects of stress will be, or how the offshore amenities compare, but some of these details can be learned in casual prerace conversations. Each well-known boat has a distinct reputation among the racing fleet's population.

Here's a conversation between crewmen you might have overheard after one of last winter's club dinners:

Dick, a sailmaker, has just joined Tom and Harry at the club bar. The latter are not in the boat business but are avid sailors. Tom asks, "Who are you crewing with in the Southern Circuit, Dick?"

Dick, after checking to see who is within earshot, confides, "I've got to choose soon between a reworked Freres 46 and a new Two-Ton. The company wants me on the Two-Tonner, but I'm still checking them both out. A brand-new design is always an unknown quantity, but nowadays so is last year's boat, even if it is improved."

"I notice you didn't say whose boats they were, Dick. Keeping the owners guessing, as usual?"

"Well, Tom, I'll let you know in a few days what I decide and then maybe I can get you on the other one in my place."

"No, I'm satisfied to stay on *Seafarer*. This will be my fifth season. We have a fine group aboard and the owner gives great crew parties. Plus, I've finally worked up to watch captain."

"Sounds great."

"Better still, we'll be in the 'old boat' division this time where it's more relaxing than that hot group you're in."

Harry was silent, but when pressed to disclose what he was up to, responded: "Not much, fellas. I've had trouble finding a good berth since my last skipper went bankrupt. I was with him so long I don't know any of the new people. Besides, with the entries down, there are fewer opportunities. Maybe I'll just go south and walk up and down the dock wearing a sign, 'crew available.' "

"There was a bit of that last year," replied Dick, "but don't get discouraged. The new owner of *Tide Rip* was in the sail loft last week and he told me he was looking for experienced people. Here's his phone number. Why not call him?"

"Thanks, Dick, maybe I will. She's a good boat, but what's the owner like?"

"Don't know much about him, Harry, except that he is from the Great Lakes and seems OK. This is his first major campaign. He's putting a lot of money into the boat. Maybe he'll spring for airline tickets, too, once he sees you've got the talent."

Does this seem to indicate that top crews are a pampered lot? This depends upon the observer. A crew member who knows his chosen specialty develops a reputation equal to his demonstrated ability. He is thus able to exercise his own process of selection of a berth from those available to him for a particular race. The better he is, the more choices he has. In the above example, Dick, being a sailmaker, is better able to keep current on where the action is.

Conversely, an owner, by keeping in touch with what is happening, can update his list of potential crew members, eliminating those whose performance is less than satisfactory and adding newcomers of promise.

Women Crew Members

Now for the matter of increasing participation by women. There is no question that many women can master a number of jobs on an offshore racer and certainly there is no intellectual or physical reason why women cannot or should not become successful navigators, watch captains or deck hands. Thousands of women have passed navigation courses and raced one-designs, so the problem is not whether they can do it but whether they will have the opportunity to practice what they have learned. However, the fact is that at the moment they do not participate in significant numbers in top offshore boats other than in the capacity of cook, which is unfortunate and misleading. Some may feel that this is an unimportant position on a boat, but how it is performed is highly significant in terms of crew morale, stamina and staying power. It takes a lot of guts to produce good meals in a rough sea when you would rather be up on deck getting the fresh air. My point here is that women can also master a tough sailing job.

For many years one-design ranks have been open and available to women sailors. The Women's North American Sailing Championship, called the Adams Cup in honor of Mrs. Charles Frances Adams, was first awarded in 1925. The small boat ranks have consistently, over the years, developed many fine offshore sailors, but few women have made the transition, whatever the reason may be. Sally Ann Langmuir, some years back, was a lone exception, an offshore woman sailor who was the successful owner and skipper of *Bolero*. It is not recorded how many members of her crew were women.

In the 1975 One-Ton Class World Championship, the yacht *Wildwood* had a female skipper named Romeyn Everdell, a three-time Adams Cup winner. Another female skipper, Pat Duane, a successful *Flying Dutchman* helmsman, appeared in the 1976 SORC aboard *Moody Blue,* and there were two woman skippers in that year's Bermuda Race, so the outlook may be improving.

Perhaps the most significant point is that a skipper of an offshore boat has the final say in selecting the crew. The problem of staffing a boat on a representative basis has to be solved on that level. Let's face it—all of the top skippers are men. Certainly there are many women who can afford to buy a gold plater. After all, the economists tell us that women control most of the money in this country. A woman skipper can promote the cause on her own boat and in her sailing area by developing women sailors who can, if they qualify, go on to skipper their own boats and serve in almost any capacity in top racers on other than a regional basis. Why don't more women do this?

Ability, motivation and performance are what a top skipper wants. If a woman has what it takes, in free competition, she will get the assignment. There is a lingering doubt as to whether women are competitive and team players because they really are brought up differently from men.

Year after year, as owners and crew members change, the crew selection process continues in its mysterious, inefficient but somehow effective way. Somehow, top boats always seem to have top crews.

There are crew members who wait to be asked. There are other crew members who through various means try to influence the skipper to select them. One obvious way to do this is to prepare a sailing résumé and distribute it to as many skippers as possible. I have often seen copies of these résumés in the chart table on boats on which I have sailed. A sample sailing résumé is illustrated. At least, this way, the skippers know that you are available.

The Factory Team Approach to Crewing

Another effective way to be considered for a crew job is to get to know the people in yachting-related businesses. They have a great influence on crew recruit-

SAILING RÉSUMÉ

EDWARD F. COTTER, Jr.
Lt. (JG) U.S. Navy   Home Address: 310 Covered Bridge Road
                                        Cherry Hill, N.J. 08034
                                        (609) 428-5145

Day Racing Experience

U.S. Naval Academy 1969-1973 (Graduated '73)

Dinghy Team Skipper, three years, Varsity Letter
"A" Skipper 1972-'73, Middle Atlantic Champs 1973
Second, Timme Angsten Regatta, Chicago 1972
Navy 44' Yawls, Kennedy Cup, McMillen Cup, Tactician
Sailing instructor and coach, 1973 dinghies and yachts
Laser Regatta Winner, Gulf Area

Offshore Racing Experience

MARADEA	62'	Deck Watch/Helmsman
1972	Chesapeake Races	
1972	Cape May-Newport Race	
1972	Newport-Bermuda Race	
OUTRAGE	50'	Skipper/Watch Captain/ Helmsman
1973	Chesapeake Races	
1973	Annapolis-Newport Race	
1973	Block Island Week	
WANDELAAR	50'	Deck Watch/Helmsman
1973	New York Yacht Club Cruise Week	
LA FORZA DEL DESTINO	51'	Deck Watch/Helmsman
1973	Marblehead-Halifax Race	
1973	Vineyard Race	
THREE-QUARTER TONNERS	32'	Watch Captain/Navigator
1974	Gulf of Mexico Races	

Technical Qualifications

Naval Flight Officer—completed Naval Flight Training 1974
Navigator—P-3, Long-range, U.S. Navy multiengine
          ASW patrol plane
          Pacific and Far East 1975
              (celestial navigation, electronic navigation, Omni, Loran, Omega
              and related computers)

3/1/76

ing. These include designers, sailmakers, builders, yacht brokers and others with a big name in the sport who have a nucleus of key people on call who can go aboard a boat as a well-functioning group.

This is useful to the members of these groups as well as to the skipper who needs to assemble a crew from scratch on short notice. But there can be pitfalls on both sides.

Here is a recent case. Skipper John Smith, through a combination of fortuitous circumstances, happens to have under construction a boat from a top designer which, based upon advance reports, is going to be a fast boat. This will come on stream before an important series and because of time constraints or unavailability of other builders will be one of the few designs of top potential ready. At this point there also happens to be a shortage of good boats entered for this event. All of a sudden, Smith is getting calls from people whom he has heard of or read about, but who previously have never given him the time of day. He is now being deluged by a variety of sailmakers who just happen to have a ready-made team (theirs) to put aboard his boat if he buys their sails. Or the designer and the builder, who both have a deep interest in seeing that the boat is well sailed, will be bombarding him with lists of *their* "hotshots" who "must be on the boat."

What does he do with this confusing choice of talent? If he opts for any of these schemes he may suspect that he is being used, but he might enjoy going up to accept the prize if the boat wins. Nevertheless he will also know that if it was won for him with little help on his part, other than financial, his ego may suffer. He can be sure that his regular crew from his last boat, who would have to be dismissed to do this, would not forgive him. For Skipper Smith there is always tomorrow's crewing problem when the heavies have departed in search of another fast boat.

For the experts there can also be problems. Perhaps the boat may not prove to be as fast as expected and their reputations may suffer as a result, if they are committed to a losing proposition.

So while the "factory team" crewing concept has come to full bloom, the fallacy of it is this: only one boat crew can win a given race or series. If one factory team wins, all the other factory teams lose. Regardless of whether Skipper Smith opts for a factory team or for his friends and regular crewmates is really not too material in the long run.

Many owners who have travelled both routes have concluded that having a boatload of semipros is not a satisfactory long-term answer. Similarly, a growing number of yachting-related businesses have come to realize that if their employees are out sailing all the time, they are not producing back at the office. Isn't it a better marketing concept to teach amateur skippers and their crews to be self-sufficient in the use of the product rather than doing it for them during the race where they really don't learn much of lasting value?

A quote from a factory team member aboard a winning boat is apropos. I asked him, "What will happen to the boat when you fellows give her back to the owner?" He said, "She will go slower and won't win as many races."

13 THE ONE-DESIGN SKIPPER FLEETS UP

You've been sailing a popular one-design in your home waters for some time now. You've been doing well and occasionally you journey to a distant area for regional and national competition. Your children have been a ready source of crew material but they are now growing up and interested in other things. Your wife is getting tired of making sandwiches and sitting around on shore waiting for the races to be over. You and your wife have just come back from a sailboat show with a possible solution. Get a cruising boat! This way she can sail with you and maybe the kids will be enticed back for newer and better things. You don't want to cruise all the time, so you have picked out a boat that also can be raced.

Should you do it? After all, the new boat is only $1,000 down and $350 a month for 84 months. You are moving ahead in your career and you can afford it. Luckily, you haven't decided yet. Here are a few things you might want to consider.

You are aware that it costs more than advertised to maintain a typical one-design boat in competitive condition but do you know what it's going to cost to keep your cruising/racing boat the same way? Have you considered the so-called "extras" which you are not going to get with the original purchase but you will soon find are necessities? What are the number and variety of sails needed? Are you going to be satisfied with a stock deck layout (winches, cleats, sheet leads, etc.) or do you want this customized? Do you want a gasoline engine or diesel? What is your budget for electronics, and can your boat's power supply furnish required current? What are the crew requirements and skills needed? Where are you going to keep the boat and how much will this cost? Do you have the time and the know-how (and the money) to take care of the post-weekend work lists to bring the boat back to shipshape ready condition for the next weekend?

At this point you may think: "I'm not going to get involved in all this. I'm going to cruise most of the time and race only once in a while when I feel like it." If this is so, you have no problem. After the first couple of races at the tail end of the fleet you can just concentrate on cruising and forget racing. But this is not usually what happens. Your competitive drive, revealed by your previous successful one-design experience, won't let it happen. You can't cruise anywhere without seeing other boats that are racing, and the old warhorse in you is not going to let you be satisfied as a spectator. You say to yourself, "Look at that guy hacking it up—I can do better than that!" Subtly, the machismo factor is working on you. You'll try again, just one more race to see what it's like, and again finish with the tailenders. You know there are a lot of things you can do that will improve your position in the fleet. Sure, these take time and money but you want to do better. You do them and you do finish better, but still you're way off the pace. Now you're hooked! You have to have a better boat. You want to be like the guys who have a winning boat and a hot crew, each outfitted in matching T-shirts displaying the name of the boat. These are the guys you read about in the boating magazines. That's really the life! But what you don't know is that's only the tip of the iceberg.

It's not like one-designs where the next mark is visible. Because now you are going into an arena where pointing the boat the right way is often more important than how fast it goes. In fact, if you're going in the wrong direction, it's better to go as slowly as possible. (More on this in Part III.)

Logistics, preparation, outfitting and manning increase geometrically in importance, the bigger the boat is. Often, unlike a one-design, where most of this is done yourself, now you have to depend on many others to help you.

A lot of skippers who "fleet up" learn this the hard way after they take the step. It's best, before you do, to ask yourself if you are willing to make the commitment. If not, set a less ambitious goal and live with it.

Care to hear more? There are at least four identifiable plateaus:
- successful one-design
- cruiser—occasional low-key racer
- hot stock cruiser/racer, no holds barred
- custom racer—new boat every second year

And if you're into it all the way will you be satisfied to win your class once in a while? Or are you after the fleet overall prize? A lot of thinking and planning is needed to answer these questions, and only you can answer them.

Here's a typical example of a fellow who has moved up through one-design and cruiser–occasional-racer to level three. He now has a stock One-Ton, well built and equipped and from the board of a well-known designer. The boat has good potential but it must be well organized and sailed to realize it. Even so, he is outclassed by the custom One-Tons, and knows it.

His first step is to do a bit of rating juggling so he can't possibly be in the custom One-Ton group. (The One-Ton rating cannot exceed 27.5, and if less you are giving an advantage away.) So our skipper can either go with 27.6 or 27. He consults his sailmaker or designer for advice as to how to do it.

Assuming the sail plan, rig and deck layout are now OK, his next step is crew organization. A way to get the picture here is to crew on another boat and observe what it has or doesn't have. He'll need a qualified navigator, an experienced foredeck boss and several good helmsmen for starters. String pullers and winch grinders can be trained from among the younger and stronger persons available, including his grown son. He never thought he'd be running a nautical talent agency! His wife is taking a Power Squadron course and hopes to work up to navigator. In the meantime, she has taken over the food planning and logistics. If he really wants the ultimate, he can arrange with a sailmaker to have an "account executive" assigned to his boat to advise on sail inventory, trim, selection and the inevitable midweek recutting.

For day racing he will find that six people can move the boat around the buoys adequately, but for longer races he really needs eight. In these, he and the navigator will "float" and there will be two watches of three persons each, including a watch captain. As a three-man watch is not enough to handle some sail evolutions, rather than waking up the off watch unnecessarily, the skipper or navigator will assist, either taking the helm or filling in elsewhere.

This means that a big and continuing job, after everything else is done, is manning—slotting in the best available people for both the day and long-distance races, having alternates available, providing info as to where the boat will be, when and how to get there and other details. Luckily, his wife can do the calling and scheduling for him from lists of potential crew members.

I saw him at the club dock recently, getting his boat ready for a race, all the preparing and organization behind him. "Would you go back to one-designs after what you've been through with your present boat?" I asked him.

"Never," he replied, "this is tougher, but the scope and challenge are unlimited. By the way, how do you like our new crew T-shirts?"

Tips and Techniques

PART III

The irony of the sport is, with everyone so obsessed with speed, how slow the boats really are. All the effort is directed at going from 10 knots to 10.2. And after sailing for hours to gain a few minutes you can lose it all with one wrong move.

—Phil Chinnock
Experienced offshore crewman

BLACK GOLD, a Two-Tonner launched in 1977.

The tips and techniques outlined here do not relate to making the boat go fast since speed is related to hull and rig design, sails used, wind velocity and sea conditions. The two former are rapidly changing components and the two latter are beyond the control of the boat's crew to change.

Rather, this part deals with such important factors as making the boat go in the right direction, finding the right marks, getting the most out of weather and current. To do this you must know not only where the boat is at all times, but where it was and where it ought to be later—in fair weather and foul. These factors are less affected by equipment, although this is important and necessary, but are more dependent upon techniques and judgment which are less prone to obsolescence.

14 OUTFITTING FOR NAVIGATION

The Instruments and Tools

How does an owner go about selecting equipment when outfitting for navigation? It is well to separate what is necessary and what is desirable in terms of cost, space, utility, power supply, maintenance and operator skills required. How actively and where the boat is raced will also affect the requirements.

The primary navigational device is a lighted steering compass (most newer boats have two, one on each side of the cockpit). This should be the best you can buy, properly installed away from magnetic influences, compensated and a deviation table constructed. Its accuracy is extremely important for maintaining a good dead-reckoning (DR) track as an inaccurate compass can be dangerous as well as inefficient. The other necessary ingredient to provide DR input is a calibrated speed-and-distance indicator, again the best you can afford. The DR plot is charted by stepping off the distances run for a stated time period in the direction of the average course steered from the last available fix. It will give you a dead-reckoning position and a basis from which to work when applying known leeway, set and drift. When a new fix is obtained, the DR plot is scrubbed and begun again from that point. Do not underestimate the value of a DR plot. Even though it is an approximation, it can be quite close to where you really are. In situations where aids and equipment are "iffy," a faithfully constructed DR plot can keep you in business.

A hand-held compass should be added next for taking visual bearings as described in Chapter 22. A chart table compass is also a nice addition. At the chart table should also be located in handy holders the tools for charting such as dividers, parallel rules and a time-distance calculator.

A good all-band radio is next. This will provide essential weather reports, accurate time signals and entertainment when the sea stories lag. In emergency, a portable radio may even be used in a rudimentary way to provide rough direction finder bearings on a broadcast station.

All offshore boats should have an adequate sextant and a safe place to stow it. When the sophisticated stuff fails, this is still the basic position-finding device offshore. Chapter 16 describes how a sextant is used. But with it, the appropriate almanac, sight reduction tables, star finder, work sheets and an accurate chronometer are required. The sextant can also be used for measuring horizontal angles in piloting and as a relative distance check on a race competitor.

After it is used for the start, a stopwatch is needed for timing aids-to-navigation

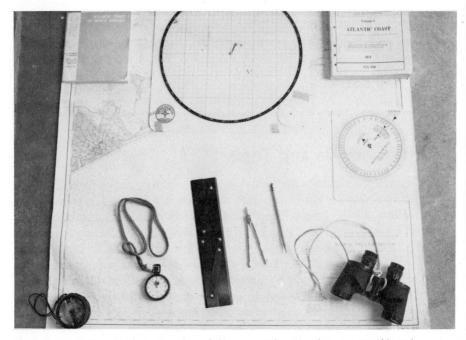

The tools for piloting *(clockwise from lower left):* compact hand-bearing compass, tide and current tables, wind and current plotter, light list, time-distance calculator, binoculars, pencil, dividers, parallel rules, stopwatch

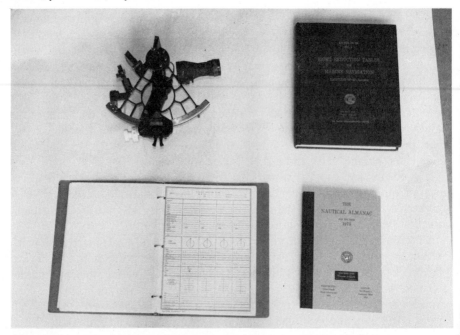

The tools for celestial navigation. *(Top)* sextant and sight-reduction tables. *(Bottom)* sight-reduction worksheet and *Nautical Almanac*

lights and can be used in timing sights in conjunction with the chronometer. Chronometers have come a long way in recent years with the advent of the quartz crystal and battery operation. For celestial observations, timing to the second is essential and these new timepieces are accurate to within one second a month. A chronometer is also used to time the yacht's daily activities such as the change of the watch, mealtimes, the timing of log entries, the timing of distances run and the like.

Binoculars (7 X 50) are vital for a number of uses.

Before electronics, a lead line was used for manual soundings of the bottom. To avoid the ignominy of running aground, you should have one as a backup for your electronic depth sounder which quickly reads the distance between the transducer and the bottom in feet or fathoms. The capacity of your depth sounder will depend upon the size of boat and power supply, but a 50-fathom maximum reader should be sought and a 100-fathom is even better.

A radio direction finder (RDF) provides lines-of-position for all-weather fixes or is used for homing on a single marine transmitting station.

An Omni is another direction finder instrument. This provides easily obtained bearings on known aircraft beacons within line-of-sight range.

Loran and Omega receivers use long-range hyperbolic line-of-position systems —the result being an all-weather fix with accuracy, depending upon the location of the receiver and the transmitting station.

These require the use of special charts upon which are printed the various position lines in relationship to the transmitting station sites.

Loran, Omni and RDF are further discussed in Chapter 15.

Radar is another very helpful electronic device for all-weather navigation in that it can give a precise, nearly instantaneous fix by means of bearings and ranges taken off the scope where the target contour can be identified. This is a great advantage over the other systems in that both a range and a bearing can be obtained from the same instrument. However, except for portable hand-held models, a radar receiver is expensive, requires a rather elaborate topside antenna system and a special power source, as well as high-class maintenance, making it practical for only the larger yachts. Radar ranges are generally more accurate than radar bearings and the preferred method of using radar for a fix is, therefore, obtaining two or more ranges on identifiable charted objects.

Radar, Omega, Loran and Omni are not permitted to be used in some offshore races, so you should check the applicable rules carefully.

Some sort of device should be available to measure progress through the water. This can range from a simple taffrail log (a line and a spinner streamed astern connected to a mechanical dial on the fantail) obviously not practical for racing boats, to an electronic direct-reading speed-and-distance indicator mounted aboard.

Other items, simple or deluxe, include an anemometer or wind velocity indicator, an apparent wind speed and direction indicator, a manual or direct reading sea temperature thermometer, an air thermometer, a barometer or barograph, a VHF weather receiver and a voice radio transceiver.

Approaching the Task

Let's look at how the outfitting task is approached in a particular case. Watt Webb, a physicist from Ithaca, New York, who sails on Lake Ontario as an owner-navigator, states his problem this way:

"Electronic navigation dominates your writings but you must live in the ideal world because your equipment always seems to deliver its rated capability. In this you have been much more successful than my friends or I have. Innocent-seeming Lake Ontario is a monster to navigate at night or in the fog with depths beyond the sounder, RDF signals good for about five miles with most receivers (due to interference), no Omni, no Loran and a 50% probability of finding certain lighthouses dark. Crossing the shipping lanes can be terrifying on a foggy night passage.

"How do I pick electronic equipment that *works* reliably? What is the *practical* performance of the available equipment? For those inlanders who seldom reach the coast, how do we choose among Loran, Omni and Omega? Can I do better than the 10 to 15% accuracy that I have now?

"I have written to you rather than to an electronics specialist because it is practical performance experience that matters in this problem—not electronic details."

Mr. Webb's case raises some very interesting issues.

Regardless of the technological advances since the days of Magellan, navigation is still an art and not a science. The key test for a navigator is the ability to discriminate among good information, mediocre information and erroneous information. The ability to evaluate is much more important than the ability to use a particular kind of equipment. There is no navigational device that is always reliable, whether it be electronic or mechanical. There is no calculation that is not subject to human or mechanical error. There is no collection of facts that is guaranteed not to mislead the observer in his analysis of them. With this in mind we can begin to come to grips with our lake sailor's problem.

A yacht navigator must know his theory, but he operates in a nontheoretical environment. He must first have an excellent understanding of the waters in which he is operating, the strengths and weaknesses of the navigational aids available in that area and must equip his boat accordingly.

To begin to answer Mr. Webb's query, let's look at Canadian Hydrographic Service Chart #2000 which covers Lake Ontario. The lake is about 180 miles long and 30–35 miles wide. The fact that the water itself is fresh rather than salt is of no concern navigationally. What is important is the bottom depth, the contour of the lake, meteorological considerations and the choice of navigational devices based upon available aids.

It should be recognized that Lake Ontario has for centuries been navigated by commercial craft and that navigational aids have evolved to meet that need. The experienced captain of a lake ore-carrier has over the years accumulated the required equipment and know-how to get through Lake Ontario from Fort Niagara to the St. Lawrence River in all kinds of weather and in any season. Therefore, we know the navigational job can be done. The only question that remains is how do we scale this down to the needs of the typical yachtsman? In particular, the yachtsman with a small cruising boat who wants to win races.

Let's look at the electronic navigational systems we can use: Omega provides full coverage in Lake Ontario. There is also full Loran C coverage in the area but not Loran A. To go all out, a separate Loran C receiver or an Omega receiver, though expensive, would give complete, all-weather coverage of the lake.

In a less expensive mode, Omni or RDF will also provide all-weather coverage, but with less accuracy. To use a marine type Omni receiver, you will need the U.S. Government Flight Information Chart Panel L-12 which shows the precise location and frequency for aircraft Omni transmitting stations around Lake Ontario. These locations are then transferred to your nautical charts for ready reference.

There are usable Omni stations at Watertown, Rochester and Toronto. Since these stations have a practical range of about thirty to forty miles with good marine equipment, by scribing an arc from each location we can determine the extent of coverage on the lake for each station. There are also several marine direction finder stations operated by the U.S. Coast Guard and the Canadian Government. By scribing arcs on the chart with the effective range of the respective DF stations, we can again evaluate the coverage available.

On Lake Ontario good frequency discrimination is necessary to use the available RDF stations, as most of them are on 302 (kHz) or on 306 (kHz). Your tuning to the appropriate frequency needs to be very accurate. A marine RDF suggestion that eliminates this problem is Vecta RDF which uses inserted modules precisely tuned to each frequency.

An examination of the depths of water in the lake shows that the deepest part is 133 fathoms. We know that there are yacht-type depth-sounders presently available that will find the bottom anywhere on the lake, but we also know that the deeper they read the more costly they are and the more power they drain from the yacht's batteries. Nevertheless, a depth-sounder with a range of at least 150 fathoms and preferably with a chart recorder can be a great help and well worth the money. This way, you would never be out of contact with the bottom of the lake and could frequently obtain lines-of-position using charted bottom contour lines. A bearing, visual or electronic, combined with a sounding can provide an adequate fix.

A good VHF radio covering the channels used by Great Lakes shipping will give you weather and merchant ship traffic information. However, as this is a line-of-sight receiver with the range depending upon the height of the transmitter and the height of your antenna, the latter should be a masthead antenna for most efficient use. Lake Ontario shipping follows a fixed track, so if you know the traffic list, this can provide a valuable navigational input. Crossing a long string of closely spaced merchant ships can be a problem in low visibility, and for safety you might want to use one of the low-cost portable radar instruments that are now available.

Electronics aside, don't discount the utility of celestial observations when in mid-lake. Whether one would use this method would depend upon such factors as the sky visibility, the horizon available, and the length of time it takes. In pilot waters other visual methods are as accurate and can be a lot simpler and quicker, but don't rule the celestial method out by not having a sextant and related publications aboard.

As to what you can expect of your electronics in the way of performance, this depends upon four factors:

1) quality of equipment
2) quality of installation of nonportable items
3) quality of maintenance
4) ability of the operator to use the instrument correctly

Cover all these bases and your equipment can deliver to its rated capacity. If not, seemingly simple but undetected causes may be at fault, such as weak batteries, loose connections, particularly those to antennae, foreign matter or tools inside equipment, loose controls, moisture in the equipment or minor maladjustments while operating.

Readers in other sailing areas can use the same analytical approach to equip their particular yacht for the conditions to be encountered.

Charts

The nautical chart, more than just a seagoing road map, is literally a gold mine of navigational information waiting to be used. Chart inventories should be reviewed at intervals and updated, particularly before venturing into new waters or starting offshore races. To identify the charts needed, consult the appropriate chart catalog.

Let's suppose you are planning to cruise from Newport, R.I., to Edgartown on Martha's Vineyard to participate in day races in that area. Nautical Chart Catalog No. 1, "Atlantic and Gulf Coasts," available free from the National Ocean Survey or your local chart dealer, will show you that you need chart Nos. 1209 and 1210 to start with.* These amply cover the cruise area. But you might also want the larger scale charts of sections within this area, such as No. 353 covering Narragansett Bay, and No. 264 covering Martha's Vineyard. No. 261, even larger still, shows the details of that Island's Vineyard Haven and Edgartown Harbors; and likewise No. 265 covers all of Nantucket Island, while No. 343 details Nantucket Harbor. Prices and chart scales are shown in the catalog, along with the addresses of authorized agents and a listing of related publications, such as coast pilots, tide and current tables, current charts, and light lists.

You may find that you have some of these charts already. But first, check their condition and the date of last change entered. Your chart may be in fine shape

---

*NOTE: NOS changed its numbering system in 1973 although NOS charts carry both old and new numbers. The catalog shows only the old numbers. Conversion tables listing old and new numbers may be found in the "Numerical Listing of Charts," published by the Defense Mapping Agency Hydrographic Center, Washington, D.C. 20390.

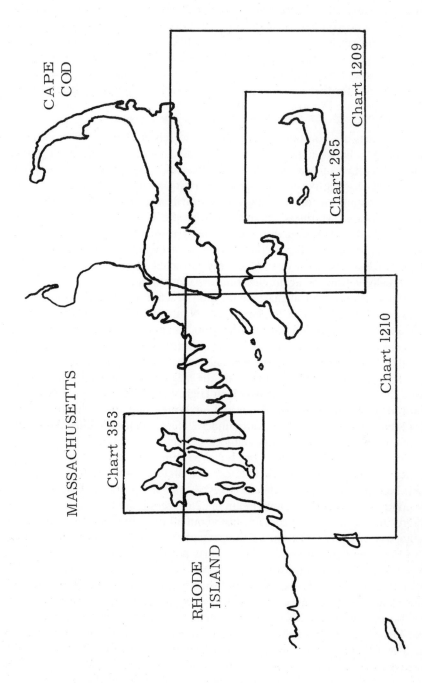

CAPE COD

Chart 1209

Chart 265

Chart 1210

MASSACHUSETTS

Chart 353

RHODE ISLAND

Excerpt from Nautical Chart Catalog No. 1

but may be badly out of date, and if so, it can be a hazard if not updated or replaced. How do you find this out? First look at the issue date, usually in the lower left-hand corner. A typical entry looks like this—"6th edition, March 3, 1975; Revised 2/20/'75." Then check this against the dates in the pamphlet "Dates of Latest Editions" (also free from your dealer). If the chart is a current edition then look for the hand stamp which indicates through what date the chart is further corrected. For example—"through 'Notice to Mariners No. 41,' October 11, '76."

Master charts are constantly being revised to reflect changes of importance. These changes, between new editions, are disseminated to interested parties through a "Notice to Mariners." "Local Notices," issued by the appropriate Coast Guard District, cover items of a temporary nature, such as a light being temporarily extinguished, or a buoy temporarily missing or off station. The weekly "Notice to Mariners" is published by the U.S. Naval Oceanographic Office. This will provide you with the information by which you can bring your usable charts up to date. Revise the "corrected through" date accordingly. You may prefer to buy the latest version, already corrected, but make sure this is what you are really getting by again checking the items noted above.

Let's look at some typical charts to see a bit of what they tell us. Sailors in the Northwest are familiar with the large-scale Nautical Chart No. 690-SC, "Lake Washington Ship Canal and Lake Washington," a "must" for the annual Opening Day Yacht Parade heralding the beginning of Seattle's boating season. The charts designated "SC," by the way, are especially created for small craft navigation.

Good items to start with habitually are the heights and depths. In this case we see that the heights are in feet above Mean High Water. The soundings below the Ballard locks are in feet at Mean Lower Low Water, and above the locks are in feet at Mean Water Level. Shoal water under 20 feet is shaded in blue. Applicable rules of the road are shown. Bridge and lock signals are indicated as are horizontal and vertical bridge clearances in the Lake Washington Ship Canal.

Scales are indicated for both nautical and statute miles. A table of public marine facilities and services offered is keyed to chart locations. True and magnetic compass roses showing a variation of 22 degrees E are conveniently placed. In short, this one document contains just about all the info needed to cruise Lake Washington in safety and to make the passage from the lake through the canal out to Puget Sound, where additional charts are put to use.

An example of a medium-scale chart is No. HO 27, "Bermuda Islands." This one, familiar to Bermuda racers, is published by the U.S. Naval Oceanographic Office, as are most foreign charts used by U.S. mariners. It has heights in feet above Mean High Water Springs, and soundings in fathoms (six feet), with those under 11 in fathoms and feet. Shoal water three fathoms and under is shaded in blue. The 10-fathom and the 100-fathom curves are indicated by dashed lines. Compass roses show a variation to date of nearly 15 degrees W.

An important caution is printed in magenta at the top of the chart—"Local magnetic anomaly exists in the vicinity of the Bermuda Islands. Differences as much as six degrees above and lesser differences below the Variation Chart values have been observed."

Small-scale charts are intended for long-distance ocean cruising. HO chart No. 16510, "Newport to Cape Romain," including Bermuda, is such a chart. Of necessity many details of particular areas are omitted. These must be picked up on the appropriate larger-scale chart. The small-scale chart identifies these chart numbers. Because the area covered has a marked change in variation, 16 degrees W at Cape Cod, compared to 2 degrees W at Charleston, South Carolina, the variation is indicated by Magnetic Variation Curves rather than a compass rose.

Medium-scale charts will contain Loran Lines. These lines are used to plot readings taken with appropriate receivers aboard your boat.

Once you have the charts you need for your purpose, take care of them. Keep them dry. Don't rest coffee cups on them. Use soft pencils for markings. Erase carefully. Fold charts twice into quarter size for storage, blank side out, and mark the chart number in a corner for easy reference.

Before you leave port, be sure you have all the charts you need—skimping on charts is poor economy—and arrange them in the order in which you will use them. And do use them. You may have been there before, and you may be a great eyeball navigator, but if you have a proper chart, put it to work.

Navigational Publications

Once you're familiar with *how* to navigate, there is an entirely different collection of publications in addition to the required charts that you should have to actually perform your navigational work on a day-to-day basis. These are available from offices of the U.S. Government or its local agents on an annual or "when revised" basis and annually in slightly different form from commercial publishing sources.

Probably the most used by the typical coastal yachtsman are the *Tide Tables* and the *Tidal Current Tables* for a specified area. The former enables you to predict high and low tides and the latter the velocity and direction of surface current. With these two publications one can avoid going aground or being caught in an adverse current.

Next you should have the appropriate volume of the U.S. Coast Guard *Light List,* a publication describing the aids to navigation for your waters. This includes major lights, buoys, beacons, fog signals and radio beacons for the area covered in the volume. For example, Volume I lists aids to navigation along the East Coast from Maine to South Carolina. For major U.S. harbors, bays and sounds, *Tidal Current Charts* are available which, when used in conjunction with specified *Tide Tables* or *Tidal Current Tables* will give you a visual picture of the direction and velocity of the current at a given time on a particular day.

The *U.S. Coast Pilot* is a nine-volume set covering U.S. coastal areas and offering a wide variety of information helpful to the navigator, including special navigational regulations, landmarks, detailed harbor and channel peculiarities or dangers, local weather and port facilities. Free annual supplements are available to update older editions.

All of the above may be obtained from the Distribution Division, C-44, National Ocean Survey, Riverdale, Maryland 20840, or from authorized sales agents.

If you are sailing offshore and intend to use celestial navigation, you will need a *Nautical Almanac* or an *Air Almanac* for the current year. You will also need sight reduction tables. HO-229, *Sight Reduction Tables for Marine Navigation,* comes in six volumes, each covering 15 degrees of latitude (north and south).

Some navigators prefer the older HO-249, *Sight Reduction Tables for Air Navigation.* These are in three volumes: Volume I, *Selected Stars,* Volume II, *Latitudes Zero to 39 Degrees* and Volume III, *Latitudes 40 to 89 Degrees.*

Other publications of interest to ocean sailors are HO-117A, *Radio Navigational Aids,* Atlantic or Pacific and *Worldwide Marine Weather Broadcasts.*

Need more? There are the various *Sailing Directions* for foreign coastal areas —70 volumes covering the entire world. These are similar to the *U.S. Coast Pilot* in content.

These foreign and offshore publications are available from the Superintendent of Documents, U.S. Government Printing Office, Washington, D.C. 20402, in case your local dealer can't supply you.

You should also have the U.S. pamphlets spelling out the *Rules of the Road* in your area of operations. There are three sets of rules: The *International,* the *Inland* and the *Great Lakes and Western Rivers.* These may be obtained free from the local U.S. Coast Guard office.

One of the problems on a small yacht is that you may not have the room for a large selection of volumes. Commercial books, available at a variety of marine dealers, can help you. These bring together the information from several Government publications, and although sometimes the reduction in the size of charts and tables makes for less readability, the facts are all there and are compacted into one volume rather than several. These all-inclusive publications can save you money and are less trouble to acquire because only one purchase is necessary. They also have extra features not found in the Government publications.

The Navigator's Station

Once the tools, equipment, charts and publications have been chosen, the place to put them is next. The approach to designing and equipping a navigator's station is highly personalized and the result often reflects the level of the owner's own interest in the practice of navigation. It is also subject to the limitations of space, cost and power supply and influenced by the type of campaigning the boat will engage in. Nevertheless, the navigators' stations in most new boats are light-years ahead of what used to be the standard only a few years ago. The improvement in ocean-racing rigs, sails and hulls, and the increased aggressiveness in the way boats are now sailed have also been reflected in the extensive array of equipment and in the more functional work platforms now available for the offshore navigator.

As may be expected, comfort, space and the amount and variety of installed equipment all increase with boat size—but a minimum level of efficiency is recognized in even the smallest racing boats with space and related equipment dedicated full time to the navigator. The optimum configuration begins to appear in boats of about 45 feet, overall.

An important consideration in location is to minimize the likelihood of rainwater and spray dousing the chart table. This would preclude being under or too near the main hatch, although a spray curtain around the chart table is a help if that location is unavoidable. A well-braced seat is a necessity for installations oriented fore and aft to minimize the enervating effects of a constantly slanted work platform. An athwartships installation, with an adjustable seat set at a different angle for each tack, can be less tiring on the navigator in a long race.

The accompanying photos show some of the various ways money and ingenuity have been combined to put a navigator's station together.

Maxi-yacht *Ondine* is one of the best equipped in the fleet.

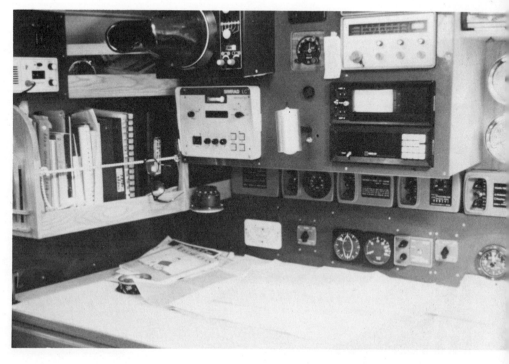

Navigator's Stations

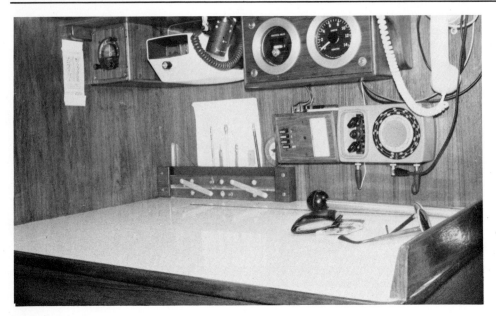

Navigator's station aboard *Rattler,* a Frers 46

Williwaw, a Peterson Two-Tonner, has a lean but well-equipped station.

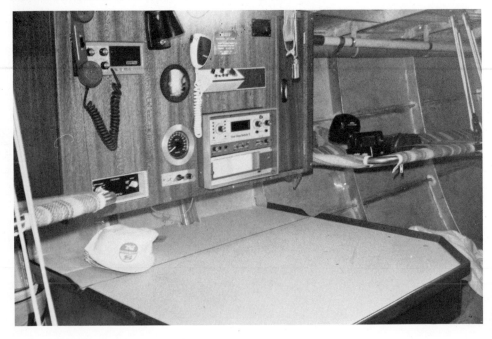

Peter Bowker's work station aboard *Scaramouche* in the 1974 Bermuda Race

Jemel, a Chance 44, has a comfortable and completely instrumented work area.

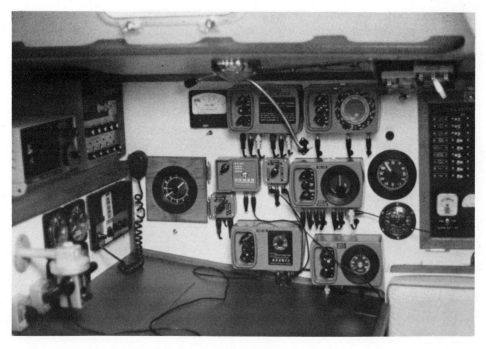

La Forza del Destino (51-foot Mull) has well-thought-out stowage for portable items.

Salty Goose, a 54-foot Derecktor design, has an athwartship arrangement with all instrumentation within easy reach of the navigator.

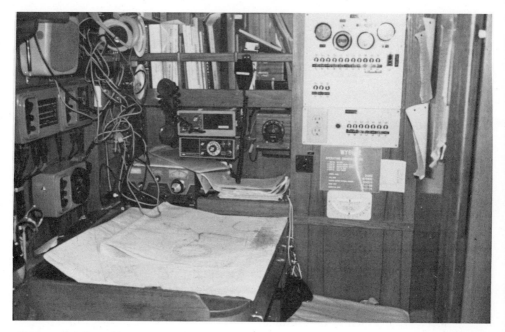

Diane, a stock Swan 44

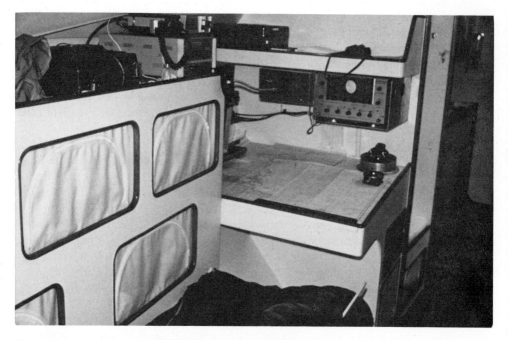

Plenty of storage space to left of 68-footer *Equation*'s chart table

15 ELECTRONIC NAVIGATION

Using the RDF

Previously we listed the direction finder (DF) as an important item of navigational equipment to consider when outfitting a cruising boat. If you have one in operating condition and know how to use it, you need never get lost in coastal waters, regardless of visibility. The DF is a radio beacon receiver and, while one of the most useful tools, is often one of the least understood by the average sailor.

A total DF system has three fundamental parts: a transmitting station to originate the signal, a receiver aboard your boat to pick up and directionalize the signal and a nautical chart encompassing both the station's location and the boat's location on which to plot results.

Bearings may be obtained on any radio signal within the frequency band and range of the receiver and are plotted on the chart the same way as visual bearings. But aeronautical beacons and commercial radio broadcasting stations, due to their inland locations, are often subject to refraction and, while useful, should be considered only for very rough bearings. Signals travelling directly over water and coming from marine radio beacon transmitting stations are best. These have a charted location, an identifying signal in dot and dash code, an assigned frequency and a specified time during which transmissions are made, all of which must be known by the DF operator. Such stations are indicated on coastal charts and described in HO-117A, Radio Navigational Aids and in Coast Guard Light Lists. A station does not need to be seen visually to be used.

Most stations in a locality are grouped, sharing the same frequency, and transmit in regular sequence. This facilitates taking a series of bearings. Ranges vary from 15 miles to 350 miles.

Though there is a great variety of receivers on the market, they all work in a similar manner. Portable DFs have the antenna on the receiver. Permanent installations have an external loop in a fixed or portable location. The receiver will give the loudest signal when the antenna is perpendicular to the station and the least distinct or no signal (null) when it is pointed directly away from or toward the station. The null is what gives you the bearing. If your receiver has a null meter, the null can be determined visually by watching the needle drop to its minimum reading.

Assuming the receiver is correctly installed and operating satisfactorily, and the station is transmitting, the quality of results depends mostly upon the skill of the operator. Perfect yours by following the manufacturer's operating instructions and by sufficient practice in positions where results can also be checked visually.

The structural features of your boat may cause inaccuracies or a weak signal. For example, a portable DF placed inside an aluminum hull won't work very well. You should check your receiver's accuracy by circling within sight of a radio beacon station and taking simultaneous DF and visual bearings. A portable DF must first be aligned fore and aft. If differences are noted make up a calibration table. This is used in the same way as a deviation table for your compass.

DF bearings are relative to the boat's heading, which must be added to convert to magnetic bearings for plotting. That is, if you are heading 045 degrees magnetic and you obtain a bearing directly on your starboard beam (090 degrees relative), the magnetic bearing would be 135 degrees plotted from your boat toward and through the position of the transmitting station. Thus the precise heading should be obtained by calling "mark" to the helmsman at the instant of finding the null. If the sum of the relative bearing and the heading is over 360, subtract 360. Some receivers have a movable compass ring by which the course steered may be set into the instrument and the bearing read directly. With this device preset, the helmsman should notify you when he is off course. Other receivers have a built-in compass to obtain the readings directly off the instrument.

Because it is possible to get two bearings, one toward the station and one away from it (180 degrees apart), you should have a pretty good idea as to the approximate direction of the station from your dead reckoning position. A receiver with a functioning vertical sensing antenna will eliminate this problem.

DF bearings are conceded to be somewhat less accurate than visual bearings due to operator technique and the longer distances involved. A rule of thumb is to allow for a minimum error of plus or minus two degrees. Where the bearings cross is therefore designated as an estimated position rather than a fix. When homing, that is, heading directly for the station, allow for this error factor until you can fix your position by other means and don't forget that you may be on a collision course with the station. Nantucket Lightship was sunk in 1934 by a ship homing on her beacon. Also a phenomenon called "night effect" can be expected around sunrise or sunset and is characterized by a lack of directional characteristics or by obscure, indistinct, swinging or multiple nulls. The receiver's sensitivity (ability to pick up signals at the rated range) and selectivity (ability to choose one frequency) are other limiting factors.

Notwithstanding these cautions, the great navigational value of the DF compared to visual bearings lies in its range, its utility in poor visibility, and the positive identification of the station heard through its coded signal.

Now let's take a bearing. Suppose we are heading NE (045 degrees magnetic) about 15 miles out in the Atlantic southeasterly from Block Island. Block Island Radio Beacon Station has a range of 20 miles. We tune the receiver to its frequency, 310, note that it broadcasts fifth in its group, and listen for its signal, the International Code letters "BI." As it should be off the port side we set the antenna fore and aft for maximum signal, then while the identification is being transmitted we rotate the antenna to port, back and forth across the null, narrowing the sector. At the end of the coded transmission a ten-second dash will be heard. This is when the null can best be determined. In this case let's imagine that the signal begins to fade at about 260 degrees relative and picks up to maximum again at about 275 degrees. We pinpoint the null at 267, call "mark" to the helmsman who reports our exact heading at that time as 047 degrees magnetic. Adding 267 and 047 gives a magnetic bearing of 314. We set the parallel rules to 314 and draw a line on the chart at this angle through the charted position of Block Island Station and to seaward. Our boat is located somewhere along that line. A DF bearing on another station crossing that line (or other navigational techniques) will tell us approximately where.

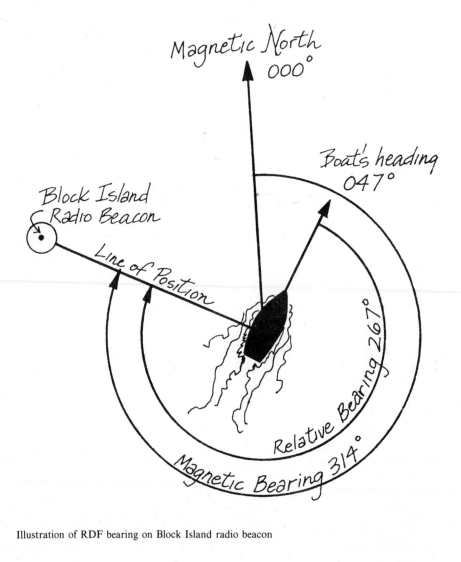

Illustration of RDF bearing on Block Island radio beacon

Loran vs. Omega

An ocean-racing skipper outfitting his new boat called me recently to discuss the relative merits of Loran and Omega, two similar all-weather, day and night, electronic navigational systems using hyperbolic lines of position. While his eventual choice was based upon his particular needs, a review of both systems may be helpful to others facing the same decision.

Omega, although under development for many years, is only recently available for yachts, while Loran (short for "long-range aid to navigation") has been on the nautical scene since World War II. For example, several of the new boats making their debut sport Omega receivers while many of the older boats still have Loran.

The issue is also of general interest to most navigators because Omega is a positioning device that can be used to provide a fix in a few minutes by persons with little or no navigational experience, while standard Loran requires a fair amount of operator skill (even with today's refined receiving equipment). Both systems are quick and highly accurate when used correctly.

Such electronic navigational devices are barred in some offshore races, but are allowed in most. Therefore, any boat that is to be campaigned extensively offshore should be equipped with some type of hyperbolic receiver. The equipment can also come in handy on ferry trips between races.

Loran

Standard Loran, now designated as Loran A, operates in the 1850 to 1950 kHZ frequency range. A line of position is obtained by receiving a coupled pair of stations (master and slave) which transmit a pulse signal. During daylight hours ground waves provide coverage from the stations up to about 700 miles in the Atlantic and 800 miles in the Pacific. This drops at night to about one-third less. For distances over that, sky waves have to be used. These are a little trickier to tune in and to read, but are usable up to about 1400 miles. The receiver is set to the desired pair of transmitting stations which is identified by letter and number (for example, 1H4). Master and slave wave signals are visually matched on a scope on the receiver-indicator, and a numerical reading is shown on dials. This reading is used to enter Loran tables to calculate a line of position which is then applied to a plotting sheet. Or, more commonly, the reading is applied to a nautical chart upon which Loran ground wave lines are preprinted and identified. The charts also show the appropriate sky wave corrections. Interpolation is used to plot a reading that is between the printed lines of position on the chart.

It should be apparent that the selection of the proper pulse signals for the area and the identification of ground waves vs. sky waves on the scope are crucial to accurate use of Loran A. Because there are four types of sky waves, only one of which is usable (the left-hand one, called a "One-Hop-E") a certain familiarity with the appearance of signals on the scope relative to the amount of gain needed

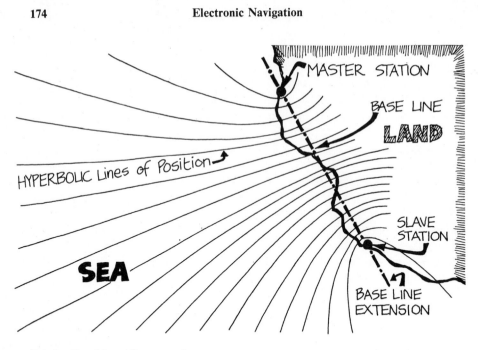

MASTER STATION

BASE LINE

LAND

HYPERBOLIC Lines of Position

SLAVE STATION

SEA

BASE LINE EXTENSION

Relationship of Loran lines to stations

is very important. Linking a ground wave and a sky wave leads to positioning errors unless correction tables are used. It is preferable to match ground waves with ground waves and sky waves with sky waves. The distance of the receiver from the stations will help to sort out the types of waves seen on the scope. If a single wave is visible it is usually a ground wave, but when several waves are seen, and if the gain is sufficient, the ground wave will be the left-hand wave of the group. The appearance of the waves also helps. Ground waves are normally steady in shape and height. Sky waves are seldom steady for more than a few minutes and are subject to changes in intensity which cause fading.

In addition to operator technique and correct plotting of the reading, accuracy in obtaining a Loran fix also depends upon the angle at which the selected lines intersect. As with any lines of position, the best results are when two lines intersect at an angle of 90 degrees. Also the position of your boat relative to the transmitting stations is important. The lines are more closely spaced along the base line between the master and slave stations. From there the lines fan out and are at a greater distance for the same charted values. This means that a one microsecond error in the reading (about 500 feet at base line) can increase substantially the farther you are from base line. The area of base line extensions should not be used.

Loran ground wave coverage is excellent along the coasts of North America, Eastern Europe, Western Asia and the Pacific Islands. Sky wave coverage is continuous across both the North Atlantic and the North Pacific.

Loran C, a newer and even more accurate system, operating on 100 kHZ and using ground waves with a range of 1200 to 1500 miles, works in a similar way. Loran C is slated eventually to replace Loran A. At present, many areas have both Loran A and Loran C coverage. Loran receivers can be obtained to pick up either Loran A, Loran C or both A and C.

Representative of the new Loran C receivers is the Simrad/Internav 101 manufactured by Simrad, Inc., Armonk, N.Y. This instrument weighs 30 pounds, is 15 X 11 ¼ X 8 inches, operates on either 115/230 volts AC or 12 or 24/32 volts DC. Signal acquisition time is two minutes, setting to full accuracy is six minutes, readout is digital to seven decimal digits. Ground wave range is over 1200 nautical miles; sky wave range is over 2500 nautical miles and ground wave accuracy is 200 to 1200 feet. It simultaneously tracks two lines of position.

The improvement in accuracy of Loran C over Loran A is due to the more precise transmitted signal and to the more sophisticated receiver which decodes and displays the signal. The numbers on the digital display can be directly plotted on Loran C charts. If what you need is a quick, relatively simple to operate and highly accurate system, the cost of $3500 for the typical receiver can be justified.

A feature of the latest and highest cost Loran receivers is automatic tracking with readout in digital form or on a recording chart. After pulse-matching of a station pair has been achieved by manual means, the receiver can be switched to automatic. It then monitors the station pair without resetting and gives continuous readings while in operation, thus showing progress across Loran lines or facilitating "homing" on a single line.

Omega

Omega navigation is similar to Loran in that a receiver is used to pick up pulsed signals from pairs of transmitting stations but it displays them directly in terms of Omega lane number and centilane position, or percent of lane position, relating to Omega charts. It differs in an important detail. Whereas the Loran receiver is turned on to obtain lines of position and then is turned off, unless tracking, the Omega receiver is turned on when leaving port and left on at all times while at sea. For each line of position it is only necessary to switch the receiver to the appropriate pair of stations and the display will indicate the reading to be applied to the chart. The receiver is constantly tracking the selected stations without further adjustments other than the initial Omega position or initial Omega lane at a known point of departure. Coverage now includes the Pacific Ocean from latitude 75 degrees N to 30 degrees S between North and South America and Hawaii, and the entire Atlantic Ocean from 75 degrees N to 20 degrees S, plus the entire Caribbean, Mediterranean and North seas. When all eight stations are operational, worldwide coverage will be provided.

Omega operates at very low frequency in the 10.2 to 13.6 kHz range. This permits extremely long-range reception, using effectively direct waves that follow the curvature of the earth and are inherently stable. Minimal corrections, due to the wide spacing between Omega stations, are handled by using Omega Propagation Tables which take into account certain highly predictable plus or minus phase errors.

Because Omega is a tracking receiver and must remain on at all times, the obvious question is what happens if the receiver loses power? Omega receivers have provisions for two power sources. If one should fail, the other will automatically take over operation. However, if the receiver is started up after being totally without power for a period of time, or if the antenna is accidentally disconnected, it must be set up again by inputting the then-current Omega position obtained by conventional means.

At the present time, an Omega receiver is considerably more expensive than the various types of Loran receivers ($4500 vs. $1000 to $3500). Both systems use charts and tables provided by the U.S. Naval Oceanographic Office, Washington, D.C. These are listed in the *Catalog of Nautical Charts* (HO publication 1-N-A) which also shows station locations and coverage areas. Weight and size of the receivers is similar. Accuracy with proper operation is similar.

In summary, the choice boils down to the coverage available in the proposed sailing waters, the skill required, the relative cost and the capability of the available power supply. These factors must obviously be analyzed for each installation.

The Wave of the Future

A recent announcement by Teledyne Systems Company of Northridge, California, describes a very highly sophisticated Omega receiver with a built-in microprocessor. This is used to make the receiver fully automatic. That is, special Omega charts and propagation correction tables are eliminated. Following the entry by the operator of estimated present position and current GMT time and date, the TDO-1000 automatically (1) synchronizes the Omega transmission format and lane identification and (2) computes the skywave correction for each Omega signal, (3) converts the received Omega information into latitude-longitude coordinates, (4) resolves initial position uncertainties up to 12 nautical miles from DR position, (5) continuously displays time and date in a 24-hour format, (6) computes and displays vessel's true speed and course in knots and degrees respectively and (7) following operator entry of a selected destination, computes and displays both Great Circle and rhumb line range and bearing to that destination.

In addition to the digital readout, a digital printer is also available as well as a remote display. The receiver size is 6 by 17 by 12 inches and weighs 30 pounds. With the first production model being delivered in the latter part of 1976 at an estimated cost of $12,000 per unit, it is still a bit beyond the reach of the average yachtsman, but it does indicate what is in store for the future.

16 THE CONCEPT OF CELESTIAL OBSERVATIONS

Choosing a Sextant

The choice of a sextant is most important in celestial navigation, the art and science of position-finding by using stars and planets. As with any product, sextants come in a variety of qualities and prices. Simple plastic sextants of the type that come with correspondence courses on navigation can be obtained for as little as $15. A bit better version of a nonmetal sextant features a micrometer adjustment and a two-power scope instead of just a sighting tube and sells in the $50 range. Simple metal sextants start at about $200 and increase in price as the design and quality improve and features are added. Also in this price range are good used sextants which can be obtained from ship chandlers in various metropolitan seaports. The Plath Micrometer Drum Sextant selling for close to $600 is the ultimate in instruments, based upon its prevalence aboard the top-notch boats in the ocean racing fleet. This sextant has a guaranteed accuracy of better than 10 seconds of arc. The horizon mirror is 50 millimeters in diameter, a significant feature, and all mirrors in the sextant and optics in the telescope are of fine quality. The preferred telescope for a yacht sextant is the 4 X 40.

So, if your objective is just to practice the technique, possibly one of the plastics might be OK until you are ready for something better. However, be prepared to live with the inaccuracies inherent in this type of instrument. For a great many sailors who cruise more than race, a new middle-range metal sextant or a used higher-quality sextant might be the answer. If price is no object and you want the greatest accuracy and easiest operation, a new Plath will fill the bill.

The Observation

A successful celestial sight, because of the observational skill required and the meticulous calculations necessary, is considered the highest form of the navigator's art. To oversimplify, what it amounts to is a two-step process; observing the altitude (angle) of a selected celestial body with the sextant, then calculating by means of tables what the altitude of that body is at a known point, using the time of the observed altitude, and plotting the difference, if any, on an appropriate chart.

If a celestial body is directly overhead, its angle from the observer's horizon would be 90 degrees. But, as the observed angle decreases, it should be apparent that the observer can be anywhere on a circle centered at the position at which

The author shooting the sun *(Mike Levitt photo)*

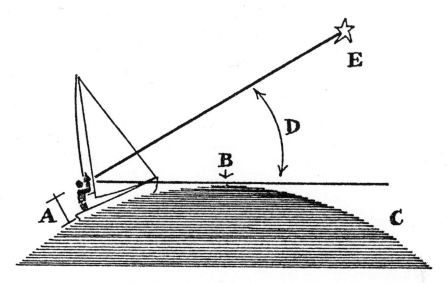

Elements of a sextant observation. (A) height of eye above sea surface, (B) visible horizon, (C) sea surface, (curvature exaggerated), (D) observed altitude (angle indicated by sextant), (E) celestial body observed.

the body was directly overhead. Let's describe it in more conventional terms. You are standing in your living room and directly over your head is a spot on the ceiling. A horizontal stripe on the wallpaper is directly at eye level. The angle formed between the stripe and the spot on the ceiling, with your eye as the apex, is 90 degrees. If you back away until the angle is, say, 60 degrees, you can circle around the room, if it is big enough, while keeping the angle at 60 degrees.

Going back to the ocean, a circle of equal altitude can cover a vast area (the lower the angle the larger the circle), so that for practical purposes only a small segment is used as a line of position and is plotted as a straight line. The navigator, though, through his DR position, has a good idea where this segment is.

The sextant functions by means of a split image, like a camera range finder, and the body observed on one image is "brought down" to the horizon seen on the other image by moving the index arm. Naturally, the horizon must be visible and distinct. A small body, like a star, is brought directly to the horizon. A larger body, like the sun or the moon, is brought down until either the bottom is resting on the horizon or the top is touching the horizon. (The entire body may not be visible.) Then the time is taken, the reading is obtained in degrees and minutes from the position of the index arm on the sextant arc and the bearing of the body is noted. Time is most important in an observation because celestial bodies are in motion relative to a position on the earth's surface.

The Corrections

Because the navigator wants to be as accurate as possible, he must make corrections in the reading obtained from the sextant. First he corrects for sextant index error. A properly adjusted sextant usually has a small residual error, measured in minutes, inherent in the instrument. This is easily found each time the sextant is used by lining up both images on the horizon and tilting the sextant a bit from side to side to ensure a good match.

The height of eye above the water surface at observation time is recorded and a correction for this is obtained from a table in the *Nautical Almanac.* In a rough sea the wave height must also be considered as the correction tables are based upon the assumption of a calm sea. The experienced navigator usually times his sight at wave top, estimating his height of eye at that point.

Other significant correction factors include refraction (on lower altitude sights), horizontal parallax (on planets; greatest with the moon as it is closest to the earth), and semidiameter which corrects to midbody of the sun or the moon because either the bottom or the top is matched with the horizon. These are all obtained from tables in the *Nautical Almanac.*

The Computation

When the observed altitude is corrected, the navigator begins step two, figuring the computed altitude. He uses the time of his observation to enter the *Nautical Almanac* and get the hour angle and declination of the body observed. With these data, and using an assumed position near the DR position, he can now enter the appropriate *Sight Reduction Tables.* Using a work sheet compatible with the Tables and designed to indicate each step of the mathematical work, he will obtain for the selected body at the assumed position a computed altitude and an azimuth (the direction the observed body bears from the observer).

Plotting the Sight

Because the assumed position, chosen for convenience in entering the *Sight Reduction Tables,* is usually some distance from the actual position at the time of observation, the navigator must plot and adjust the results obtained. He draws the bearing line through the assumed position and compares the computed altitude and the observed altitude, as corrected. If the computed altitude is the greater figure, he measures the actual altitude difference (at one minute per mile) from the assumed position in a direction away from the body—if the computed altitude is less, he measures toward the body. A line perpendicular to the bearing line is then drawn through that point and this becomes the line of position for that observation.

If the navigator has taken a good observation with a good horizon and has properly identified the celestial body; if the watch time is accurate; if the recorder

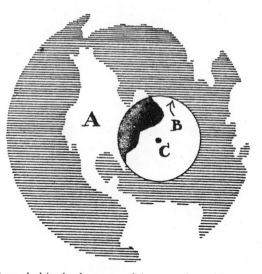

Circle of equal altitude shown on globe, covering wide area of
North Atlantic. (A) North America, (B) circle, (C) center of
circle or geographical position (G.P.), the point directly below
the celestial body.

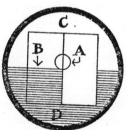

View of sun with bottom edge touching the horizon, as seen
through the sextant. (A) sun, (B) horizon, (C) sky, (D) water.

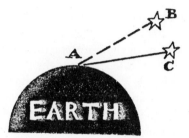

Illustration of refraction. (A) observer's position, (B) star's apparent position, (C) star's actual position.

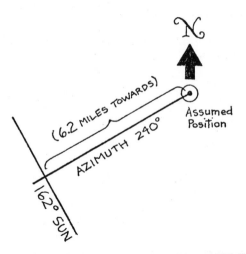

Plot of a line of position using the sun at 1620 (4:20 p.m.) azimuth 240 degrees, computed altitude less than observed altitude by 6.2 minutes of arc.

has not made any errors in reading the watch or in recording the data and if the navigator has made all his calculations without error using the right tables, the yacht was somewhere on that line at the time of observation. The navigator can tell how good the line is by comparing it with the DR position.

Readers who want to pursue this subject in more detail are referred to the many excellent books on the subject, but here are a few hints applicable to ocean racing yachts:

  • Practice and patience are necessary for accurate observations from a small yacht lurching in a seaway.
  • Wear a safety belt when sighting in rough weather. The skipper needs you aboard.
  • Check out the assistant who reads and records the sight time and data to minimize inaccuracies.
  • Don't hesitate to change the yacht's heading momentarily to bring the celestial body in a better relative position for observation.

The recent development of programmable calculators and miniaturized computers has made possible the mechanization of sight reduction by pushing buttons rather than using tables, pencil and paper. Since this is only a part of the total celestial navigation process, the potential time saving is minimal and if the basic observation is incorrect or the results are not properly plotted, inaccuracies are still possible. Still, with inexperienced navigators, sight reduction can be very time-consuming and is the part where most errors are made.

Only the practitioner can decide whether the additional cost of the calculator or minicomputer is worth it in terms of time saved and errors eliminated. Many race committees still prohibit the use of programmable calculators and minicomputers for sight reduction.

17 WEATHER AND STRATEGY

To be successful, an offshore sailor has to have more than a passing interest in the subject of weather. The ability to assemble data, analyze them and to come up with a good judgment of what the weather will be during a race is vital to a winning strategy. Anything better than a guess can be a real advantage.

What is "weather" in this context? Basically, it is wind direction and velocity. But more than that, it is an understanding of why wind is blowing from a certain direction, why it is as strong or as weak as it is, and what happens to the ocean, sky, temperature, barometric pressure and the visibility. It is not our intention here to give a short course on such a vast subject that has puzzled and confounded not only mariners, but nearly everyone else on the face of the globe, including highly sophisticated forecasters. The latter, both governmental and commercial, function in a more scientific way than most, but often their results are as inexact as those derived by the arthritic farmer whose aging joints tell him it is going to rain tomorrow.

Suffice it to say that it is possible, within the constraints of allowed or feasible equipment, for the crew of a modern racing boat to record at regular intervals, either manually or on a recording device, atmospheric pressure, sea temperature, air temperature, wind direction and velocity, sky, sea and swell conditions and to receive by radio plain-language local and wide area forecasts on a variety of frequencies and from a variety of sources. In conjunction with radio weather forecasts, weather observations, the recently recorded weather data actually experienced at a selected group of stations, are also broadcast. One must distinguish, in wind directions, whether they are reported in true direction or magnetic. This can make a difference in areas of high magnetic variation.

With all the above information faithfully received and logged on a recurring cycle and adding in the data obtained at your yacht's location, it is not difficult to construct a rudimentary weather map which, when compared with readily available weather maps collected before the race, can tell you when to expect a change in conditions on the racecourse or tell you that conditions will remain the same for a predictable period. Once you know this, you can determine what sails you probably will use, how you will trim and sail the boat and where you want to be in relation to the straight-line course from point to point (rhumb line) when the predicted weather materializes. Of course, there's no problem figuring what to do about the weather you are suffering or enjoying at your yacht's location.

Let's illustrate with some specific examples . . .

One of the distinctive features of the 635-mile Newport–Bermuda Race is that the first leg of the course from the start to the turning buoy at Kitchen Shoals

Buoy is 630 miles long in a straight line. Rarely, if ever, does the fleet experience wind from the same quadrant as it moves along this line, and certainly never of a consistent velocity. More often than not there are three weather systems: one between the start and the north edge of the Gulf Stream, a second and highly localized system in the Gulf Stream and the third, another local weather system in the vicinity of the Bermuda Islands. Because of this, it is very important for a yacht to be positioned on, to the east or to the west of the rhumb line when making the final approach to Bermuda in consideration of the winds expected in the latter 100 miles of this leg.

Assisting or hindering this effort is the effect of the Gulf Stream current at the time of crossing. Chapter 30 has more about this factor.

Sometimes in this race the wind direction allows for a reach directly along most of the rhumb line. This was the case in 1968, when after a day of beating in a southeasterly generated by the coastal weather system, a sudden shift of wind to the southwest allowed a reach directly to the islands. In 1970 it paid to stay moderately east of the rhumb line under a wide variety of wind conditions. In 1972, because of a building southeast gale off Bermuda, it was important to get as far east as possible, using the continental weather system and a southeasterly Gulf Stream meander well to the east of the rhumb line. Those who used this approach were able to lay the turning mark at Kitchen Shoals on the port tack. Those who went to the west had to beat into the gale for a day to a day and a half. In 1974 it was necessary to go 40 to 60 miles west of the rhumb line to intercept a favorable meander. But with the southwest wind prevailing at Bermuda, this meant that it was not difficult to get back to the rhumb line at the turning point. In 1976 the opposite occurred. This time a favorable meander, similar to the one in 1972, was present to the east of the rhumb line, and to take full advantage of it meant going 90 to 100 miles east of the straight-line course. Further, it was relatively easy to get back to the rhumb line at the turn because of the easterly wind prevailing in Bermuda for that period. Again, those that went the right way slid in on a single tack. Those who did not had to beat many miles directly to windward. In these instances, information on the Bermuda weather, both present and predicted, was most important in determining whether the departure from the rhumb line track was worthwhile. The only possible way to do this was to have plenty of weather information collected as described previously and analyzed in connection with other key factors such as current, sea conditions, the boat's best sailing angle in relation to the wind, the sails favorable for increased boat speed, the distance traveled over the bottom and the like.

Not all legs in a race are as long as the one just described. Naturally, the shorter the leg the less elaborate weather data need be. In a 50-mile leg the weather may not change at all and local knowledge may be more important than the latest weather information. For example, at one time in Long Island Sound one could almost set his watch by the afternoon southerly which came in at about 4:00 P.M.

In the wintertime SORC races in Florida and the Bahamas a rich yield of weather data can be used to advantage by a racing yacht.

A series of U.S. weather maps illustrated on the following pages show a

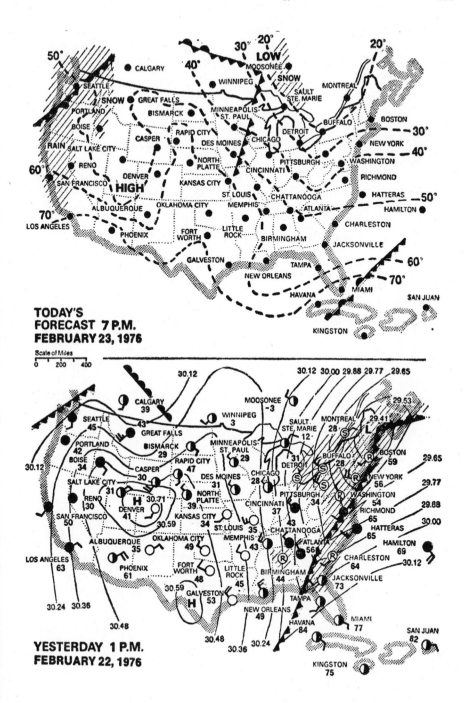

TODAY'S FORECAST 7 P.M. FEBRUARY 23, 1976

Scale of Miles
0 200 400

YESTERDAY 1 P.M. FEBRUARY 22, 1976

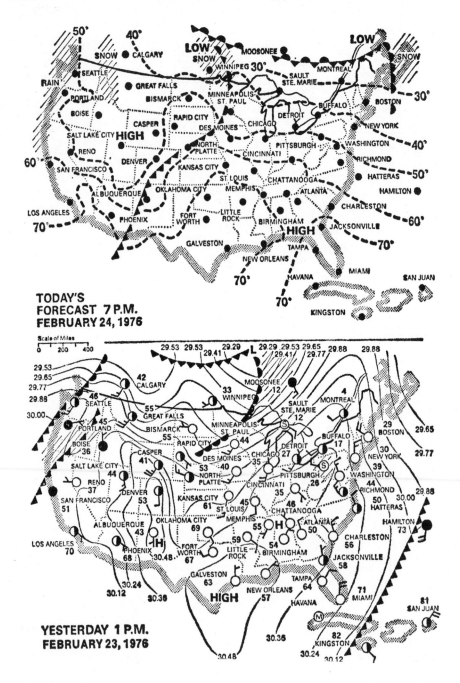

TODAY'S
FORECAST 7 P.M.
FEBRUARY 24, 1976

YESTERDAY 1 P.M.
FEBRUARY 23, 1976

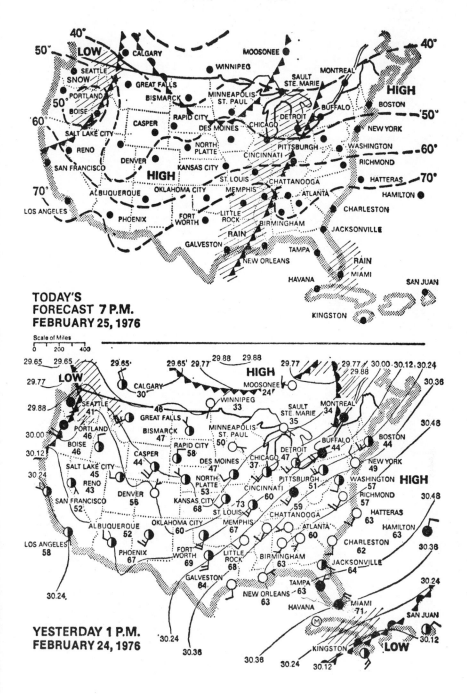

TODAY'S
FORECAST 7 P.M.
FEBRUARY 25, 1976

YESTERDAY 1 P.M.
FEBRUARY 24, 1976

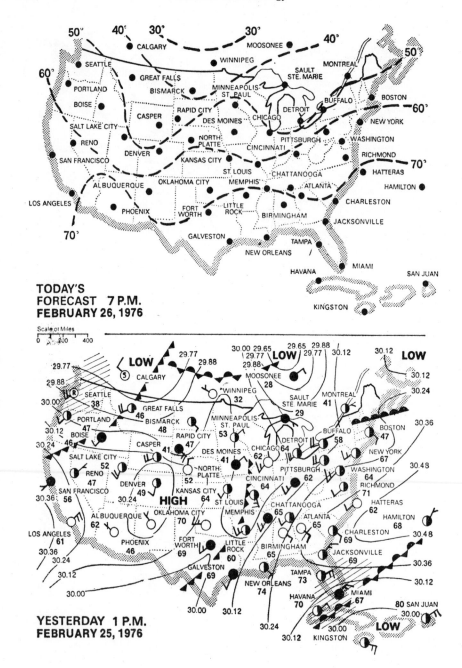

**TODAY'S
FORECAST 7 P.M.
FEBRUARY 26, 1976**

**YESTERDAY 1 P.M.
FEBRUARY 25, 1976**

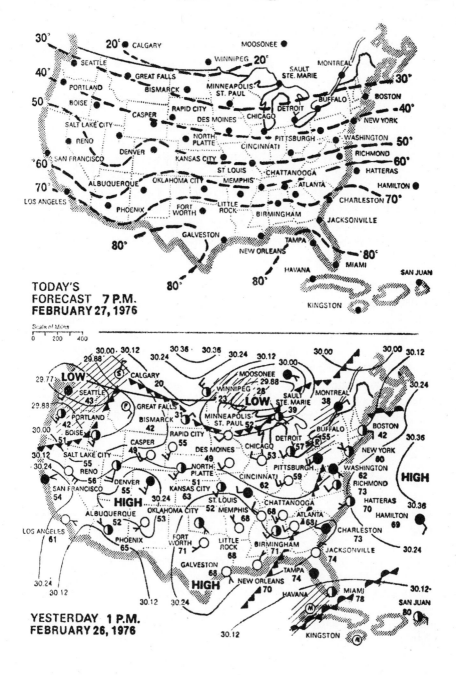

TODAY'S
FORECAST 7 P.M.
FEBRUARY 27, 1976

YESTERDAY 1 P.M.
FEBRUARY 26, 1976

sequence of weather over a five-day period during February. The forecast is at the top of each illustration and the actual weather from the day before is shown at the bottom. The actual weather from February 22nd shows a large frontal system extending from the Florida panhandle on up to Boston along the East Coast. The forecast above it indicates that this front will have passed quickly through Miami by the following day. The actual weather for February 23rd confirms this forecast and also shows an additional frontal system building in the Great Lakes area.

Following this next sequence we find on the 25th another frontal passage in the Miami area, which on the 26th has passed Miami but has moved very slowly and is now passing through central Cuba. From this sequence we can see that the weather in the Florida area is influenced on a regular basis by cold fronts during February. Some pass through rapidly and some move very slowly. In between, local weather predominates. We can also conclude that, in the absence of a large overriding weather system, the winds will be influenced between fronts by local thermal conditions. In the Tampa area on the Gulf of Mexico these local conditions take the pattern of a southeast breeze in the morning, swinging around as the day progresses through south, southwest, west, northwest, north and about midnight into the east. In the absence of a front, the sequence will be completed the next morning.

In the Miami area the prefrontal winds are normally from the southeast as indicated in the actual weather for February 22nd where we see winds from nine to 14 miles an hour from the southeast. After the frontal passage, the winds will be in the opposite direction—that is, from the northwesterly quadrant until the prevailing wind again dominates with the same clocking pattern through north and east and ending again in the southeast. An additional local pattern is evident between Miami and Fort Lauderdale and the Bahama Banks off the east coast of Florida in the absence of the prevailing southeasterly winds. Winds will be light to moderate offshore along the Florida coast, that is, from the west, and light to moderate off the Banks from the east with the transition point being along the axis of the Gulf Stream. These winds are light during the night and gradually build to a peak about midafternoon, then gradually subside again as sunlight wanes.

Most of the SORC racecourses are within range of VHF plain-language weather broadcasts, which give regular forecasts as well as observed weather in the forecast location. For example: If you are racing along the Florida Keys, Miami VHF Weather Report will tell you what is expected for the next several hours as well as what has actually been observed prior to the broadcast. In addition, there are a number of airports scattered along both coasts of Florida and the Bahamas, all of which transmit weather forecasts over the Florida–Bahamas area and in addition give meteorological data previously observed at a series of stations. These are extremely valuable in tracking the progress of an expected front. They can tell you whether a front has passed Tampa and Jacksonville, but has not yet arrived in Miami. This kind of information is valuable in the long St. Petersburg–Fort Lauderdale Race which begins in Tampa Bay, passes through the Florida Keys and finishes on the east coast, and in the Miami–Nassau Race. On the long legs of these courses accurate weather information can help you decide, as in the Bermuda Race example, whether to stay on the rhumb line or to deviate one side or the other from it in order to make use of the anticipated wind directions and velocities when combined with data on currents.

Additionally, one can often pick up local weather from broadcast band stations although in a less sophisticated form. I recall one instance during the 1970 St. Pete–Fort Lauderdale Race when we were about 10 miles south of Marathon in the Florida Keys enjoying the beautiful southeast breeze and speeding along under chute. We knew this would not last because, using the aviation weather reports, we were tracking a cold front coming down along the Florida peninsula. On the chance that we might get something locally, we tuned in to the Marathon broadcasting station. Sure enough, the disk jockey interrupted his music to exclaim, "Wow! all of a sudden it is blowing hard and raining like cats and dogs outside." The front was about to hit us. We quickly made preparations to douse the chute and shift to #2 jib in anticipation of a quick change of wind from the southeast to the northwest and an increase in velocity. Two other competitors were nearby. Very soon the front swept over the water and we were ready for it. But our two competitors were taken by surprise and were knocked over on their beam ends before they could douse their chutes and make the appropriate sail changes. By that time we were long gone. . . .

Two good publications to start with in your search for radio weather information are: *Aviation Weather Services,* published jointly by the Federal Aviation Administration (FAA) and the National Oceanic and Atmospheric Administration (NOAA) and *World Wide Marine Weather Broadcasts* published jointly by NOAA and the Naval Weather Service Command.

The former explains in great detail what reports consist of while the latter lists times, frequencies and types of broadcasts for all ocean areas around the world.

But it is well to consider the advice of Lynn Williams of Chicago, skipper of *Dora IV,* and several times winner of the Mackinacs, who retired in 1976 after 50 years of offshore racing. "If you'll agree not to be discouraged, I'll pass along a dark secret of offshore racing vouchsafed to me before a Bermuda Race a few years ago by a well-known and very successful old-timer: 'Take all weather predictions with liberal amounts of salt.' "

Brenton Reef Tower, the other end of the starting line, was not visible from Committee Boat end in 1974 Bermuda Race, due to fog.

18 TAKING ADVANTAGE OF FOG

The onset of fog during a race can be a great competitive advantage if you know how to cope with it. If you don't, it can be a disaster. How are you handling it?

Some recent instances are a reminder that fog is more prevalent throughout a year's racing campaign than might be supposed. One was at the start of the Ocean Triangle Race in mid-February in the 1975 SORC, in which the boats had to go on instruments right after the gun. Others were at the start of the 1974 and 1976 Bermuda Races when it was impossible to see one end of the line while at the other end. There were Committee suspicions that the yachts in the middle and not visible were taking advantage of both the fog and the situation. Still another was at the end of the October 1974 Skipper Race on Chesapeake Bay when, after the fleet unexpectedly encountered dense fog about 10 miles from the finish in restricted waters, a couple of dozen boats went hard aground on an outgoing tide. Fog can also be expected often in the West Coast and New England areas of the U.S. and in northern European waters.

One of a mariner's greatest pitfalls can be self-delusion, defined in this context as the ability to convince oneself that things are other than they really are. Sailing in a fog can do this to you if you let it. Have you ever dismissed available facts when they didn't compare with what you wanted to believe? Have you ever refused to admit to yourself that something didn't add up, when it didn't? Have you ever been reluctant to ask for assistance when you needed it in a tight situation?

Part of the reason this is a problem for skippers is that they must have confidence in themselves and project it. If this is shaken, credibility, that most prized asset, can be lost with others in the crew.

When fog is present, or imminent, a navigator needs all the help he can get because the normal inputs available are severely restricted and the work load can be increased. Without frequent fixes and solid information as input, particularly in coastal waters, disorientation can easily occur. The best way to stay on top of the situation when positioning is critical is to set up a fog emergency procedure, which we will illustrate later.

Navigating in fog differs little from the approach used in good visibility as far as maintaining the plot is concerned. The great difference is in how you arrive at the information to construct the plot. On the open ocean, in races where you would normally use celestial observations, the lack of available horizon or inability to see the celestial body in poor visibility will eliminate the use of this method to fix your position. If Omega or Loran is not allowed in the race, one has to fall back on the depth sounder (provided it is capable of reaching the bottom) or the direction finder when within range of transmitting stations. Failing these, an accurate and continuous DR plot will help significantly (see Chapter 14).

With the use of direction finding and depth sounding, fairly accurate fixes can be obtained by combining a direction finder station line-of-position with a sounding; or a sounding may be used to verify the point at which two direction finder bearings cross. When homing on a direction finder station, progress toward the shore can be measured using the depth sounder as various bottom contour lines are crossed. This technique was particularly helpful to many boats at the finish of the 1972 Bermuda Race when all that was available at the height of the gale and reduced visibility was RDF at Kindley Field and Gibbs Hill until the boats were close enough to cross the 100-fathom curve close to Bermuda's coral reefs.

Basically, the crucial points in a poor visibility race are when nearing the turning points in the racecourse and when approaching the finish. As these are usually in coastal waters, the navigator is not only concerned with the shortest course to find the mark or finish, but also with keeping the boat off the bottom. Navigational aids are equipped to emit audible signals that can be very useful with low visibility. Lighthouses and other prominent aids have diaphones that sound a very loud signal, heard many miles away. Bell buoys and whistle buoys can also be heard quite a distance. All of these have distinctive tones and some have a distinctive characteristic. All are described in the appropriate light list and indicated on larger-scale charts. It is very important to have the latest edition of these coastal charts because you can't use something that is no longer there, and if a newly placed aid is not on the chart you have, it can't help you much.

Sightings in a fog are better than audible signals. But remember, when buoy-hopping, that these are only guides and can be missing or off-station, so use whatever additional means are available to verify your position further.

Taking an actual illustration from the Skipper Race mentioned above, the accompanying diagram illustrates the situation at the finale of that contest. This is an annual 100-mile race—50 miles down Chesapeake Bay from the Annapolis Sea Buoy and back. Aboard *Running Tide,* we were in the fleet lead and thus ran into the fog first as it crept silently down the bay from Annapolis. At the time we were on the starboard tack, hard on the wind and on a course that would take us close aboard Flasher #73. When we ran into the white curtain, with resultant 100-foot visibility, we set up a fog emergency procedure; a crew member to call out soundings, another crew member to man a stopwatch, two lookouts forward, Bo Van Metre, starboard watch captain and a fine helmsman, at the wheel, crew members stationed at all positions needed for quick sail handling; port watch captain, Norm Raben, assisting me with the navigational plot inputs and relaying the results to the cockpit and Skipper Al Van Metre overseeing the entire operation from the afterdeck.

The first step was to transfer the plot to the largest-scale chart available and stand by for the sighting of Flasher #73. This was sighted close ahead, and when it was abeam the stopwatch was started and the log reading and depth reading were taken and transferred to the plot. The course and speed made good were thus confirmed from the last fix before entering the fog and extended from Flasher #73 on the chart. Our tacking angle was known so that the tacking point could easily be established on the chart. The time to tack was calculated using the known boat speed and the time interval needed in the tacking evolution. At the appointed time the tack to port was made to the new heading, as log and depth sounder readings were taken and recorded and the stopwatch restarted. The new heading would put us on top of Can #75 off Thomas Point Light.

Since we had other inputs to position the next tack, to be made at Can #75, the run time to the Can was not as crucial, for we were now able to use also the horn at Thomas Point Light and the difference in bottom depth on either side of the Can (13 feet on the north side and 40 feet on the south side). The lookouts spotted the Can looming up right on the nose—in fact we almost hit it! Our tack to starboard was made flawlessly by the ready crew members and the log and depth sounder read and recorded and the stopwatch restarted again for the next leg. This heading put us slightly inside the 18-foot curve so that we now had another verification of our progress over the bottom when we crossed outside the 18-foot curve into deeper water. The next tack had to be made solely on a timed basis and had to be accurate so that the next port tack heading would put us within visual distance of Bell #77. This had to be left to port as a mark of the course, as was Thomas Point Light, previously passed. At the appointed time we tacked to port, repeating the procedure in previous tacks. The depth sounder readings were now critical. Just as it dropped to 33 feet we sighted the Bell #77, ran out to 40 feet and tacked to starboard on a heading calculated to put us between Can #1 and Bell #2, the latter being the finish buoy. The point here was not to overstand and be caught in the strong, adverse current and not to lose frequent visual contacts. After a short tack to port, Bell #2 was sighted and a short tack to starboard brought us over the line before noon—first to finish!

With the help of the fog we saved our time on our competitors and we were declared the overall winner on corrected time. Late that afternoon we learned that a number of boats were still aground on Bloody Point Bar. A glance at the diagram will show what happened to them. With the water depth changing from 70 feet to 6 feet in a couple of hundred yards, boats heading into Eastern Bay to escape the mid-Chesapeake current lost their plot continuity because of the few available aids, fetched up on the bar and had to await the next high tide to get free.

When you are heading for a mark in poor visibility and are not too sure about exactly where it is, try an old coastal pilot's trick. (This assumes that there is an adjacent direction finder station and you have an RDF aboard.) Set a course that will definitely put you to seaward of the mark by using soundings and continue on until the bearing of the radio beacon crosses the position of the mark, then turn and run down the bearing line until the mark is located visually.

A final point. When enveloped in fog, stay cool. The comforting knowledge that many of your competitors will not stay cool is a great tactical advantage. Navigation must be unemotional and logical, and all the more so under low visibility conditions. Knowing what to do, how to do it and doing it well will get you through even the most adverse conditions.

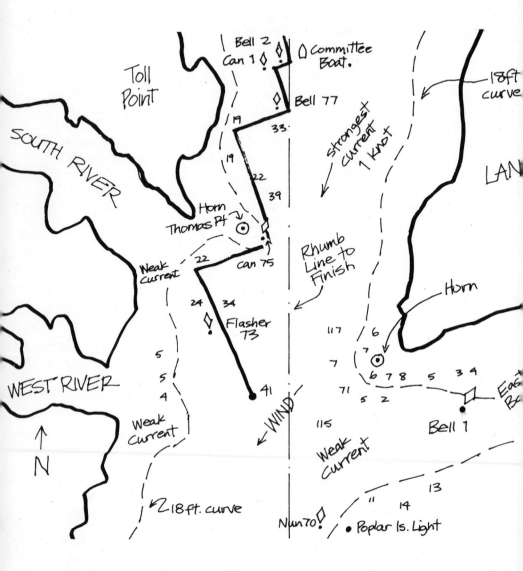

Running Tide's track at finish of 1974 Skipper Race

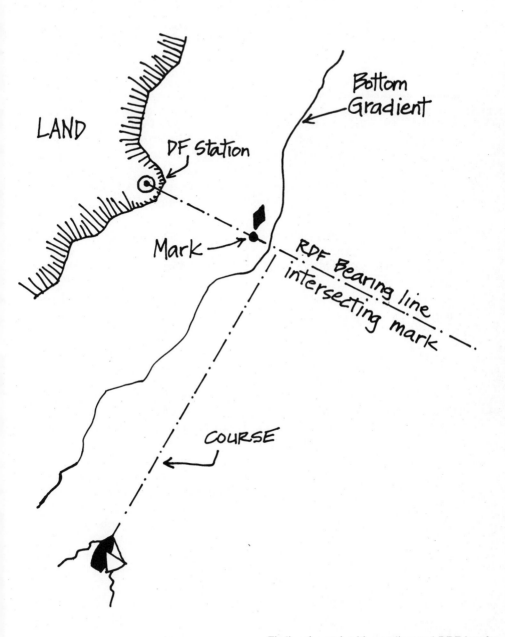

Finding the mark with soundings and RDF in a fog

19 WRITE IT DOWN

The recording of data is a constant preoccupation of the racing sailor. Much data will be placed on the appropriate chart, some will be written in notebooks or in logs for future reference and some will be jotted on a convenient piece of paper to be discarded when the purpose has been served.

Get in the habit of writing info down in a manner and form that can best be retrieved and used. In the heat of competition, memory can be unreliable and forgetfulness is costly.

With this in mind equip yourself accordingly. Trying to make notes on a soggy pad with a broken pencil stub at a crucial time can be frustrating. Have a pencil rack near your chart table that holds at least a half-dozen new and well-sharpened pencils. Keep more in reserve. Find a dry spot for your scratch pads, bound and loose-leaf notebooks as well as your charts and publications. A small pencil sharpener, a couple of gum erasers, some felt-tipped pens in various colors and a roll of Scotch or masking tape will complete your recording kit. The tape is used to tab pages in your publications for quick look-up and to post notes for ready reference by the crew.

Considerable extra data can be added to your charts well before race time and done comfortably and without deadline pressure. Here are some suggestions. Danger areas can be noted. (One skipper I know outlines in color the waters too shallow for the draft of his particular boat.) Prominent landmarks and navigational aids can be located and circled. Additional info extracted from cruising guides and coast pilots can be pencilled in. Arcs of visibility of major lights and maximum ranges of DF stations can be described. Special start and finish instructions can be footnoted. Omni station locations and frequencies can be added.

If you are using tidal current chart booklets, look up the appropriate data in the *Tidal Current Tables* and note on the applicable pages of the booklet the date and time they are effective. If tidal current charts are not available for the sailing area, construct the current data on a conventional chart using the reference station positions in the tables. This prefigured info on currents will help in determining your starting tactics and overall race strategy.

Extract DF station frequencies and characteristics for those you expect to use —write the info on a piece of paper and tape this near the DF receiver. Write the dots and dashes for signals rather than letters, which have to be converted. Determine and record watch or chronometer error and record it in your notebook.

Locate and designate on the chart the course marks described in the race instructions—then double-check your work to be sure. If you are in the lead you may be the one who has to find them for the fleet. Some instructions list a large number of marks with three or four to be used as designated from the Committee Boat just before the start. Write these down when they are displayed but check again after your warning gun to be certain they have not been revised. When the race course is firm, plot and label the base course and distance to each mark.

Whenever possible, the skipper and the navigator should attend the prerace skippers' meeting, and come equipped with pads and pencils for taking notes. Some skippers now use a tape recorder to record important data for later playback. This eliminates guesswork as to what was heard. Often, important changes, additions and additional information are announced at these proceedings. It helps to get them at first hand.

If the marks are offshore aids, check them in the latest light list for any changes and amend your chart accordingly. In the 1971 Storm Trysail Club's Race to the Chesapeake, from Sandy Hook, N.J., to Hampton Roads, Va., two turning marks were described in the original instructions as "lightships" but actually had been changed to large navigation buoys at race time as part of a U.S. Coast Guard replacement program. This made a big difference as to what to look for.

The race instructions will also indicate any prohibition on the use of equipment, such as Loran. Tape a piece of paper appropriately labelled across the face of the prohibited instrument so it will not be used inadvertently.

After the start, here are a few typical recording chores:
- Record the time of rounding each mark and the time other navigational aids are passed close aboard. This will provide input for speed-over-the-bottom, a point of departure for the next plot and a tentative ETA at the next mark.
- If competitors are nearby, time and record the interval between your mark roundings and theirs so that gains and losses can be figured.
- Record your boat's position frequently on the chart and label the positions by time and date and according to accuracy: i.e., Fix, Running Fix, Estimated Position, Dead Reckoning Position.
- Record a series of bearings before plotting them for greater accuracy. If doing this from memory, digits can be transposed.
- On the wind, record the wind speed and the boat's heading on each tack in various wind velocities to determine tacking angle (degrees through which the boat tacks) for future use in determining the lay line as well as to read the patterns of wind shifts.

On a long race, record and post navigational data of interest to the crew, such as miles remaining, distance and speed past 24 hours. This is not only informative, but also saves answering a lot of repetitive questions.

For celestial observations it is helpful to keep a loose-leaf notebook containing work sheets, both blank and filled in, and a small bound notebook for time, altitude and azimuth data.

Facts and figures are useful only if you have them readily available in readable form. In competition it's better to have an embarrassment of riches than not enough.

20 FINDING THE MARK

Racing marks can be a challenge to both committees and contestants. Omitting for this discussion the considerable factors of shape, size and color, the common denominator is the navigational aspect. Is the location of each mark described in clear, understandable terms? Is each mark placed where the committee says it is? Can marks be found with confidence by a contestant using readily available methods? If the answer to any of these is no, there's trouble ahead.

The committee's role is to be precise in the choice, description and setting of a course so that finding marks does not assume such overriding importance that racing tactics suffer.

In the 1975 One-Ton North American Championships off Newport, R.I., there were two long-distance races in which the turning marks were lighted buoys well off shore. These were selected without apparent regard for the yachts' ability to find them (electronic equipment is restricted in One-Ton yachts to RDF and depth sounder). Fog and low visibility made the marks invisible day or night and the lack of nearby RDF stations or distinct bottom gradients in the vicinity of the marks chosen required blind navigational rather than visual roundings. This caused the yachts extra sailing miles and shuffled the positions unnecessarily at each mark.

Placing an experienced navigator on the race committee and listening to his suggestions can minimize this sort of unhappy situation.

Occasionally, marks will go adrift after a race starts, or a committee will forget to set one. These things happen in even the best planned regattas. But our concern here is for the elimination of all possible ambiguity in a *properly* set course.

The now notorious first mark in the Lipton Cup Race in the 1971 SORC is a near classic in this regard. In spite of a conscientious committee that had put a lot of thought and effort into designing the course, and a large fleet carrying some of the finest offshore racing talent in any ocean, most boats badly oversailed that mark, giving away four to 12 additional miles on what was intended to be about a 12-mile spinnaker run. Skippers were apoplectic and navigators fell into disrepute. What led the fleet to chase a mirage?

This 26-mile round-the-buoys course, rated at 27 miles for handicap purposes, had a straight first leg starting just north of Miami's Government Cut (Coast and Geodetic Chart #1248) on a heading of 006 degrees to a manned stake boat, thence a 14-mile zigzag around three other stake boats back to the finish. Visibility was excellent. Miami Beach was close aboard and navigational aids for figuring speed-of-advance were plentiful. The stake boats marking the return legs were plainly visible to the boats sailing the first leg.

The course was described in the race circular as if it were an overlay on the chart keyed to the committee boat location, which was only approximately described. This is normally the approach taken in describing courses for small one-designs, where in most cases all the marks are visible from the starting line. Thus, the distance of the first mark off the beach was not given in the circular, as this depended upon where the committee boat was in fact positioned at the start of the race. The other marks, in turn, were charted in relation to the committee boat and the first mark. This introduced a significant variable. If a contestant's plot of the committee boat was off, so was his plot of the first mark and the rest of the course. If those committee members aboard the stake boats did not have the actual location of the committee boat, there could be an unintentional element of inaccuracy in their positioning, also.

The Lipton Cup Committee has, long since, abandoned this approach to setting an offshore course.

Another variable was the use of the word "approximate" without further definition. What should the allowable margin be for a 12-mile leg? Fifty yards? One mile? The consensus of most navigators was that the mark was off, to the westward, by a half mile or more. This could make a difference of two degrees in the base course to the mark.

Coupled with this, most boats held high of the course to the east to benefit from a better sailing angle and more push from the Gulf Stream current. Class A, the first of five classes, passed well east of the mark, and all but a few boats in the rest of the classes followed.

In retrospect, the obvious approach for this kind of race should be to describe the position of each mark independently of all others because of the distances involved, define the allowable error in its location and place it as close to the position as navigational tools will permit.

Often, government aids to navigation are used to define a racecourse. These have advantages. They are accurately charted, have readily identifiable characteristics and are precisely positioned. The crew of a Coast Guard buoy tender may use all of the following to fix the position of a buoy, usually in the order listed: horizontal sextant angles, true bearings by gyro repeater, fathometer readings and radar plot. Buoys over 25 yards from charted position are reset closer, preferably within 10 yards.

But as before, they should be chosen with regard to other aids in the area so that they can be found in poor visibility with available equipment.

A word of caution. If you prepare your race instructions well ahead, make sure that the government marks you select are still there when race day dawns. Changes in buoyage are sometimes made and buoys are sometimes temporarily missing or off station.

Once the course is set, finding the mark as a contestant can be simple or it can encompass all the skills of the navigator's art, especially in poor visibility. If the mark is a charted fixed object, such as Buzzards Tower, used in the Vineyard Race, or an accurately placed and clearly described floating mark, the approach is straightforward. By keeping a continuous and accurate position plot a mark

can be found without undue difficulty, while still paying full attention to strategic and tactical considerations. Whether the boats are small or large, the method is the same.

But where the contestant feels that the mark may or may not be where it is supposed to be, a new element is introduced. This uncertainty can influence the racing tactics considerably.

Going back to the Lipton Cup situation, conditions were ideal for maintaining an accurate plot. When the 12 miles had been run by Class A, the mark should have been discovered or radical course changes should have been made to find it. Suppose this race had not had a history of marks being far off station, though not relevant in 1971, and suppose "approximately" had been defined as, say, "one-half mile." Would the entire class have charged unhesitatingly by the unseen mark, a 45-foot motorboat?

In Class B, when their distance had also been run, an additional factor was present. The Class A boats ahead were seen either still sailing north, or apparently turning and tacking back from an assumed mark well to the north. Class B skippers were torn between facts, reason, and what they could see, as were skippers in later classes, some of whom sailed all the way to Fort Lauderdale before turning around! Mob psychology? Perhaps. Just remember that at 10 knots, with spinnaker drawing and the Gulf Stream behind you, a delay of 15 minutes to think it over puts your boat two-and-a-half miles farther along your heading.

Most racing sailors have been in this position more than once. Do you ignore the rest of the fleet or do you go along—particularly if your closest competitor in the point standing is doing the same thing the rest are?

Pinpoint accuracy by the committee in describing the course and laying it out will eliminate a lot of later confusion. Proper understanding by contestants of the committee's efforts, including asking the right questions at the skippers' meeting to clear up uncertainties, will also help.

←

Buzzard's Tower is a mark that's not hard to find.

21 FIGURING THE CURRENTS

Many racing sailors feel that accumulating and using information about currents encountered along the racecourse are troublesome facets of yacht racing. Some ignore currents and wonder why they don't do better, and others are overly concerned with this factor to the neglect of race strategy. But those in between who do use currents wisely are usually at the top of the fleet when racing in tidal waters.

Figure it out. A one-knot current helping one boat and hindering another in one hour can put two more miles between the boats even though they are of equal speed through the water.

Fortunately currents are predictable to a remarkable degree, the information needed to predict them is readily available and most of the work can be done ahead of time. But like any other aspect of yacht racing you must be accurate and meticulous. There is no room for error.

To work up current data you need the appropriate chart plus *Tidal Current Tables* for the particular year. Don't confuse the latter with *Tide Tables* which tell you the times and heights of high and low waters, although these are necessary for other reasons.

The *Tidal Current Tables* predict when it will be slack water (no current) and when the maximum flood and ebb currents will occur as well as the expected velocities and direction. These cover rivers, bays, sounds and shoreline areas along the coasts. In addition, special *Tidal Current Charts* usable year after year can be obtained for certain large areas such as Long Island Sound, Chesapeake Bay, San Francisco Bay, Puget Sound and the English Channel. For example, the charts for Long Island Sound give you a comprehensive visual picture with arrows of direction and the velocity already marked for each hour of the tidal cycle when coupled with the times of flood or ebb at the reference station called "The Race," obtained from the annual *Tidal Current Tables.*

You can construct similar information on conventional nautical charts by plotting selected reference or subordinate stations obtained from the tables and applying the appropriate current data.

But first, let's illustrate the effect of current. Place a piece of paper on your chart table. Visualize the paper as the surface of the water and the table as the bottom.

Place a coin on the paper. Imagine that is your boat and it is becalmed. Now, without touching the coin, slide the paper slowly along the table. The top of the water is moving due to current, and though your boat is not moving on the water surface, it is moving over the bottom in the direction the paper is moving.

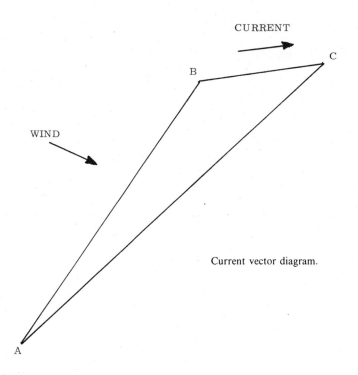

Current vector diagram.

This tells us that when current is present, speed over-the-bottom counts, as well as speed through the water.

Now let's be a bit more detailed. Draw a wind arrow on the piece of paper. Locate your boat with a point marked **A.** Draw a line from this indicating your boat's heading consistent with the wind (assuming a speed of five knots and the scale 1 inch to 1 mile) and make another mark five inches along the course line and label it **B.** Hold a pencil, point down, above but not touching the paper at **B.** Move the pencil about two inches in any direction, simulating a current of two knots. Drop the pencil and mark the paper again, labelling this point **C.** Draw a line from **A** to **C.** This line represents your actual course and distance over the bottom versus your intended course and distance as shown by the line from **A** to **B.**

Now draw a line from **B** to **C.** The length of this line represents the drift and the direction of the line is the set.

In other words, as you are going along the surface of the water on your compass heading and at your recorded speed, the current has caused a different course and speed over the bottom. When you left **A** if you knew the velocity and direction of the current you would encounter in the next hour, you could possibly have steered a corrected heading, wind permitting, to make good the intended heading.

A further factor is that when the current is strong, the actual speed and direction of your yacht over the bottom, compared with its speed and direction through the water, will affect the apparent wind on your sails at the surface. For example, if you are going to windward with a favorable current, the apparent wind will increase in velocity vs. the true surface wind. Endless variations in apparent wind are possible and may further refine the choice of heading to get the most out of both wind and current.

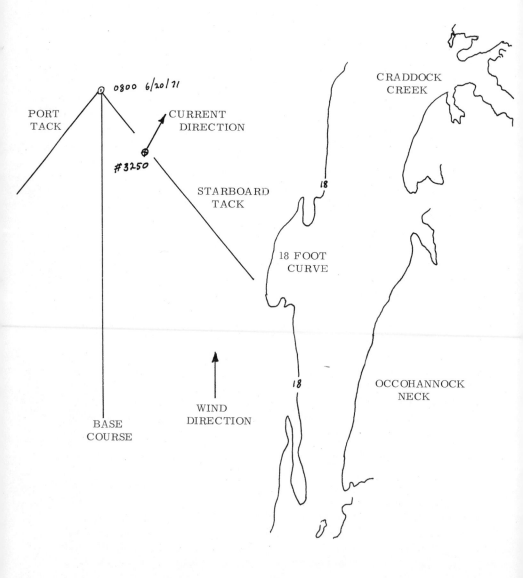

Let's discuss a real example of predicting current.

We are competing in the Annapolis–Newport Race, tacking down Chesapeake Bay. Our 0800, 20 June 1971 position is 37:35N 76:03W, about five-and-a-half miles west of Craddock Creek. Base course is 180 degrees true, speed through the water is six knots. We are on port tack heading 220 degrees true. Wind is steady from the south at 15 knots.

We are using NOS Chart 1223, Chesapeake Bay, Wolf Trap to Smith Point. The *Tidal Current Tables, 1971 Atlantic Coast of North America* is our reference book.

Our first step is to locate subordinate stations near our position and along the projected course line. Wolf Trap Light is on the chart so we look that up and find it on page 200 of the *Tables* in the index. Turning to Table 2 which has stations listed in numerical order, we find the entry for Wolf Trap Light station #3240 at the bottom of page 155, noting its position is 12 miles to the south. We also select 3250, the easterly of two stations off Stingray Point. This one is less than two miles from our 0800 position. As these entries are differences to use as corrections, the major heading "Chesapeake Bay" in midpage tells us where to look for the Reference Station's daily prediction data. We mark stations 3240 and 3250 on the chart and label each with its number. (This preferably should have been done before the race, along the expected course.)

Now we turn to Table 1, under "Chesapeake Bay Entrance, Va." and find the columns for June 1971 on page 66. Opposite Sunday, June 20, we note that maximum flood is indicated at 0618 and slack water at 0400 and 0836. Remembering to convert these 75-degree W. meridian times to Eastern Daylight Time we add an hour to each, giving 0718, 0500 and 0936 respectively.

Our next step is to correct these Bay Entrance times for our local subordinate stations. At station 3250 we add one hour 40 minutes to the 0500 slack water time and get 0640. For maximum flood we add the correction two hours five minutes, giving a time of 0923 with current flowing toward 030 degrees true at .7 knots.

Doing the same for station 3240, using its correction of plus one hour 45 minutes, we get a time of 0903 for maximum flood toward 015 degrees true. The velocity is .9 of that listed for the Bay Entrance. As that is .7 knots the resultant is .63 knots. The next slack water figures out to be 1111.

We are now ready to apply these data. Obviously, if the wind remains steady and if we hold our port tack to the SW, we will encounter increasingly stronger adverse currents on the windward bow. It would be better to tack to starboard, putting the current more on the beam and favoring the shallower water and less flood current along the Eastern Shore, working out again at slack water, to take full advantage of the oncoming ebb current after 1111.

This should give you an idea of how it works. Don't forget that these are predictions, and varying influences may make the actual current a bit different from the prediction. Get in the habit of double-checking your figures against the tidal flow past buoys, lobster pot markers and the like, if they are available.

Let the current work for you whenever possible consistent with overall race strategy. The lighter the wind, the more significant it becomes.

In Part IV currents experienced on actual racecourses are further discussed.

TABLE 2.—CURRENT DIFFERENCES AND OTHER CONSTANTS

No.	PLACE	POSITION		TIME DIFFERENCES		VELOCITY RATIOS		MAXIMUM CURRENTS			
								Flood		Ebb	
		Lat.	Long.	Slack water	Maximum current	Maximum flood	Maximum ebb	Direction (true)	Average velocity	Direction (true)	Average velocity
		° ′	° ′	h. m.	h. m.			deg.	knots	deg.	kn
	DELAWARE BAY and RIVER—Continued	N.	W.								
				on DELAWARE BAY ENTRANCE, p.58							
				Time meridian, 75°W.							
3055	Fisher Point------------------	39 59	75 04	+5 45	+5 25	0.8	0.9	40	1.4	225	1.
3060	Torresdale, west of channel------------	40 02	74 59	(¹)	+5 50	0.5	0.8	45	0.9	225	1.
3065	Rancocas Creek, off Delanco------------	40 03	74 58	+6 15	+6 15	0.6	0.5	90	1.0	270	0.
3070	Bristol, south of--------------------	40 05	74 52	(²)	(²)	0.7	0.8	25	1.3	200	1.
3075	Burlington Island, channel east of----	40 06	74 50	(³)	(³)	0.5	0.9	20	0.9	205	1.
3080	Whitehill--------------------------	40 08	74 44	-----	⁴+7 00	----	0.7	----	----	235	1.
	DEL., MD. and VA. COAST										
3085	Indian River Inlet (bridge)-----------	38 37	75 04	+0 10	+0 10	1.0	1.1	265	1.8	85	2.
3090	Fenwick Shoal Lighted Whistle Buoy 2--	38 25	74 46	See table 5.							
3095	Winter-Quarter Shoal Buoy 6WQS⁵-------	37 55	74 56	See table 5.							
				on CHESAPEAKE BAY ENTRANCE, p.64							
3100	Cape Charles, 70 miles east of--------	37 05	74 51	See table 5.							
3105	Smith Island Shoal, southeast of------	37 05	75 43	-2 10	-2 10	0.3	0.3	300	0.3	70	0.
3110	Chesapeake Light, 4.4 miles NE. of----	36 59	75 42	(⁶)	(⁶)	----	----	----	----	----	---
3115	Cape Henry Light, 2.2 miles SE. of----	36 54	75 59	-1 15	-1 30	1.0	0.6	345	1.0	165	0.
	CHESAPEAKE BAY										
3120	Cape Henry Light, 1 mile north of-----	36 56	76 00	0 00	-0 25	1.1	1.3	280	1.1	90	2.
3125	Cape Henry Light, 1.8 miles north of--	36 57	76 00	-0 05	-0 15	1.2	1.0	290	1.2	100	1.
3130	CHESAPEAKE BAY ENTRANCE--------------	36 59	76 00	Daily predictions				305	1.0	125	1.
3135	Cape Henry Light, 4.6 miles north of--	37 00	75 59	-0 35	-0 50	1.3	0.9	295	1.3	105	1.
3140	Cape Charles Light, 9.5 mi. WSW. of---	37 04	76 05	+0 10	0 00	1.5	0.9	320	1.5	125	1.
3145	Cape Henry Light, 8.3 mi. NW. of------	37 02	76 07	-0 05	-0 10	1.0	0.7	330	1.0	135	1.
3150	Lynnhaven Roads----------------------	36 55	76 05	-0 35	-0 40	0.8	0.6	280	0.8	70	0.
3155	Lynnhaven Inlet bridge---------------	36 54	76 06	-2 05	-2 35	0.6	0.9	180	0.6	0	1.
	Chesapeake Bay Bridge Tunnel										
3160	Chesapeake Beach, 1.5 miles N. of--	36 57	76 07	-0 15	-0 20	0.8	0.6	305	0.8	100	0.
3165	Thimble Shoal Channel---------------	36 58	76 07	-0 40	-0 40	1.4	0.9	310	1.4	95	1.
3170	Tail of the Horseshoe--------------	37 00	76 06	-0 25	-0 40	0.9	0.7	300	0.9	110	1.
3175	Middle Ground, channel west of-----	37 03	76 05	-0 25	-0 10	1.6	0.9	335	1.6	150	1.
3180	Chesapeake Channel-----------------	37 02	76 04	-0 15	-0 15	1.8	1.0	335	1.8	145	1.
3185	Fisherman I., 3.2 miles WSW. of----	37 04	76 02	-0 55	-1 05	1.2	1.1	330	1.2	135	1.
3190	Fisherman I., 1.4 miles WSW. of----	37 05	76 00	(⁷)	-1 15	1.8	0.7	330	1.8	140	1.
3195	Fisherman I., 1.8 miles south of---	37 04	75 59	-0 45	-1 10	1.6	0.9	320	1.6	120	1.
3200	Fisherman I., 0.4 mile west of-----	37 06	75 59	-0 45	-1 10	2.0	1.3	5	2.0	175	2.
3205	Fisherman I., 1.1 miles NW. of-----	37 06	76 00	(⁸)	-0 40	1.8	1.1	355	1.8	165	1.
3210	Cape Charles, off Wise Point-------	37 07	75 58	(⁹)	(⁹)	0.7	0.1	305	0.7	75	0.
	Little Creek										
3215	North of east jetty---------------	36 56	76 11	-1 50	-2 00	0.9	0.7	280	0.9	75	1.
3220	0.5 mile north of west jetty-------	36 56	76 11	-1 10	-1 15	0.9	0.6	275	0.9	110	0.
3225	Old Plantation Flats Light, west of---	37 14	76 04	+1 10	+0 50	1.2	0.9	5	1.2	175	1.
3230	York Spit Channel---------------------	37 13	76 09	+0 55	+0 55	0.8	0.7	10	0.8	195	1.
3235	Wolf Trap Light, 0.5 mile west of-----	37 23	76 12	+1 05	+1 05	1.0	0.8	15	1.0	190	1.
→3240	Wolf Trap Light, 5.8 miles east of----	37 23	76 04	+1 45	+1 45	0.9	0.9	15	0.9	175	1.
3245	Stingray Point, 5.5 miles east of-----	37 35	76 10	+1 50	+2 20	1.0	0.6	345	1.0	180	0.
→3250	Stingray Point, 12.5 miles east of----	37 34	76 02	+1 40	+2 05	1.0	0.5	30	1.0	175	0.

¹ Flood begins, +6ʰ 55ᵐ; ebb begins, +5ʰ 00ᵐ.
² Flood begins, +6ʰ 55ᵐ; maximum flood, +5ʰ 30ᵐ; ebb begins, +4ʰ 55ᵐ; maximum ebb, +6ʰ 10ᵐ.
³ Flood begins, +7ʰ 30ᵐ; maximum flood, +5ʰ 45ᵐ; ebb begins, +4ʰ 15ᵐ; maximum ebb, +6ʰ 45ᵐ.
⁴ Data for ebb only. Flood is usually weak and of short duration. A weak ebb or flood current occurs about 6 hours after maximum flood at Delaware Bay Entrance.
⁵ Tidal current is weak and rotary, averaging less than 0.1 knot.
⁶ Current too weak and variable to be predicted.
⁷ Flood begins, -1ʰ 45ᵐ; ebb begins, -0ʰ 40ᵐ.
⁸ Flood begins, -1ʰ 15ᵐ; ebb begins, -0ʰ 05ᵐ.
⁹ Flood begins, -0ʰ 30ᵐ; maximum flood, -0ʰ 20ᵐ; ebb begins, +0ʰ 25ᵐ; maximum ebb, +0ʰ 50ᵐ.

CHESAPEAKE BAY ENTRANCE, VA., 1971

F-FLOOD, DIR. 305° TRUE   E-EBB, DIR. 125° TRUE

MAY

DAY	SLACK WATER TIME H.M.	MAXIMUM CURRENT TIME H.M.	MAXIMUM CURRENT VEL. KNOTS	DAY	SLACK WATER TIME H.M.	MAXIMUM CURRENT TIME H.M.	MAXIMUM CURRENT VEL. KNOTS
1 SA		0130	0.9F	16 SU		0042	1.1F
	0448	0818	1.0E		0354	0724	1.1E
	1148	1348	0.3F		1054	1300	0.5F
	1554	2018	1.2E		1512	1924	1.4E
	2348				2254		
2 SU		0230	0.7F	17 M		0142	1.0F
	0542	0918	1.0E		0448	0824	1.2E
	1254	1454	0.3F		1154	1406	0.6F
	1706	2124	1.1E		1630	2036	1.3E
3 M	0054	0336	0.7F	18 TU	0000	0248	1.0F
	0636	1012	1.0E		0542	0924	1.3E
	1348	1600	0.4F		1248	1512	0.7F
	1824	2230	1.1E		1748	2148	1.4E
4 TU	0154	0436	0.6F	19 W	0112	0348	0.9F
	0724	1106	1.1E		0642	1024	1.4E
	1436	1700	0.5F		1348	1618	0.9F
	1930	2324	1.2E		1912	2254	1.4E
5 W	0254	0524	0.6F	20 TH	0212	0448	0.9F
	0806	1148	1.2E		0736	1118	1.6E
	1512	1748	0.6F		1436	1724	1.1F
	2030				2024	2354	1.5E
6 TH		0012	1.2E	21 F	0318	0548	0.9F
	0342	0606	0.6F		0824	1212	1.7E
	0848	1230	1.2E		1530	1824	1.3F
	1548	1830	0.8F		2130		
	2118						
7 F		0054	1.3E	22 SA		0054	1.6E
	0424	0648	0.6F		0412	0636	0.9F
	0918	1306	1.3E		0912	1300	1.8E
	1624	1906	0.9F		1618	1918	1.5F
	2200				2230		
8 SA		0136	1.3E	23 SU		0148	1.6E
	0506	0718	0.6F		0506	0730	0.9F
	0948	1342	1.4E		1000	1348	1.9E
	1700	1942	1.0F		1706	2006	1.5F
	2242				2324		
9 SU		0218	1.3E	24 M		0242	1.6E
	0542	0754	0.6F		0600	0818	0.8F
	1018	1412	1.4E		1042	1436	1.9E
	1730	2018	1.1F		1800	2054	1.5F
	2324						
10 M		0254	1.3E	25 TU	0018	0330	1.5E
	0618	0830	0.6F		0648	0906	0.8F
	1042	1448	1.4E		1124	1524	1.8E
	1806	2054	1.1F		1848	2148	1.5F
11 TU	0000	0330	1.3E	26 W	0106	0418	1.4E
	0700	0906	0.6F		0742	0948	0.7F
	1112	1518	1.5E		1206	1612	1.7E
	1842	2136	1.2F		1936	2230	1.4F
12 W	0042	0412	1.2E	27 TH	0154	0506	1.3E
	0736	0942	0.6F		0830	1036	0.6F
	1148	1554	1.5E		1254	1700	1.6E
	1924	2218	1.2F		2024	2318	1.2F
13 TH	0124	0454	1.2E	28 F	0236	0554	1.2E
	0818	1018	0.5F		0918	1124	0.5F
	1224	1636	1.5E		1342	1754	1.5E
	2006	2300	1.2F		2118		
14 F	0212	0536	1.1E	29 SA		0006	1.0F
	0906	1106	0.5F		0318	0648	1.2E
	1312	1724	1.4E		1012	1218	0.5F
	2100	2348	1.1F		1430	1842	1.3E
					2212		
15 SA	0300	0630	1.1E	30 SU		0054	0.9F
	0954	1200	0.5F		0406	0736	1.1E
	1406	1818	1.4E		1106	1312	0.4F
	2154				1530	1942	1.2E
					2306		
				31 M		0148	0.7F
					0448	0830	1.1E
					1200	1406	0.4F
					1630	2042	1.1E

JUNE

DAY	SLACK WATER TIME H.M.	MAXIMUM CURRENT TIME H.M.	MAXIMUM CURRENT VEL. KNOTS	DAY	SLACK WATER TIME H.M.	MAXIMUM CURRENT TIME H.M.	MAXIMUM CURRENT VEL. KNOTS
1 TU	0006	0242	0.6F	16 W		0218	1.0F
	0530	0924	1.1E		0506	0854	1.4E
	1254	1506	0.5F		1218	1454	0.9F
	1736	2142	1.1E		1742	2124	1.3E
2 W	0106	0330	0.6F	17 TH	0048	0318	0.8F
	0618	1012	1.1E		0600	0954	1.5E
	1342	1606	0.5F		1318	1600	1.0F
	1848	2236	1.1E		1900	2236	1.3E
3 TH	0206	0424	0.5F	18 F	0154	0418	0.8F
	0700	1100	1.1E		0654	1048	1.6E
	1424	1654	0.6F		1418	1706	1.1F
	1948	2330	1.1E		2018	2342	1.4E
4 F	0300	0512	0.5F	19 SA	0300	0518	0.7F
	0742	1142	1.2E		0748	1148	1.7E
	1506	1748	0.8F		1512	1806	1.3F
	2042				2124		
5 SA		0024	1.1E	20 SU		0042	1.4E
	0348	0554	0.5F		0400	0618	0.7F
	0818	1224	1.3E		0836	1242	1.7E
	1548	1830	0.9F		1606	1906	1.4F
	2136				2224		
6 SU		0106	1.2E	21 M		0136	1.4E
	0430	0642	0.5F		0500	0712	0.7F
	0854	1300	1.3E		0930	1330	1.8E
	1624	1912	1.0F		1654	2000	1.4F
	2224				2318		
7 M		0148	1.2E	22 TU		0230	1.4E
	0518	0718	0.5F		0548	0800	0.7F
	0930	1342	1.4E		1018	1424	1.8E
	1700	1954	1.1F		1748	2048	1.4F
	2306						
8 TU		0230	1.2E	23 W	0006	0318	1.4E
	0554	0800	0.5F		0636	0848	0.6F
	1006	1418	1.5E		1106	1506	1.7E
	1742	2036	1.2F		1836	2130	1.3F
	2348						
9 W		0312	1.2E	24 TH	0048	0406	1.3E
	0636	0842	0.6F		0724	0936	0.6F
	1048	1500	1.5E		1154	1554	1.7E
	1824	2118	1.3F		1918	2212	1.2F
10 TH	0030	0354	1.3E	25 F	0130	0448	1.3E
	0718	0924	0.6F		0806	1018	0.6F
	1130	1542	1.6E		1236	1642	1.6E
	1906	2200	1.3F		2006	2254	1.1F
11 F	0118	0436	1.3E	26 SA	0206	0530	1.2E
	0800	1006	0.6F		0848	1100	0.6F
	1218	1624	1.6E		1324	1724	1.4E
	1954	2248	1.3F		2054	2336	1.0F
12 SA	0200	0524	1.3E	27 SU	0242	0612	1.2E
	0842	1054	0.7F		0930	1142	0.6F
	1312	1712	1.6E		1406	1812	1.3E
	2042	2336	1.3F		2136		
13 SU	0242	0612	1.3E	28 M		0018	0.9F
	0930	1148	0.7F		0318	0654	1.1E
	1406	1812	1.5E		1018	1230	0.6F
	2136				1500	1900	1.2E
					2230		
14 M		0024	1.2F	29 TU		0100	0.7F
	0330	0700	1.3E		0348	0736	1.1E
	1024	1248	0.8F		1106	1318	0.6F
	1512	1912	1.5E		1554	1954	1.1E
	2236				2318		
15 TU	0118	0800	1.1F	30 W		0142	0.6F
	0418	1124	1.4E		0424	0824	1.1E
	1348	1624	0.8F		1154	1412	0.6F
	2018	2342	1.4E		1648	2048	1.0E

TIME MERIDIAN 75° W.   0000 IS MIDNIGHT.   1200 IS NOON.

22 VISUAL BEARINGS

A quick, easy and dependable way to fix your boat's position in good weather is by means of visual bearings on three known objects about 60 degrees apart. But, like everything else in offshore racing, it is simpler to say than to do.

The one-design skipper uses much of this technique, but applies the information mentally. The cruising boat skipper or navigator has more of the tools aboard and is able to complete the process of recording and plotting the information. Therefore, if you are fleeting up from, say, a Lightning to one of the offshore designs, you are already well on the way to mastering these important skills.

The racing skipper who knows exactly where he is at all times has, even in a short "round-the-buoys" race, a great advantage over a competitor who is just "eyeballing" it. This was dramatically illustrated at a recent Chesapeake Bay day-race for cruising boats when one of the craft, manned by a crew familiar with the area, nestled gently into the mud off Thomas Point while on the wind on the first leg. Only the speed needle dropping to zero told them they were aground. Not a single bearing had been taken after the starting gun although objects upon which bearings could have been taken were visible all around the horizon. Moral: You do not need to have a navigator, as such, but somebody aboard must be assigned to do the navigating!

In most races visual bearings can be taken. A bearing is the horizontal direction from boat to object, and is expressed as the angular difference between north and the bearing line, measured clockwise through 360 degrees. Because yachts have magnetic compasses, the bearing is measured from magnetic north. It is essential in plotting that you be able to locate on a nautical chart the object on which you are taking the bearing, and a glance at a chart will show that there are two compass roses. One is oriented to true north—the other, superimposed on it, is magnetic—the difference, if any, being "variation." This changes from place to place on the earth's surface. For example, the variation off Miami Beach is zero while the variation off Block Island is 14 degrees 30 minutes west. This need not concern the skipper because the bearings obtained from the boat's magnetic compass are plotted on the chart using the magnetic rose. But if deviation (a boat-induced error) is present in the compass, it must be corrected for.

A common method used to take a bearing is to sight across the steering compass toward the selected object and obtain the compass reading of an imaginary line from the center of the compass to the object. A preferable method is to use a hand-bearing compass, which normally will give a more precise reading. In taking a series of bearings, sight first the objects having the greatest rate of bearing change. That is, on a moving boat the bearing of an object on the beam would change more rapidly than an object broad on the bow, while a bearing on an object ahead or astern would change very little. Record the time the first bearing is taken so that you can mark the time of the resultant fix on the chart.

Picking the appropriate object is important. A lighthouse, tank, steeple or tower (provided they are charted) or a point of land dropping steeply to the water, all make excellent objects. Buoys are not recommended because they are not always floating on their exact charted position.

A single bearing plots as a line of position, which means that your boat was at that time somewhere along that line. To obtain a fix, at least one other bearing crossing that line, preferably at about 90 degrees, must be obtained. This will completely define a position if the bearings are taken in quick sequence. But an additional line or lines can dispel any doubt as to its accuracy. If three objects are available, try to get them about 60 degrees apart. If everything goes well, these should intersect at the same point. Occasionally they will form a small triangle with the usual case being that the position is in the center of the triangle—but it could also mean a constant error in all three bearings if this situation persists with subsequent fixes. Similarly, four or more bearings could result in a pinpoint fix or in other geometric shapes. It is possible in a multiple-bearing fix that the quality of individual bearings may differ. If this is known, a suspect bearing should be discarded.

Another source of a bearing is when two fixed objects are in line relative to your position. This is known as a range and can be obtained without reference to your compass by merely noting the time when you see the objects lined up. The direction of the range is obtained from the chart. Add a visual bearing on another object at the time you are on the range and you have a fix.

How do we select the objects we will probably use? Ideally, study the chart before the race. See where the prominent objects, aids and ranges are located and how they are described. If they are navigational aids, additional details can be found in the appropriate U.S. Coast Guard light list. At night, bearings are usually taken only on navigational aids which have lights of a specified color and characteristic so that you can positively identify what it is you are looking at. But don't guess! If the chart or the light list indicates that the selected light is flashing every six seconds, time it with your stopwatch.

From your chart or your light list you can also extract the limit of visibility which is given for sea level. So if you are 16 miles away, you, at deck level, would not expect to see a light that was visible only to a maximum of 10 miles. It is helpful to circle on the chart these prominent objects, pencil in the arcs of visibility and highlight the characteristics.

Although this discussion has been limited to visual bearings it is not intended to imply that other types of bearings cannot also be used. Combine visual bearings with those obtained by using a direction finder or an Omni receiver. Add depths shown on your depth finder. The key word in navigation is "redundancy"— superimposing all available methods to confirm the reliability of the end result.

In spite of the multitude of navigational aids available to racing navigators for use in piloting, there are times when there is not a great deal to work with. In situations like this, be resourceful and exploit what you have. Even a single, fixed, identifiable object can provide a great deal of help, but you must know some of the tricks to make the most of it.

Two cases in point come to mind in a recent SORC aboard *Sorcery*. One had to do with the technique of obtaining the distance away by means of timed bearings when passing a single object off the beam. The other had to do with tacking toward a single object while at the same time avoiding obstacles on either side of the rhumb line. Both were at night, when light characteristics (timing and color) can be clearly identified.

The first occurred in the St. Petersburg–Venice Race. The turning mark, Boca Grande Sea Buoy, was a lighted buoy with a visibility of about four miles, located some distance offshore. The Florida shoreline was approximately parallel to the southerly course to the buoy. Only one major aid was available, Boca Grande Light, visible 16 miles and located on shore well north of the turn buoy. This meant that this light was visible to port a long time before the turning buoy hove into sight. A textbook approach in a case like this is to take two preplanned bearings at calculated angles to the course steered, and from their geometric relationship figure your distance from the light.

If the speed is fairly constant and known, you can take bow and beam bearings. The first one is taken at an angle of 45 degrees between the course and the object, and the second at 90 degrees. The distance run between bearings equals the distance away from the object when the 90-degree bearing is taken. Other angles may be used: for example, 30 and 60 degrees, in which case the distance off the object will be about 7/8 of the distance run between bearings. If using 63 1/2 and 90 degrees, this will give a distance off of about twice the distance run.

Unfortunately, a racing sailboat does not always have a predictable rate of advance. While assuming a certain speed, you may run out of wind after the first preplanned bearing and your plan will go down the drain. It is often more practical to take two bearings while you can, regardless of their angle to the course, timing them so that the distance run between them can be estimated. Plot the bearings on the chart, set your dividers for the distance run and set your parallel rulers to the course line. Adjust the rulers away from the object and measure with the dividers until the distance run is just intersected by the two bearings along the course line.

It would be reassuring here to take a sounding also at the time of the second bearing, and if this confirms your distance off as plotted, you are in business. We used this method and picked up Boca Grande Buoy right on the nose—much to the delight of the foredeck crew who had noted a competitor to leeward making three tacks to lay the mark.

The Miami–Nassau Race provided an example of the second instance mentioned above. Due to a combination of circumstances we made a landfall on Great Bahama Bank north of Bimini, but well south of Great Isaac, after crossing the Gulf Stream in light weather on the port tack. The wind was out of the NNE, which meant that if we tacked to starboard we would have the southerly counter-current close along the edge of the shoals on our windward bow. It was a bright moonlight night; the sea was calm and the wind had enough heft to drive us at about six knots.

As our competitors peeled off, we chose to continue on a port tack over the shoals with a steady three fathoms under the bottom. Although the skipper was later accused in some quarters of being a "gambler," it was a calculated decision with little risk and much to recommend it. We had good water and we were lee bowing a northerly flowing current across Great Bahama Bank. Great Isaac Light was fully visible, although North Rock Light had faded out of sight. There were several wrecks and rocks to avoid, but these were clearly marked on our large-scale British Admiralty chart of the area. The problem: how to avoid them with

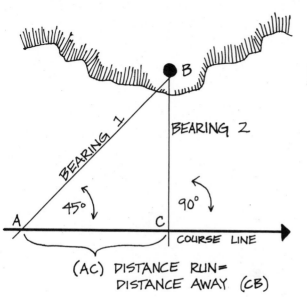

Bow and beam bearings with precise angles.

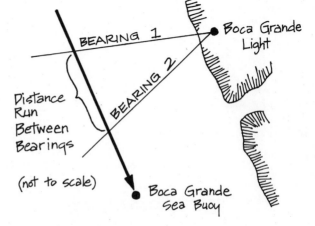

Timed bearings regardless of angle.

only a single object on which to take bearings, particularly since we were tacking toward that object and could not steer a straight line to it. The solution: use danger bearings on each side of a safe area. In this case the rhumb line was constructed from a bottom gradient about south of the light. By plotting the tacks so that they were contained within the danger bearings, we successfully threaded our way between Hen and Chickens Rocks and a wreck to the eastward, rounding Great Isaac boat-for-boat with race leaders *Charisma* and *Bonaventure,* who prior to this maneuver were well ahead, and went on to overtake them.

Even though your navigational information may seem limited, if it is dependable, you can use it with confidence and aggressiveness. What may seem like a gamble to your competitors is really only the best route to the finish.

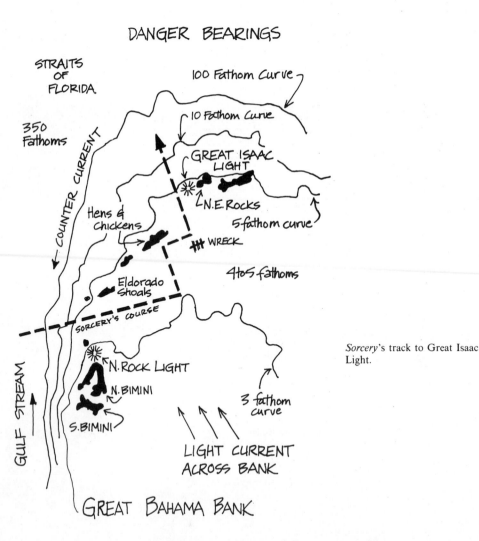

Sorcery's track to Great Isaac Light.

The Races

PART IV

Winning any race is a thrill. To bring Robin *to the Admiral's Cup course already a transatlantic winner was among the finest moments of my life.*

—Lee Van Gemert
Skipper of *Robin*, 1975
Transatlantic Race Winner

In any given week there is an offshore race somewhere in the world, and the list is constantly changing. New races appear in response to demand, some established races are discontinued due to lack of entries, still others are updated with course or rule changes and may be renamed. Some are short, like the San Diego–Ensenada Race, or, like the Capetown–Rio Race, span long distances across open seas. The St. Petersburg–Fort Lauderdale Race is highly competitive with much at stake. The St. Petersburg–Isla Mujeres Race is mostly fun and fresh air. The Fastnet Race will attract hundreds of entries, while others never draw more than a dozen or so yachts. The 3,571-mile Los Angeles to Tahiti Race is beyond the reach of most owners.

The scene may be the coast of North or South America, Western Europe, Southern Africa or Australia, the English Channel, the American Great Lakes, the Gulf of Mexico, the Caribbean Islands, the Mediterranean, or points in between. Races have been run from ocean to ocean and around the world.

Sometimes races have been combined into a series with the selected races given different weights in the series' score based upon length, degree of difficulty or importance. Examples are the Admiral's Cup, Onion Patch and SORC series.

Campaigning worldwide is possible only by the fortunate few who have the energy, time, money and a yacht suitable for that purpose. Most offshore skippers are content to stick to nearby waters, with an occasional foray into other areas.

It is not possible to cover all the available races here, so I have selected a representative cross section to describe in detail, and your favorite may be among them.

Although these are among the more competitive, popular and better established contests, they are still quite different from one another and illustrate a wide range of sailing conditions. In sum, they do encompass the wide-ranging nature of the sport.

23 THE ADMIRAL'S CUP AND THE FASTNET

National flags of the Admiral's Cup teams displayed at Cowes

The Admiral's Cup Series

The Admiral's Cup is a generous-sized, two-handled covered bowl decorated with suitable ornamentation. It rests on a silver base and its color is bright gold. Unlike the America's Cup, it has a bottom. What is not apparent at first glance is the Cup's magnetic quality. Every two years since 1957 it has drawn top-notch offshore yachtsmen to race in British waters—some from halfway around the world. In 1975 there were three-boat teams present from 18 nations to match skills in this four-race series designed to provide "an exacting test of racing tactics, seamanship and navigation." Truly, this contest is the pinnacle of ocean racing.

It is one of yachting's greatest honors to compete against a sparkling array of the world's finest yachts, manned by an international amalgam of crews who never let up, and to navigate some of the toughest racing courses man and Nature

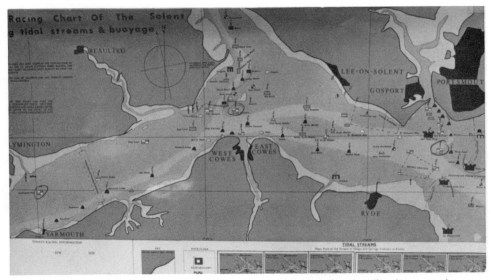

Marks for the races in the Solent are selected from this chart based on the wind direction at starting time.

Boat Basin at Plymouth is without water at low tide.

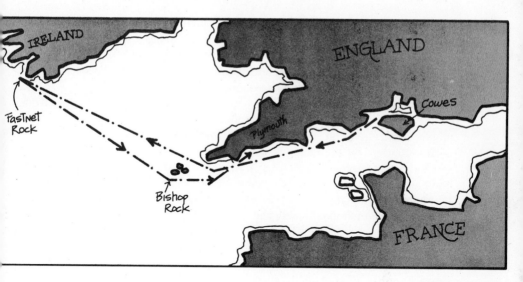

Fastnet race course.

Channel race course.

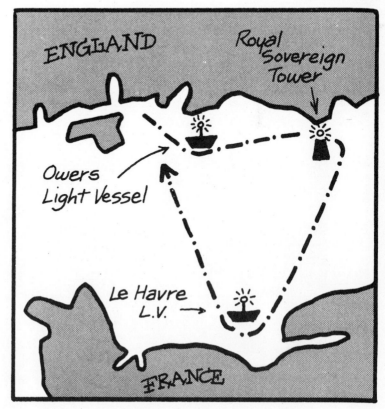

can contrive—all put together in a setting replete with maritime history.

The first event is a triangular race of 225 miles, along England's south coast, then across the English Channel to Le Havre, France, and back. Next come two round-the-buoys day races in the Solent, a tricky body of water between the Isle of Wight and the mainland. The windup is the challenging Fastnet Race—a 605-mile marathon west from Cowes around Lands End to lonely Fastnet Rock off the south coast of Ireland, then around the Scilly Isles to the finish at Plymouth, departure point of the Pilgrims' *Mayflower* in 1620.

Headquarters for the racing is at Cowes on the Isle of Wight, a small island south of Southampton and the British naval port of Portsmouth, the permanent home of Lord Nelson's flagship HMS *Victory*. The Admiral's Cup races are scheduled intentionally to coincide with the Cowes Week daily racing for many classes, and unintentionally with the month in which all England goes on vacation, resulting in an unbelievable jam of boats and people. Crews and their retinue, press representatives, spectators and holiday seekers engulf the population of this rustic, nautically flavored community of 18,500 permanent residents. What with spectator craft, TV boats and helicopters and some 800 actual contestant boats in Cowes Week, starts eclipse in magnitude the Battle of Trafalgar and shoreside activities are so hectic that to get a meal in a restaurant is sometimes tougher than

Main Street in Cowes

the actual racing. How all this is managed is a tribute to British organization and efficiency. Races go as scheduled, boats are duly recorded, protests handled and results announced promptly and accurately, while social events, both formal and impromptu, proceed apace, and repair crews toil round-the-clock to keep competitors in the battle.

However, at least two factors beyond the control of the Committee are the weather and the relentless currents that sweep inexorably in and out of the English Channel and connected waters with velocities as high as six or seven knots in certain areas. The range between low and high tide can be 25 feet or more.

Despite the difficult sailing conditions, navigational restrictions are very stringent. Electronic aids such as Loran, Omni, Omega, radar and automatic direction finder are prohibited. Depth sounders, simple radio direction finders and Consol (similar to our discontinued Consolan) are OK. In practice the depth sounder is the only instrument that can be relied upon. Direction finder reception is good during the daytime, but very poor at night. Consol has a reliability of five to 10 miles in this area. Fog, haze and cloud cover often prevent celestial observations. Navigational errors are commonplace and groundings routine. At least 30 nautical charts and a dozen related publications are needed for the racing.

Sailboat racing is a spectator sport during Cowes Week.

Polished brass starting cannon and signal flagpole of the Royal Yacht Squadron mark one end of the starting line.

Close racing around Brambles Buoy

Yachts are hauled for bottom cleaning and repairs between races.

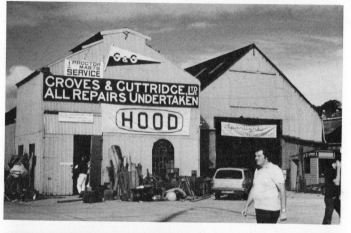

Temporary repair shops are available.

French Team members making sail repairs

Guide to the Fastnet

Take any three or four of the toughest, most frustrating offshore races you have experienced, mix them all together and you have an idea of what you're up against in a typical Fastnet Race.

The length, 605 miles, is enough to provide a variety of weather conditions and to reduce most crews to an understandable state of weariness. The combination of coastal and offshore sailing is exquisitely designed to prevent falling into a regular on-board daily routine, and the swift and ever-present currents add just the right amount of uncertainty at each point of land or turning point in the course. Fog and low visibility may be encountered at any time and the weather is quite changeable. Add the requirement that only rudimentary navigational instruments may be used (sextant, direction finder and depth sounder) and you begin to get the picture.

The Fastnet is one of the oldest offshore races in yachting history. Sponsored since its inception by the Royal Ocean Racing Club of Britain, it was first run in 1925 and continued annually until 1931. Thereafter it has been run every other year, alternating with the Bermuda Race. The legendary Sherman Hoyt, sailing the 50-foot schooner *Nina* in 1928, was the first American to win this classic. In 1931 Olin Stephens in *Dorade* and in 1935 his brother, Rod Stephens, Jr., sailing *Stormy Weather* were the next Americans to win. America's fortunes then languished until Dick Nye's two successive corrected time victories in 1955 and 1957 with a former *Carina*. In 1971 Ted Turner was first to finish with his *American Eagle* and racked up a new elapsed time course record. But for most of the races since the beginning of the Fastnet, Great Britain has dominated the winning circle. This is understandable when you consider what a non-British yacht owner has to go through just to get his boat to the starting line.

The time, effort, money and logistics are monumental, and preparation must begin months ahead. For example, to get *Salty Goose* from Long Island Sound to England in 1973 as a member of the three-boat U.S. Admiral's Cup Team required a transatlantic voyage of over three weeks by co-owner Wally Frank and a ferry crew assembled for the task. Meanwhile, back in the U.S., our other co-owner, Bob Derecktor, was busy handling such necessary items as arranging for prerace yard work to be done on arrival, having sails recut, ordering new ones (nonracing sails were used for the trip across), shipping necessary backup gear and making final racing crew appointments. Crew housing in Britain, provisioning, entry forms and rating certificates were other items needing attention. Crew members had to adjust their personal schedules, book space on airlines and take care of related details to be on the scene ready to go. All this, it is hoped, falls into place on the day of the start.

That year, a record 294 boats were entered in competition for an impressive array of 24 interestingly named trophies, ranging from the Fastnet Challenge Cup for the overall winner on corrected time to the Iolaire Block for the oldest yacht to complete the race. Included in the fleet, of course, were Admiral's Cup yachts for which this race was the grand finale of a four-race international series.

The race can be divided into several stages. From the start, a 13-mile leg leads out of the narrow, boat-clogged, current-swept Solent to the Needles, at the southwest tip of the Isle of Wight. Then comes a coastwise leg of 166 miles along England's rocky south shore and past the rugged bluffs of St. Albans Head, the Bill of Portland, Start Point and Lizard Head to Lands End. Next come two offshore legs. It's 179 miles into the Atlantic to Fastnet Rock close to the southern tip of Ireland, then 152 miles back to Bishop Rock, marking the southwest part of the Scilly Isles which lie 30 miles off Lands End. The final coastwise leg from Bishop Rock back around Lizard Head to the finish at the breakwater off Plymouth harbor entrance is 95 miles.

The first step in preparation is to get English Channel Chart NO-36000, or British Admiralty Chart 1598. Either will give you an overall picture of the entire racecourse and will also show prominent navigational aids such as major lights and direction finder stations as well as useful bottom gradients. Mark range arcs from lights and DF stations to show their coverage along the track line. Note that some of the DF stations operate only during periods of fog. Their operator's idea of what is fog may differ from yours, so don't be surprised if they are not transmitting. I also found that the actual DF reception ranges varied up and down from those listed, the French stations being more powerful than their listed distance. For position finding with the depth sounder, you will need to know the range of tide (difference in feet between high and low water) at the various locations and times. These can be found on pages 15 to 17 of HO-700, Section I, Tides and Currents, which also contains tidal current charts for the area on pages 52 through 64. Consol, a hyperbolic system using a direction finder to pick up dots and dashes, provides coverage, but is not accurate enough for pinpoint navigation.

It seems almost academic to say that all your allowable navigational instruments should be working to perfection in this league. Compasses should be compensated, depth finder and direction finders (more than one should be aboard) calibrated, sextant and timepiece should be in top condition and ready. You will need a good radio receiver to pick up time signals and the frequent BBC Channel 2 area weather forecasts that are most helpful in getting a line on conditions influenced by the low-pressure areas sweeping frequently across the North Atlantic and into the British Isles. Your distance and speed indicator should be as accurate as you can make it, or the error should be known and recorded for various speeds. An accurate hand-bearing compass is also a necessary item.

Putting together your chart portfolio requires a bit of thought. Wally Frank and I spent a couple of hours poring over U.S. Naval Oceanographic Office Chart Catalogue for Region Three and its British Admiralty counterpart, NP-131. We came up with a list of 20 charts for this race plus four tidal current chart booklets. (To use these you need the tables for high water at Dover.) Once in England we added a few more items such as a full-color, plastic-coated chart of the Solent, showing all the buoys used for racing. Naval Oceanographic Charts and the British Admiralty charts are similar in detail as both systems are based on British Admiralty surveys, so take your choice. A basic premise is to get the largest-scale charts available for *all* coastal areas as you don't know where you may have to feel your way along the bricks to stay out of adverse currents.

Reed's Almanac, available in England and similar to our *Eldridge's Tide and Pilot Book,* is a good buy as it contains a wealth of valuable information on all sorts of navigational data for the area. Your kit should also include Consol charts, a nautical almanac and sight reduction tables.

On the coastwise legs timing is everything. In 1973, with the smaller classes starting first and a favorable current in the Solent, the fleet was able to beat past St. Albans Head before the current turned east. But at the Bill of Portland where the easterly current can be as high as six knots, it was another matter. There are basically two choices under these conditions to minimize the effects of the current —either hide in the bays and cut close to the points of land or go well out into the English Channel where currents are slower, and hope for a better wind. Two years before it paid to stay offshore. That year it paid to hug the beach. *Charisma* and *Salty Goose,* having worked through the fleet, sailed in close and traded the lead back and forth as *Sorcery* opted for the Channel. The result was that *Sorcery,* at the top of Class I which had started 15 minutes before these two Admiral Cuppers, was still behind them boat-for-boat when the three converged between the Lizard and Lands End. So you can't depend upon what has happened in previous races, although previous experience can be of help if properly used. Aboard Robin Aisher's high-placing *Frigate,* among the crew there totaled over a dozen previous Fastnets. At each important decision point in the race the Fastnet veterans were consulted and their recommendations synthesized to arrive at a reasonable course of action. This approach also prevents the inevitable second-guessing when this experience is not utilized.

On the offshore legs, the current, rather than being east or west, flows across the course. The problem now is to estimate the exposure time, determine how many tidal cycles are involved, then calculate the *net* amount of set for the distance and apply this factor to the base course, making adjustments as a leg is actually sailed. Bear in mind that the tidal current charts are only an average.

Fastnet Rock lies 3 1/2 miles west-southwest of Cape Clear. Nine miles northwest and beyond the Rock is Mizen Head, on which is located a radio beacon station. Fastnet Rock has no radio beacon, in clear weather is visible 18 miles and in fog is supposed to sound a fog signal. The 50-fathom curve snakes along the Irish coast about 10 miles out, crossing the rhumb line to the Rock at an angle and running nearly parallel a couple of miles south of the rhumb line.

With normal visibility, homing on Mizen Head beacon should put you in visual contact with the Rock during the daytime or with its powerful light at night. But in 1973 many of the lead boats had problems. As the large boats cleared Lands End, the wind turned aft, bringing with it a dense low-lying fog. Occasional patches of sky above seemed to indicate eventual clearing and led to a sense of optimism—false, as it turned out—for visibility actually encountered at the Rock was less than a mile when the leading boats arrived.

Early into the leg, *Sorcery,* making good use of her notable downwind capability, had disappeared ahead of us. *Charisma* was next to open out, followed by

Saga, which also disappeared into the soup. The seas were calm, the wind held, and it was a smooth uneventful crossing until we tried to find the Rock. A southwesterly set was indicated on the tidal current charts. Consol, not being accurate enough close in, was no longer usable. Depth sounder information was inconclusive outside of the 50-fathom curve. We detected, by direction finder, that we were being set south of the rhumb line and made heading corrections based upon that info. But we had no firm way of determining how close we were or what the actual set was.

Meanwhile, *Sorcery,* aided by hearing the fog signal, rounded the Rock in first position at 1030. *Charisma,* next in line and south of the rhumb line, fortunately sighted *Sorcery* on the return leg, corrected to sail the reciprocal of *Sorcery*'s heading, and rounded at 1145.

Saga was doubly fortunate. When an estimated four miles out, she sighted *Sorcery* about a half-mile to leeward and corrected accordingly; then two miles closer, sighted *Charisma* returning. Even with both of these checks, when the Rock came in view at less than a mile, it was 20 degrees on her starboard bow, indicating a greater set than predicted.

Aboard *Salty Goose* we saw no competitors and we were becoming concerned. When the DF bearings on Mizen Head suddenly began to climb in spite of successive course corrections, instead of dropping, and the 50-fathom curve had not been crossed, we knew we were close but were being swept south. It was a classic dilemma. DF bearing accuracy was plus or minus three degrees, our distance log was reading ten to 15 percent low and we were making eight knots under chute. A crucial decision had to be made quickly with few reliable facts. Our DR time ran out. We crossed the 50-fathom curve—but where? Only dousing the chute, coming hard on the wind and heading to the north brought the radio bearings back. But the problem now was which side of the Rock were we on. As it turned out, we had actually passed it to the west by about a mile and a half in the fog without seeing it or hearing any fog signal.

In retrospect, under these conditions, a better approach would have been to stay deliberately a couple of miles north of the rhumb line rather than trying to run in on it. Then, after crossing the 50-fathom curve, about 13 miles from the Rock, try to keep the direction finder bearing on Mizen Head steady at 306 degrees magnetic. To do this would mean assigning a qualified crew member to take successive DF bearings on Mizen Head (the station transmits every six minutes) posting lookouts, recording continuous soundings and maintaining a continuous plot with all available information. It also means being ready to make whatever sail changes are required to maintain the right heading. In other words, an emergency fog navigation procedure. Some boats intentionally made an even more conservative landfall to the north at Cape Clear—but this was better than missing the Rock to the south and winding up at Mizen Head, as happened to still others.

A similar problem presents itself on the return leg. Bishop Rock has no direction finder station, but Round Island, eight miles to the northeast, does. You know you are getting close when the bearing starts backing rapidly, swinging

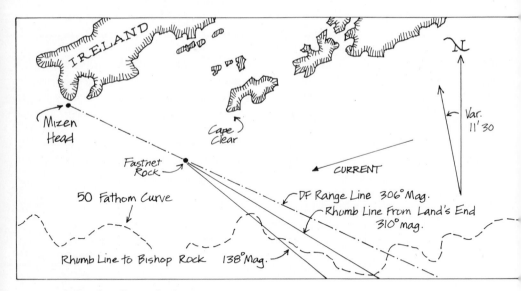

Approach to Fastnet Rock

from the southeast toward the northeast. When the bearing passes 046 degrees magnetic (Round Island and Bishop Rock are then in line with your position) and you are still in deep water, you have cleared Bishop Rock to the south. Many boats never saw the Bishop in the 1973 race. Beating into a light easterly, some passed it as much as 20 miles to the south. Albert Buell, the skipper of the West German Admiral's Cup boat *Saudade,* made a particularly bold maneuver. Sailing on port tack toward the French coast, he passed about ten miles south of Bishop Rock, continued out into the English Channel to the lay line for the finish and tacked, making it to Plymouth on that tack and finished well up, while other competitors fought their way in light winds and strong currents around the Lizard and along the Cornish headlands. His tactic paid off. There *was* more wind in the Channel at this point. *Ginkgo,* as an example, taking the inshore route, was eight hours ahead of Admiral's Cup teammate *Apollo II* close to Lizard Head, but lost seven of these in the 46 miles to the finish. *Saga* was 8 3/4 hours ahead of us at the Lizard, 5¾ hours at Eddystone Light and 3 hours, 25 minutes at the finish. Other yachts anchored as the wind died (or kedged, as the English call it) and those that didn't wished they had when the current took over.

The caliber of talent in the Admiral's Cup boats was highlighted in this 280-boat fleet by their taking the first six corrected-time fleet positions in this Fastnet's tricky conditions, as *Saga,* the overall winner, was followed by *Recluta, Charisma, Salty Goose, Safari,* and *Quailo.* The first non-Cup boat was first-to-finish *Sorcery* in seventh place.

But even a fast boat, superbly sailed and headed most of the time in the right direction, isn't enough. It helps to have a four-leaf-clover, a horseshoe, and a rabbit's foot aboard . . . just in case.

Salty Goose sails the 1973 Fastnet.

Salty Goose leaves Cowes for the starting line.

Yachts crowd the line moments before the gun.

Lonely Fastnet Rock, navigators' nemesis

Taking departure on the Needles, a rock cliff jutting into the English Channel

Goose hugs the shoreline at Portland Bill to avoid an adverse current.

Nearing the finish at Plymouth, Bob Bavier and Ken Bechell show the strain of nearly five days of tense racing as *Safari,* a dot on the horizon, closes distance.

Safari, now close astern as the wind dies to a whisper and Eddie Kajak watches the cigarette smoke for wind direction.

Yards from the finish, *Safari* was nearly abeam.
Moments later, *Salty Goose* finished in fourth place. *Safari,* caught in a tidal swirl at the breakwater, lost speed, had to anchor and finished 29 minutes later.

24 THE SYDNEY–HOBART RACE

The Sydney–Hobart Race is the high point of the Australian racing season. It traditionally starts each year on Boxing Day, December 26, which is the summer season in the Southern Hemisphere. Performances are closely watched in even years as part of the selection process for Australia's Admiral's Cup Team. In odd years, the race is part of the four-race Southern Cross Cup Series, attracting teams from the various Australian states, as well as Great Britain, the United States, New Zealand and Hong Kong.

The sailors from down under are a rugged group, spawned in the gale winds and heavy seas of the Roaring Forties. They are in demand as offshore crews and are often seen racing aboard yachts of other nations as well as their own. Australian yachts have done well in worldwide events. The yacht *Foxy Lady* won the World Half-Ton Championship in 1975. The yacht *Bumblebee 3* narrowly missed winning the 1976 Bermuda Race, finishing a close second. The maxi yachts *Ballyhoo* and *Buccaneer* have competed in the Transpac and U.S. racing. Much of this expertise comes from the challenging Sydney–Hobart experience.

G. N. Evans was 1976 Commodore of the Cruising Yacht Club of Australia, organizer of the race in cooperation with the Royal Yacht Club of Tasmania. In greeting the race participants that year, he had this to say: "In Bass Strait many a skipper vows never to put to sea again. In Storm Bay he might even try selling the boat to the crew. But as he enters Constitution Dock to the ever-present applause and welcome, he looks for next year's entry form."

Rob Mundle, an eminent yachting writer and sailor from Sydney, provides us with the following detailed account of the Sydney–Hobart:

> What started out to be just a Christmas cruise is now one of the world's major ocean racing classics. The 630-mile dash from Sydney, Australia, to Hobart, capital of Tasmania, the island state south of the continent, crosses some of the world's toughest and most demanding waters and regularly attracts 75 to 100 yachts of Half-Ton size and up.
>
> In 1945 ocean racing was in its embryonic stages in Australia. A group of nine yacht owners decided that instead of spending Christmas in Sydney, they would cruise south, in company. After some deliberation, it was proposed by the noted offshore yachtsman, Capt. John Illingworth, that the group race instead of cruise. Thus, on December 26, 1945, as the nine yachts set out for Hobart, Tasmania, began Australia's first major ocean race. Their efforts received much publicity. When a southwesterly gale plastered the fleet on the second day out of Sydney, the newspapers sank their teeth into the story. All except Illingworth's 32-foot cutter, *Rani*, sought shelter or hove to in the gale. One competitor is reported to have anchored

The maxi-yacht *Ballyhoo* leads fleet out of Sydney Harbor in 1976 Race start. This 72-foot sloop, skippered by Jack Rooklyn of Sydney, went on, through winds of 70 knots and 25-to-30-foot seas, to win line honors in what Rooklyn described as his toughest race in 30 years of offshore racing. *(courtesy Wide World Photos)*

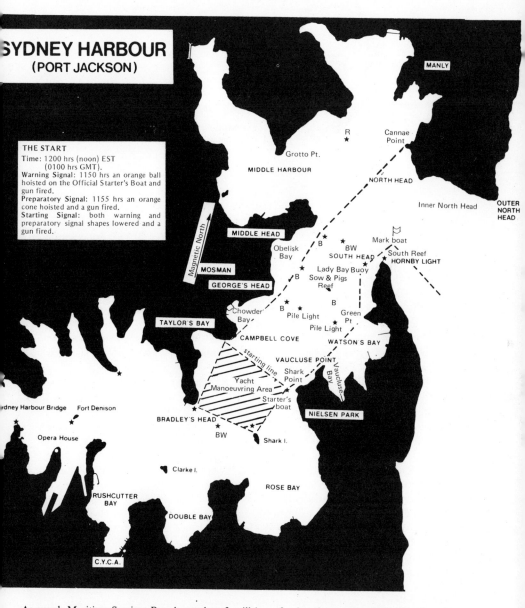

As usual, Maritime Services Board patrol craft will be enforcing the spectator limit line (see above broken line); patrol craft marking the spectator limit will exhibit a large yellow flag and all vessels must pass inshore of the broken lines. To give all Race participants a fair and even chance without interference by wake or obstacle, spectator craft are requested to stay well clear of the fleet at all times and especially until it has manoeuvred into open sea beyond and clear of the Heads. For spectators onshore, the natural amphitheatre foreshores of Nielson Park, Chowder Head and Ashton Park provide ideal viewing of the actual start, while the north and south headlands provide grand views of the fleet heading out to sea. (*Courtesy Cruising Yacht Club of Australia, and Hitachi Ltd.*)

Rob Mundle
(Drawing by Bob Smith)

in a small bay and gone rabbit hunting until the gale passed.

Headlines announced: "Plea to Royal Australian Air Force for Full-Scale Search for Missing Yachts" . . . "Boats May Have Been Dismasted" . . . "Two Missing in Race to Tasmania" . . . "Steamer Goes to Help of Missing Yacht." Then came the headline that staggered everyone: "Missing Yacht Turns Up, Wins Big Race." Illingworth and his six-man crew had pushed *Rani* through the gale and, just when everyone was becoming very concerned for their safety, they arrived in Hobart to take both line and corrected time honors.

Illingworth commented after the race: "I can't believe we were considered lost for five days. We had a fine and safe trip. It's funny to say we were lost. The crew never lost one hot meal."

The race had captured the imagination of Australian yachtsmen and the public. In 1946 the fleet had swelled to 19 and in 1975 there were 102 starters. In 1945 *Rani* had an elapsed time of six days, 14 hours, 22 minutes. In 1975 the giant American ketch, *Kialoa,* sailed by Jim Kilroy, set a course record that is going to be as easy to break as jumping over the moon. She sped down the New South Wales coast, across Bass Strait and on into Hobart in an incredible two days, 14 hours, 36 minutes and 56 seconds, breaking the Australian yacht *Helsal's* 1973 record by nearly 11 hours.

The conditions for the 1975 fleet were those you dream about. After clearing Sydney Harbor, the yachts had a sleigh ride for almost the entire course. For the leaders, the only time they tacked was when they cleared Sydney Heads and turned south. That race was an exception. The course for this event takes the fleet into the "Roaring Forties" and it is not unusual for the fleet to get a thorough dusting. The famed Southerly Busters have destroyed many a yacht's chances over the years. These ugly, sausage-like gray clouds roll in from the south and turn a near calm into a painful 70 mph gale in a matter of seconds.

In 1970 there was a southwest gale that blew for 50 hours. Huge seas and wind in the 50 mph-plus range created havoc. A record 14 retirements came in that race with one yacht, Graham Nock's *Rum Runner,* being knocked down to about 120 degrees by a massive wave. In 1963 there was a 70 mph gale in Storm Bay, near the finish. John Farren-Price's *Lolita* was rolled over by a wave and dismasted. The Royal Navy submarine, *Trump,* went to the rescue.

The Sydney–Hobart Race has to be experienced to be believed. The progress of the race is followed closely by a news-hungry public. Race reports and the end results make headlines in Australia's newspapers. The start for the uninitiated is the experience of a lifetime. Thousands of spectator boats on the beautiful waters of Sydney Harbor escort the fleet to the open sea. Tens of thousands of people cram the headlands which make the harbor a natural amphitheatre and millions watch the start on nation-wide television.

The race took on an international flavor in 1958 when Englishman Geoffrey Pattinson took his cutter, *Uomie,* to Sydney for the race. He finished third across the line and fifth on handicap, an achievement which prompted more overseas interest. In 1967 the race went truly international with the introduction of the Southern Cross Cup Series, a team event not unlike Britain's Admiral's Cup. Contested biennially, it now attracts teams from all over the world. The Cup event consists of four races, with the Hobart race being the climax.

In 1969 former British Prime Minister (then leader of the Opposition) Edward Heath represented Britain in the Southern Cross Cup Series. He won the Hobart race that year with his Sparkman & Stephens designed 32-foot sloop, *Morning Cloud.* In 1972 that colorful American, Ted Turner, became the only competitor after Illingworth to take a double win. Turner steered his converted 12 Meter, *American Eagle,* to line and corrected time honors in that race.

The 1976 event was the 32nd consecutive race and it was the 26th time that three of Australia's best-known ocean racing men, Magnus Halvorsen, Stan Darling and Peter Green have competed. The name "Halvorsen" is the most famous in Australian yachting. Magnus, with brother, Trygve, steered their powerful sloop *Freya* to three consecutive corrected time wins in 1963, 1964 and 1965.

The Hobart race has seen the introduction of a very successful age allowance handicapping system which has made the race far more interesting for all competitors. This allowance applies to all boats more than three years old. However, this doesn't daunt the newer yachts, as 40 of the 92 entries in the 1976 race were built in 1975 or '76. The fleet is divided into two divisions for non level rating yachts and also has divisions for Half-, Three-Quarter and One-Ton Cup class yachts. However, the fleet starts as one, making it one of the greatest spectacles to be seen in ocean yacht racing.

The track is virtually a straight line after the start, with the final swing west into Storm Bay then up the Derwent River, being the only major course change. That makes for an interesting race with numerous alternatives open to helmsmen and navigators. In general it is the yachts that tend to stay east of the rhumb line that do best. This applies to races where both running and beating are experienced. The fleet usually starts in a northeasterly, giving the yachts a run down to Bass Strait, then headwinds and sometimes light and variable conditions can be encountered. In 1975 the race was run all the way and the 40-foot *Rampage,* excellently sailed by Peter Packer and his young West Australian crew, won through hard driving and a course straight down the rhumb line. In the 1970 race, Sir Robert Crichton-Brown steered his yacht, *Pacha,* farther to the east than anyone in the strong running conditions that prevailed for the first two days. When the gale moved in from the south, *Pacha* was in an excellent position for a port tack lay-line into the Tasmanian coast. She won on handicap from Syd Fischer's well-known sloop, *Ragamuffin,* by less than six minutes.

The finish in Hobart has been acclaimed by international yachtsmen as the best in the world. No matter what time the first yacht crosses the line, day or night, there will be thousands of people cramming the vantage point at Battery Point to see her get the gun. The reception is unbelievable—every crew that finishes gets a reception as though they were aboard the winner. The yachts are guided into Constitution Dock at the foot of the old city and are moored there for all to see. The parties there are something else, but the highlight has to be "The Quiet Little Drink," organized by Tony Cable and John Dawson. At that function, happy yachtsmen cram into the waterfront pubs for some yarn telling, song and dance acts and to partake of copious quantities of beer which each crew combines to buy in lots of hundreds. What cash is left over goes to a childrens' home after the last, very relaxed yachtsman is put on an erratic course back to the dock. The record for total consumption currently stands at 9,450 bottles.

Sydney–Hobart race course

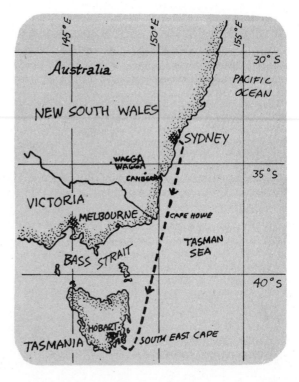

25 THE ANNAPOLIS–NEWPORT RACE

The biennial Annapolis–Newport classic, alternating in odd-numbered years with the Bermuda Race, has been an East Coast fixture since 1957 and is an interesting combination of sailing conditions. It begins in the northern reaches of Chesapeake Bay, a body noted for its frequent calms, changeable winds, strong currents and abundance of shoals upon which many a sailing craft has come to grief over the centuries. The track leads south down the Bay, through the Chesapeake Bridge-Tunnel entrance, around the offshore-positioned Chesapeake Tower, then north-easterly out to sea across the big ship traffic lanes leading to New York, on into Rhode Island Sound—and ends 473 miles later close aboard Castle Hill Light at Newport. In actuality there are two races: one a Bay race where piloting skills are at a premium, and the other an offshore race where accurate deep-sea navigation is required. Often, a third race begins in the tricky currents and vagrant winds off Montauk Point and Block Island, near the finish. Here's the story of a record-breaking passage.

Ever dream of sailing a perfect race where the wind, weather and current cooperate, the boat is always moving at top speed and the crew functions flawlessly? That dream became a reality for the fortunate sailors manning Jack Potter's *Equation* in the 1973 Annapolis–Newport Race. As watch captain George Hinman, a veteran of many nautical contests, expressed it for all of us, "If we had it to do over again, there's nothing we'd do differently."

And the results could not have been better. The speedy, Chance-designed, Derecktor-built aluminum ketch with the 68-foot destroyerlike hull not only took all the marbles by a wide margin, but also pared four hours and 19 minutes from the previous elapsed time record set by Peter Grimm's 73-foot *Escapade* in 1965. (This new time, 57 hours 18 minutes, was again shattered in 1975 by *Kialoa II.*) Getting out of the Bay in good shape is the name of the game, and 1973's weather conditions helped make this possible.

Five classes start at half-hour intervals, with the smaller boats leading off. *Equation,* rated at the top of Class I, was not only the scratch boat (we gave *Bulldog Drummond,* the lowest-rated boat in Class V, 18 hours and 40 minutes) but with her 10,000-pound 14-foot-long centerboard down, she also had the deepest draft in the fleet. This meant that we had to be particularly aware of shoal water at all times, could not hug the shoreline to minimize an adverse current, as could smaller boats, and the crew had to keep the boat moving to overcome a rating difference on all 80 competitors. On the other hand, the ability to finish

The start—Annapolis Harbor entrance buoy

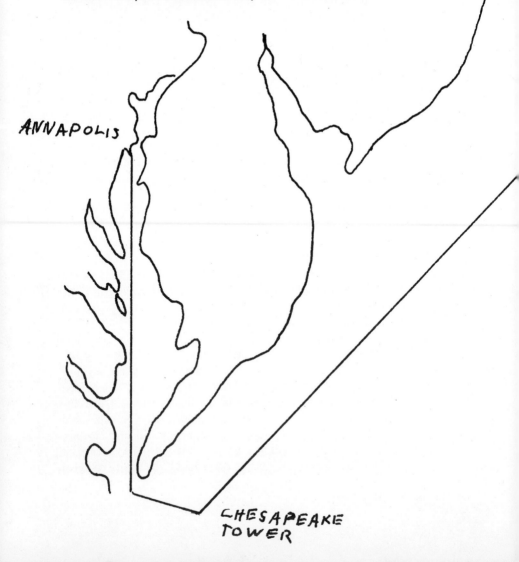

ANNAPOLIS

CHESAPEAKE
TOWER

NEW-
PORT

G ISLAND

Annapolis–Newport race course

The finish—Castle Hill Light

first could be an advantage if fully utilized and Skipper Jack Potter had assembled a crew of offshore veterans worthy of the task.

The toughest possible situation for us would be a beat out the Bay in light weather. Sure enough, at Friday's prerace skippers' meeting, the local weatherman announced that there would probably be little or no wind for the start. To compound the problem, page 72 of the 1973 *Tidal Current Tables,* necessary for entry into the Tidal Current Charts for the upper Chesapeake, contained a significant misprint on race day, June 16, which made it appear that the current was flooding (heading north) for the entire 24 hours.

By starting time both problems were resolved. A brisk south-southwesterly wind developed and, by taking visual current readings on nearby buoys and by continuing the sequence of ebb and flood from previous dates in the Tables, we were able to reconstruct the correct ebb-flood sequence for the 16th. I later checked with the National Ocean Survey, publisher of the Tables, and an official there confirmed that the 1973 book was indeed a poor printing job. In many instances "E" for ebb came out looking like "F" for flood. Later years' versions, using a different process, were better.

The Current Charts for the upper Chesapeake now showed that for at least the first few hours after starting, currents would be favorable or a negligible factor, allowing us to stay in deep water where the afterguard played the wind shifts well to take an early lead in Class I.

Past Poplar Island, *Equation* tacked through the smaller classes, crossing the bow of *Mary Lee* in Class II, then forging quickly through the lee of *Beau Geste* in Class III as her owner, Tony Cassedy, gave a resigned shrug. Off James Island a 30 MPH squall lifted us on starboard tack so that we could sail rhumb line close to Cove Point. From here on no further tacks were necessary, and as darkness fell Class V, paced by Ted Turner's *Lightnin',* was left well to leeward as we shook loose from the fleet. Our chief Class I rivals, *Running Tide* and *Sorcery,* faded astern in the haze off our port quarter. VHF weather forecasts had the breeze clocking to the west. As our track favored the west side of the Bay and kept us somewhat out of an adverse current on the stretch between Smith Point and Wolf Trap, we stayed high but not hard on the wind, passing close to Smith Point Light. Navigationally, visual bearings on charted objects combined with frequent soundings and Omni bearings on Patuxent when in range, kept us on our planned track line. The wind velocity and direction held throughout the night, defying the usual Chesapeake conditions, making possible an unexpectedly fast arrival off Cape Charles.

At 0350 Sunday morning we were logging ten knots over-the-bottom as *Equation* quietly slipped through the Chesapeake Channel entrance of the Bridge-Tunnel with the help of a strong ebb current. Helmsman Don Browning bore off to the southeast for Chesapeake Tower and the watch set the chute. At 0545 we had covered the 19 1/2 miles to the Tower, rounded and jibed to port onto the rhumb line track for Block Island. Reveille had not yet sounded for the Tower crew, so no one there saw us pass in the early morning haze in spite of our hails and horn-tooting. Twenty minutes later *Sorcery* rounded, was erroneously reported as "first," creating a temporary mystery for race followers. Where was *Equation?*

At this point we were three miles up the rhumb line to the northeast riding a long easy swell from the starboard beam and anticipating a smooth, uneventful downwind glide for the ocean part of the voyage. Special limitations on equipment for this race included a ban on automatic steering, facsimile weathermap makers and teleprinters, but all types of navigational tools were allowed. Celestial observations were not possible due to overcast skies, but we were not handicapped. Our wide selection of electronic position-fixing gear included a deep-reading depth sounder, Omega, Loran direction finder and Omni.

In the absence of any overriding weather information, the plan was to stay as close as possible to the rhumb line, making minor heading corrections to compensate for set and leeway as frequent fixes so indicated. But this plan was short-lived.

Shortly after 0900 Sunday we were progressively headed as the breeze came around through northwest and north and settled in the northeast. As the wind veered, watch captain Bob McCullough called for a quick succession of sail changes from chute to starcut and then jib; and finally a tack to starboard, settling on a heading below our intended course. The wind and sea steadily increased. The new seas, short and choppy from the northeast, driven by occasional gusts up to 40 miles an hour, competed with the long southeast swells, causing a rather uncomfortable motion. Appetites noticeably diminished. By this time VHF weather had caught up with what was happening and was broadcasting an advisory message warning of strong northeast winds along the coast.

Equation, now down to double-reefed mainsail and number four genoa and pointing as high as possible, sliced steadily through the seas. Father's Day was celebrated quietly, with crewman Steve Kasnet hoping that we would beat the stork, imminently scheduled to deliver his first-born to Marblehead, Massachusetts.

We were sagging to the west, away from the rhumb line, making good a track that was gradually closing with the Maryland shore. Loran rates 3H4 and 3H5 provided excellent fixes. Off Ocean City, Maryland, we were 15 miles east. Off Indian River inlet we were even closer and the situation began to be critical. In a couple of hours we would run out of sea room and have to tack onto an unfavorable heading in relation to the finish. But the wind gods smiled again! Off Cape Henlopen at the entrance to Delaware Bay we sailed into a large lift at about 2130 and could again head for Block Island.

Wind and seas moderated during the night and by 0700 Monday we were well off Barnegat Inlet and making good our track. As we crossed the Ambrose to Nantucket Traffic Lane 68 miles east of Ambrose Light at 1330, fixes indicated a decided set to the west. Again the wind obligingly lifted us sufficiently to correct appropriately. Wind and seas had calmed considerably, but the big "E" was still charging along at a steady seven and a half to eight knots. Loran rate 1H7 was now coming in well, to provide a good crossline with 3H4.

Passing the Hampton beaches on the fashionable eastern end of Long Island, as we sat down to dine on New York–cut sirloins, excellently prepared by hardworking cook Jane Forsberg, Bucky Weekes and Jeff Hammond conjectured whether we could stay ahead of the existing record for the course. The skipper cautioned against such talk, remembering a previous race where he had spent 16 hours becalmed off Montauk Point.

Our turning point for the final leg to the finish was set at a mile and a half to the east of Block Island Light, and this track would take us eight miles to the east of Montauk, a wide enough berth to avoid possible calms and the developing flood current flowing across our course and into Block Island Sound. At 2045 we were there and the foredeck crew under Vic Romagna eased sheets for the 20-mile slide to the finish. We were to learn later that *Sorcery* and *Running Tide* were at this time close together and about 20 miles behind us. Night was falling and so was the wind. New Englander Sam Wakeman, wise in the ways of Newport Sound, had one more favor to ask of the wind gods. "Give us enough breeze to finish," he wished aloud. It worked! Setting the starcut off Point Judith we ghosted steadily past Brenton Tower and crossed the line at 2318 Monday, first to finish, averaging 8.2 knots for the voyage.

Now the waiting began. We needn't have worried—the breeze was dying fast. *Running Tide* took an agonizing hour to sail the last two and a quarter miles from Brenton Reef and while stalled near the finish line her skipper had even considered anchoring, as the ebb current had begun. The door had been closed on the fleet. By 1300 Tuesday, when I made a predeparture check with Race Committee Headquarters at Newport's historic Ida Lewis Yacht Club, only eight boats had finished and, fortunately for us, they were comfortably back on corrected time. At 1800, as I retraced the course by airliner on the way home, the white sails of smaller classes still dotted the track line.

26 LONG ISLAND SOUND, THE VINEYARD RACE

Long Island Sound is a large body of water open to tidal influences at both ends. Being located in an area of dense population which has served to support the foremost yacht designers and builders from the beginning of yacht racing as it is known today, it early became a testing ground for new ideas in ocean racing. Here the season opens in the northeast with the Block Island Race from Larchmont to and around Block Island and return on Memorial Day weekend at the end of May. A full season of day or overnight races and club cruises overlapping into Block Island Sound and the New England area is scheduled, running on until the Vineyard Race held on Labor Day weekend.

Since the latter race takes in the entire area and is the longest in distance of those scheduled, a description of two successive Vineyard Races will illustrate the conditions in the area.

The Stamford–Vineyard Race, traditional windup of the offshore season in the northeast, has been a Long Island Sound fixture since 1932. A 238-mile course from Stamford, Connecticut, to the Buzzards Bay Entrance Tower, then around Block Island and return to Stamford, combines all of the vagaries of the area's fickle weather and strong currents. The fastest elapsed time since the beginning of the Vineyard Race, 27 hours, 56 minutes, set in 1953 by W. H. Wheeler's 71-foot yawl *Cotton Blossom IV,* was finally shattered in 1975 when Eric Ridder's 79-foot ketch *Tempest* sailed out and back in 24 hours. *Cotton Blossom IV* still holds the slowest first-boat-to-finish time with a 70 hour, 10 minutes passage in 1959.

From a navigator's standpoint, the Vineyard Race is a round-the-clock session in piloting. Navigational aids are plentiful and, in good visibility, visual fixes are readily obtainable. In addition, strategically located marine radio beacons and Omni stations are usable regardless of visibility. Bottom gradients are well defined and make the depth-sounder an excellent navigational tool. Thus, position finding is not a problem, but a continuous plot is a necessity.

The big question marks are the weather and current. Over the period of the race as many as eight changes of tide may be encountered. Long Island Sound and Block Island Sound have strong currents up to two knots in velocity and the narrow openings between them (Plum Gut and The Race) act as venturis to generate five to six knots of maximum current. Currents swirl around Block Island in a variety of directions, depending on the stage of the tide. All these currents are fortunately quite predictable in direction and velocity using the *Tidal Current Tables* and *Tidal Current Charts* for Long Island Sound and Block Island Sound.

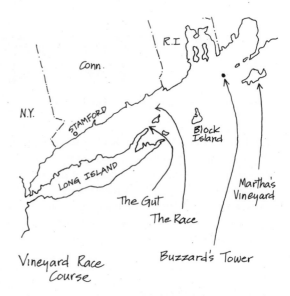

Vineyard Race
Course

The weather is often another matter. The capricious winds in Long Island Sound are legendary. In 1972 tropical storm Carrie, positioned in the Atlantic well south of Nantucket, contributed a rather predictable weather pattern, a northeast blow, which, for the first day, was steady in direction. Then, as the yachts finished, the wind gradually backed to the north. What this produced was a rugged thrash to windward all the way to the Buzzards Tower, then a fast downwind slide home.

Aboard *Equation* that year we were concerned navigationally with making the most of the current, and as it turned out, our timing could not have been better. After a fine start at 1730 Friday, with clear wind against a decreasing flood tide, we short tacked up the Connecticut shore where the diminishing current was weaker than that in the middle of the Sound. Then, as it waned further, we crossed the Sound to Smithtown Bay to pick up the first of the ebb currents which sluice around Crane Neck Point at high velocity. Our timing was right on schedule.

As the ebb progressed, we took a long hitch across to the Connecticut shore, another long hitch back to the Long Island shore, then back out into the middle of the Sound to get the most benefit out of the strong ebb current flowing northeastward. The midnight wind was dropping slightly in velocity and our calculations showed that we could not make Plum Gut, the entrance to Block Island Sound, before the current turned against us. Along the north shore of Long Island there is some shelter up close to the beach against a westerly flowing flood. We tacked in below Rocky Point on Long Island for insurance.

Tacking out again into the Sound just after the current turned, we got a 15-degree knock similar to our experience in previous probings to the north. Immediately tacking to port, we were now able to lee-bow the freshening flood coming through Plum Gut which helped us make the entrance on that tack.

Equation short tacks up the Connecticut shore with Skipper Jack Potter at the helm.

The currents at Plum Gut have to be correctly anticipated.

Equation nears Buzzard's Tower.

Block Island Light atop the cliffs at the southeast end

Behind us in the darkness, we could barely make out the closest Class A yachts, *Baccara* and *Running Tide*. *Equation* had worked through the smaller classes which had started up to two and a half hours earlier.

Once through the Gut, where the current was increasing against our nearest competitors, we continued on the port tack, receiving a lee-bow effect from the current sweeping in from the Atlantic into Block Island Sound, so that we were able to make to the northward of the southern tip of Block Island. Near the island we tacked to starboard to take advantage of a northerly flow along the west side of Block Island, then tacked back to port to ride the easterly flow around Sandy Point on the northern end of Block Island. Then it was a matter of short tacking along the Rhode Island shore to minimize the chop building from Buzzards Bay. We tacked again to port near Sakonnet Point on our final approach to the Tower and rounded at 1240 Saturday.

The course from the Tower to the south end of Block Island was dead downwind and after trying a port jibe which put us broadside to the Atlantic Ocean swells, we jibed to starboard and carried this in to three miles from Block Island. After jibing back to port on a better heading in relation to the wind, we started to move in a freshening breeze and rounded Block Island in time to pick up the new flood current. As the wind increased, *Equation* reveled in the conditions for which she was designed—slicing through the water with little disturbance. The Kenyon needle rose—11, 12, 13 knots, with the following seas creating brief surges to 16.

The combination of downwind slide and favorable current put us back through Plum Gut at slack water just before the current again turned eastward. A condition plainly indicated on the *Tidal Current Charts* showed that although the current had turned east at Plum Gut, it was still westward in Long Island Sound for another two hours. This meant that we would enjoy a favorable push while our competitors were taking it on the chin.

Once back in the Sound, the usual question is which way to go; down the middle, along the Connecticut shore or along the Long Island shore? The weather prediction had been fulfilled. The wind was backing. The current would soon turn against us. The skipper, after evaluating the alternatives, decided to steer for boat speed. Maintaining speed, we edged gradually to the south of the rhumb line in a lessening breeze. As the current turned east, we were closer to the Long Island shore in the least of the new current, and also in a position to lee-bow the ebb to Stamford. We set a course close to the south of Stratford Shoal, thus avoiding the strong currents off Oldfield Point; and as the wind backed on schedule to the north we dropped the chute and continued reaching at nine knots to finish at 0047 on Sunday, first to finish and first on corrected time.

The following year's Vineyard Race, a marked contrast, had enough variables to shuffle and reshuffle the fleet several times. The first four boats to finish were *La Forza del Destino, Running Tide, Kate* and *Equation*. From the logs of the first three we obtained data to compare them with our own track aboard *Equation*. Because these boats vary in rating from 57.6 (*Equation*) to 37.1 (*Kate*), their relative positions in the various segments of the contest tell a lot about the nature of this kind of racing. At one point both *La Forza* and *Kate* seemed completely out of it, but when the final results were in they not only stood first and second on elapsed time, but also first and second in the corrected time standings in the fleet of 74 finishers.

Six classes crossed the starting line in a light southeasterly on Friday between 1430 and 1730, with the smaller boats first. *Equation,* as scratch boat, slowly worked out to the head of Class A and began to grind down the rest of the classes in the light running conditions. A stagnant air mass over the northeast states indicated a challenging weekend for both amateur and professional weather forecasters and a good possibility of isolated thundershowers.

Sure enough, just after dark, a local thunderstorm came screaming into the fleet from the northwest and caught many boats with their chutes up. It was lively going in the 35- to 40-mile gusts in the darkness. *La Forza* took a knockdown that put her spreaders in the water and forced some green water down the main hatch. All around us boats were broaching and blowing chutes, but *Equation,* with the advantage of bigness, was screaming along under good control. One Class D boat made a vivid picture as we slid by her while she wallowed with reefed main and the flogging remnants of her chute streaming straight out from the masthead over the bow.

Finally, nearing Plum Gut, we were free of the fleet, but the slowly diminishing storm had enabled most of the boats to make a rapid passage up the Sound from Stratford Shoal. At 0048 on Saturday we passed through the Gut against a weakening flood current. *La Forza* sailed through 45 minutes later but close enough behind us to see our stern light. *Running Tide* was next, and *Kate* was well back at this point.

The course requires that Block Island be left to starboard on the way to Buzzards Tower. Block Island Sound that night was a frustrating experience with light, fickle winds and strong currents. As we headed for the bell marking the Block Island north shoal, we made slow progress under chute, not the best conditions for Jack Potter's rugged ketch which comes to life in a good sailing breeze.

The light of dawn showed that we were not alone. Off to the south and behind, but closing, by virtue of a bit more breeze and a better sailing angle, were *La Forza, Running Tide* and *Kate.* Passing the bell at 0624 with *La Forza* close behind, we had an hour and a half on *Running Tide* and *Kate.* On the run to the Tower the breeze improved as the morning progressed, we opened our distance and for the second time in two years were first to the Tower, rounding at 1005. *La Forza* was next, 12 minutes later, followed by *Running Tide* and 45 minutes later *Kate* rounded. At this point, by hanging on well, they had all saved their time on us so we had to get going. It was on the wind back to Block Island (the course requiring it to be passed to the south this time) in a steadily increasing breeze. Norm Raben, *La Forza*'s skipper, gave us points for sailing this leg better than he did as he battled with *Running Tide. Kate,* according to navigator Peter Quinn, "... lost ground on the leg to Block Island by virtue of the fact that we were leading Class B on a boat-to-boat basis. Since the entire group was let up as we approached Block Island, *Kate* wound up to leeward."

Equation continued to open out as we passed the south end of Block Island, intentionally holding to the north to escape adverse currents, and at 1800 we were five miles north of Montauk Point. The rest of the fleet had faded into the haze as the day breeze dropped to a whisper. Only *Running Tide* and *La Forza* could be seen, but they were several miles behind and closer to Montauk Point. Quoting Norm Raben: "Our horror show was as we closed with Montauk. You and *Tide* were a little north of us, but it was enough. You kept moving but we got caught by the current and had to anchor for 45 minutes."

Meanwhile, *Kate* continued to suffer in the light air south of Block Island and in the waters between Block Island and Montauk Point and fell back with the rest of the pack. Aboard *Equation* we were feeling a lot better as we drew away from *Running Tide* in the flukey air near Gardiners Island. As *La Forza* when last seen was anchored in three knots of foul current close to Montauk Point, all we had to do was shake *Running Tide*.

We went back to the *Tidal Current Tables* and the VHF weather reports. The westerly flowing current would soon be building, but the news about the breeze was bad. Stations all around the area from Point Judith to Execution Rocks were reporting the same thing—"calm."

By 2100 we were off Gardiners Island, tacking into a light westerly with about seven miles to go to Plum Gut. By 2300 we had literally been jetted through the Gut and into Long Island Sound by the high-velocity flood current. It was a weird feeling. What little breeze there was, was against us, yet the force of the current slamming us to windward filled the sails and created the drive to keep us moving. The hissing of tide rips was the only sound to break the stillness of the night.

And what of the others? *Running Tide* was able to catch the fair current through the Gut. *Kate* began a comeback. As Peter Quinn commented, "Our crew sailed the boat extremely well in the zephyrs from Montauk to Plum Gut and we regained a good bit of the ground that had been lost." "Raben's Raiders" finally got moving again and fought their way past Gardiners Island, also arriving at the Gut with still a fair current.

But in the Sound it was a new ball game with only a wisp of a norther in evidence. *Equation* and *Tide* sagged off to the Long Island shore and encountered nothing but doldrums through sunrise. As morning progressed, the heat and calm increased. Al Van Metre, *Tide*'s skipper, said, "The only thing we got by sticking with you fellows was a horde of flies off the Long Island shore." At this point we both felt that we were fighting it out for "first to finish" until, with about five miles to go, a powerboat put-putted out of the haze and announced that there were two boats ahead of us. We didn't find out till later that they were *La Forza* and *Kate*. Quinn explained: "The key to our success in this race was that we sailed a course down the middle of the Sound after passing through the Gut. We held northwesterly breezes during the daylight hours and passed close aboard Stratford Shoal. From then on the airs were very light and we favored the Connecticut shore."

We never saw her go by. Norm Raben began by playing the Long Island shore but then deliberately pointed higher to keep his apparent wind up. He was able to stem the adverse current and passed *Tide* about five miles west of Horton

Point. He also reported sighting us about three miles east of Stratford Shoal. "I elected to stay high. I didn't believe the southerly would come in. As we passed Stratford I tacked north to get over to the Connecticut shore. Within 15 minutes we were lifted on the port tack to 270 degrees. We sailed on this tack to the finish."

Both *Kate* and *La Forza* beat us by hours.

Sunset often brings calms to Long Island Sound.

27 THE TRANSPACIFIC RACE

As this is being written, the Transpacific Yacht Club is well along with plans for the 29th biennial race from Los Angeles to Honolulu in 1977. This is one of the best organized, and at 2,225 miles, one of the longest of the major races. It regularly draws 50 to 70 boats, ranging in size from 37 feet on up to 83 feet. The maximum number is limited to 75. Part of its popularity is the "aloha" spirit with which competitors, their families and their friends are greeted at the finish. Each competing yacht is assigned a welcome host and hostess. An information center at the finish point provides a chart showing the daily progress of the race and estimated time of arrival of each yacht, loudspeaker announcements are made when a yacht crosses the finish line and the famous Honolulu hospitality is unrestrained.

In 1936 the Transpacific Yacht Club agreed to hold its races in odd-numbered years so as not to conflict with the even-year Bermuda Race. Although the first Transpacific was run in 1906, the Transpacific Yacht Club did not come on the scene until 1928 when it was formed for the sole purpose of organizing and running transpacific races. Prospective members must be amateurs and must have taken part in either the Pacific Coast to Honolulu or the Pacific Coast to Tahiti races. There are no dues and no clubhouse. While both men and women are eligible for membership, it is still a male domain. Members reside both on the Pacific Coast and in the Hawaiian Islands, so that handling the start and finish of the race is not a big problem for the Club.

On occasion, the Club also sponsors a race to Tahiti, which is about 3,600 miles.

I am indebted to Club members Cy Gillette in Honolulu, and to Ben Mitchell in Los Angeles for the pertinent information on this race. Both of them are long-time active committee members and participants.

The elapsed time record was set by Mark Johnson in the 73-foot *Windward Passage* in 1971 with a time of nine days, nine hours, six minutes and 48 seconds, but the race is more often than not won by a small boat on corrected time. Good navigation is a major input because the optimum course and the strongest winds are not necessarily along the great-circle track.

Californians know this one best and Ben Mitchell, who describes this race for us below, is one of the best of the Californians, not only in the Pacific, but in the Atlantic. In 1975 he was the navigator of *Stinger,* winner of the SORC, went on that summer to navigate *Ragtime* to line honors in the Transpac and then came back east again in the fall to help *Pied Piper* win the One-Ton Championship at Newport, Rhode Island.

Ben Mitchell   Cy Gillette *(courtesy Transpacific Yacht Club)*

Ben was a flyer in the Navy, has raced in one-design Dragons and Solings and now specializes in navigating top offshore boats, when not working as a real estate consultant. Here is his story of the classic Transpac.

The Transpac was conceived by the late Clarence MacFarlane of Honolulu and, after much correspondence in 1904 and '05 with interested yachtsmen on the Mainland, he finally put together the first race in 1906. This was scheduled to start from San Francisco but because of the Great Fire and earthquake there, the start was rerouted to Los Angeles, finishing at Diamond Head.

In 1925 the race was the longest in Transpac history, starting from San Francisco and finishing in Tahiti. Commencing in 1941 all races have started at San Pedro (Los Angeles Harbor) on the Fourth of July and have finished at the Diamond Head Buoy in Honolulu, Hawaii. Since 1955 the west end of Catalina has been a mark of the course.

The number of entries is limited to 75 by berthing facilities available at Honolulu, and except for last-minute dropouts, the fleet has nudged the entry limit in recent years.

Since 1951, the year crewman Ted Sirks was lost overboard (he was picked up some 36 hours later by a Navy destroyer), a major emphasis has been on safety. Basically, the race is a downwind passage skirting around the southern semicircle of the Pacific High. But the fleet starts hard on the wind and beats to the west end of Catalina, then enjoys a two-to-three-day close reach before reaching the favorable Pacific trade winds. Here, spinnaker gear becomes of prime importance with special attention given to the problems of minimizing chafing.

Halyard block, shackles and hangers along with spinnaker sheets and guys must endure eight to 12 days of heavy wear and tear. A good secure bos'n's chair for inspection and repair trips up the mast is a must.

Communications are conducted on single side band by the race escort vessel and consist of daily position reports, an encoded weather map (more on that later) and an evening bed check. Daily position reporting is mandatory with a penalty being assessed for failure to report.

Although the variable coastal winds experienced in Southern California during the month of July can cause problems in departure from the coast, race strategy revolves around the capricious Pacific High. That blob on the weather map with a capital H in the middle, has in recent years done strange things—it has broken into two or more highs, rebuilt, had a tropical storm cross its isobaric pattern, sucking all the wind out of the ocean, and has been assaulted by local low-pressure systems as well as other "unusual conditions."

Of paramount importance is the proper analysis of the daily weather information supplied the fleet during the race. From the beginning racers realized that the weather was an important factor in the outcome of this great event. However, it was not until the advent of the 1949 Transpac that anyone did anything about it. Robert M. Allan, Jr., a top skipper in his own right, was signed on *Morning Star* as a crewman and meteorologist. Bob had served during World War II in the Air Force as a meteorologist and had made a thorough study of the weather characteristics in the Pacific. His theory was simple—given the information as to the daily location of the Pacific High and its surrounding isobaric pattern, the optimum course (not necessarily the shortest, but the fastest) could be plotted. The necessary radio equipment was installed which received the morning weather map in Morse Code; and the result was a new record which stood until 1965, when the late Bob Johnson's *Ticonderoga* broke the record in a down-to-the-wire race with Cornelius Bruyn-zeel's *Stormvogel*.

As a result, the Transpacific Yacht Club asked Bob Allan to be chairman of its Weather Committee, and requested that he set up a system by which all participants could receive the same weather information. Accordingly, a daily map is now encoded by the Los Angeles Weather Bureau and broadcast by the Coast Guard or the race escort vessel each morning prior to roll call. This enables each navigator to construct his own map.

It might be expected, in a yacht race of this distance, that a Great Circle course would be the shortest and fastest course. In practice, this course has rarely been sailed successfully. The rhumb line course skirts the eastern Pacific High and the prudent sailor even sails below this line. Unfortunately, the position of this High is influenced by several factors, resulting in considerable movement and change as to form, intensity and location. In several of the races, the High has broken into two or more cells, creating a large area of light winds along the northern edge of the course. In the middle of the 1971 race, a tropical storm invaded the course causing strong breezes for the Class A boats, but leaving nothing for the rest of the fleet.

Also to be considered are the local weather conditions existing in the channel area between Los Angeles, Catalina Island and San Nicholas Island, which affect the initial part of the race, and the local weather conditions existing near the finish in the famous Molokai Channel, with the exhilarating or wild ride (as the case may be) down its great waves.

Weather instruction sessions are held at Los Angeles and San Francisco to instruct race participants. Just prior to the start of the race, the Weather Committee

256

Skipper's instructions for
Honolulu finish *(courtesy
Transpacific Yacht Club)*

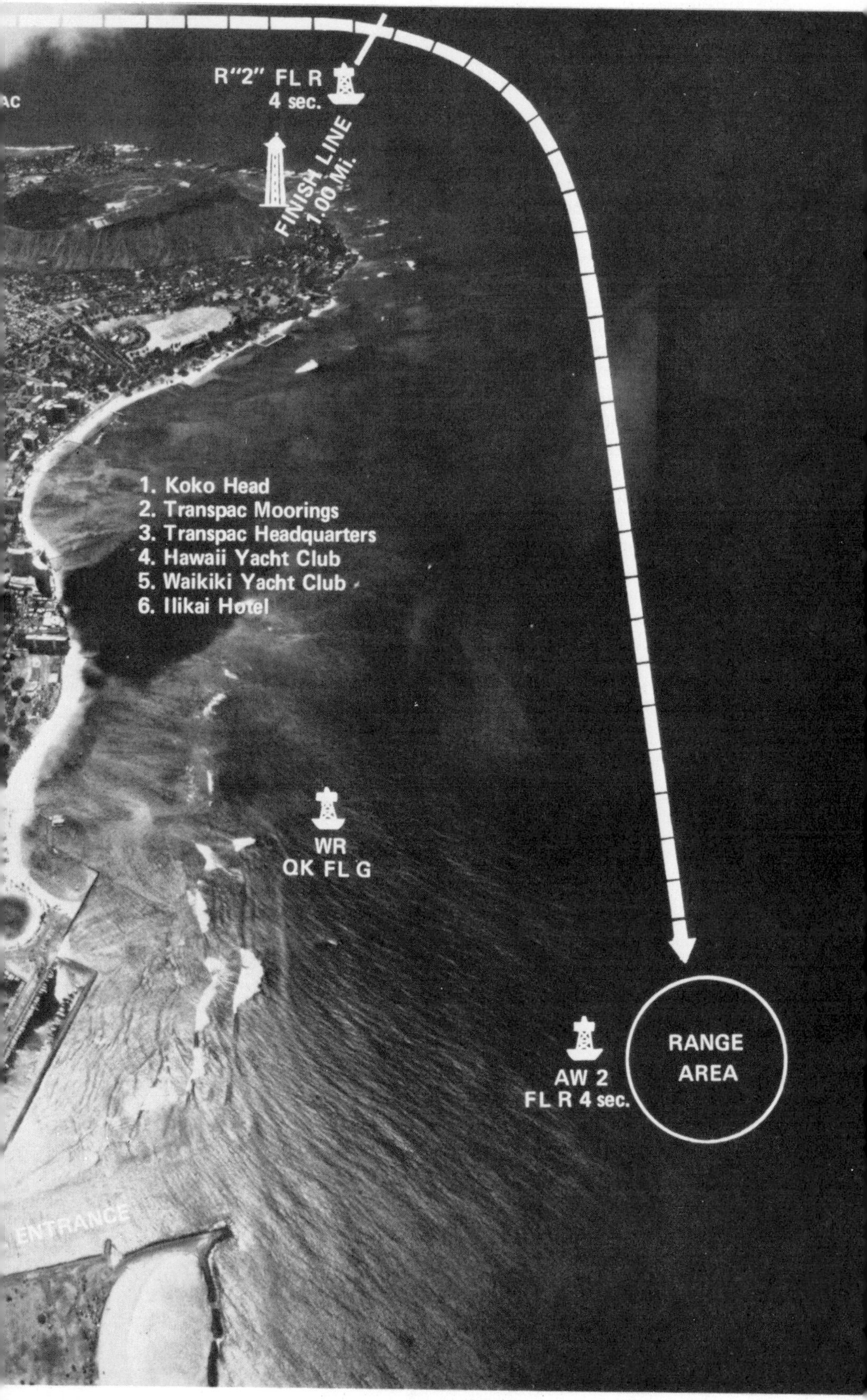

R "2" FL R
4 sec.

FINISH LINE
1.00 Mi.

1. Koko Head
2. Transpac Moorings
3. Transpac Headquarters
4. Hawaii Yacht Club
5. Waikiki Yacht Club
6. Ilikai Hotel

WR
QK FL G

RANGE
AREA

AW 2
FL R 4 sec.

ENTRANCE

and the Los Angeles Weather Bureau conduct a two-day session devoted to the local conditions at the start and finish, and in preparation and interpretation of the daily weather map. This is done to ensure that all participants are able to use the weather information received during the race to the best advantage.

The daily weather reports enable the (forgive the term) "amateur" weathermen aboard each yacht to plot the location of fronts, high and low pressure areas and the isobaric lines of equal pressure surrounding highs and lows.

Except for one year, no electronic navigational aids other than Omni and RDF were allowed. The matter comes up for decision again in 1977 with the larger boats "for" and the smaller boats "against." Good celestial navigation is a must under the present rules.

The Committee is continually grappling with the problem of trying to handicap all entrants equitably. Since normal handicapping assumes beating, reaching and running, the trend to lighter boats in general complicates this task. Cal 40's won the race on corrected time in 1965, '67, '69 and there were dark threats of dissolving the "40's" with acetone until 1971 saw the clean sweep by the maxiboat, *Windward Passage*. *Chutzpah Magic*, a 35-footer weighing about 7500 lbs. won in 1973 and *Ragtime*, a plywood 61-footer, now owned by Bill Pasquini and Bill White, was first-to-finish in 1975.

Ultralight displacement boats provide a fast and exciting passage with less damage to gear than the average. In 1975 *Ragtime* recorded a point-to-point passage across Molokai Channel at over 15 knots, and for the last 10 minutes of the race her speed was never under 17 knots!

Notwithstanding the length of the passage, the miles and miles of downwind sailing, sometimes exciting, sometimes monotonous, the squalls, the endless chafing, the blown-out chutes, the reception at Honolulu at the "end of the line" makes it all worthwhile.

When Cy Gillette was Race Chairman in 1975 he wrote:

The Honolulu Transpac is a race that is unique in many ways. It is the oldest of the world's regularly scheduled long-distance races. It is the only ocean race which, at its conclusion, finds the entire competitive fleet moored side by side, a sight to behold, in which Hawaiians, tourists, competitors and spectators alike take special relish. Transpac was the first major yachting event to provide a host and hostess for every entry, a tradition introduced into a number of other races in recent years.

You'd have trouble convincing the thousands of people who've been involved in this prestigious event over these last 69 years that the 2225-mile run to Hawaii is monotonous. Far from it. From the initial few challenging days off the California coast, through the daily attempts to outmaneuver the infamous Pacific High, out-naviguess the rest of the fleet and, through daily position reports, outfox the other tacticians, to the final and often hellacious sleigh ride down the Molokai Channel to the Diamond Head finish, and on into the Ala Wai, where a delirious lei and Mai Tai–laden throng awaits at dockside—if this be monotony, then they'd best be rewriting the meaning of the word.

All Hawaii loves Transpac. Bumper-to-bumper crowds line Diamond Head Road to overflowing, watching the historic finish; boats of every size and description hover off Diamond Head buoy; and thousands of people wander up and down Transpac

Mole for days after the race, admiring the cream of the world's yacht racing machines, reflecting the thrill and recapturing the romance of seafaring days long past.

And Hawaii's sealoving community turns out en masse to put it all together. For the five or six hundred actual racing participants, it takes about half that number on the Honolulu Committee alone to provide the type of greeting, hospitality and related activities that have made Transpac what it is.

Timeworn though many say the word has become, there's still only one which best expresses our welcome to Transpac—and we extend it to you all with heartiest good wishes: ALOHA!

28—THE TRANSATLANTIC RACE

The Transatlantic Race is one of the tougher ocean racing classics. The first race of record was in 1866. Three large schooner rigged yachts competed. The winner was *Henrietta,* owned by James Gordon Bennett, Jr. She sailed the course from Sandy Hook, New Jersey, to England in 13 days, 21 hours and 45 minutes.

The race has been sailed at irregular intervals, but when held in the even-numbered years it follows the finish of the Bermuda Race and serves to make the passage back to Europe more interesting for those boats which have come from there to participate in the Bermuda Race. In the odd-numbered years, it serves as a feeder for the boats coming from the United States to participate in the Admiral's Cup and the Fastnet, and in those years usually starts from Newport.

The finish point varies and has been anywhere between Sweden and Spain, depending upon the year and the situation. Thus it differs from the other classics in that it seldom has the same course. But whatever the starting or finishing point, it is a long race—two to three weeks—and as such can bring a wide variety of weather and sea conditions to the contest.

The 1975 race from Newport, Rhode Island, to the Nab Tower in the eastern entrance to the Solent off the Isle of Wight, England, was a duel with Hurricane Amy, making it a memorable passage for those who participated. Lee Van Gemert skippered Ted Hood's *Robin* to victory in that race. Lee normally sails as crew member, but in this case he was ferrying his boss's boat to England as part of the U.S. team for the 1975 Admiral's Cup series and turned it into the most memorable victory of his career.

He was born and brought up on the south shore area of Boston (Quincy, Mass.) and sailed the local one-design classes in his youth. Later, after graduating from the Massachusetts Maritime Academy School Ship, he served as a tanker officer in the Atlantic in World War II. For the past dozen years he has been a Sail Consultant with Hood Sailmakers as well as an active ocean racer.

The 79-foot *Kialoa III* was first to finish after 14 days, eight hours, 47 minutes and 12 seconds while *Robin,* a 40-footer, still had about 700 miles to go. The finish was a cliff-hanger with *Robin* saving her time by only one hour, five minutes and 17 seconds. Here are some of Lee's first-hand impressions of that race:

> Our rhumb line to England bent around the edge of Cape Cod and clipped Point Alpha, a spot safely south of the iceberg line, designated as an official mark of the course. The typical transatlantic is a reaching/running dash across the modified great circle. 1975 was not typical.
>
> Three days out, we had run down the numbers of our windward sail inventory,

and were now slamming off square-cut waves under a double-reefed main and a solid little high-aspect number four genoa. Worse, we were bent well south of the course, being pushed by a northeasterly gale into the path of a hurricane.

Navigator George Kiskaddon braced himself beside the radio. It was 2:00 A.M. and he had slipped below, wet clothes plastered on him like barnacles, to pick up the regular weather broadcast. On deck, Walter Greene and young Teddy Hood struggled to keep *Robin* sailing on her bottom and around the worst of bad bunches of seas.

The watch below—Phil Steggal, Rickie Hood and I—were only slightly less wet than the watch on deck. The 50-knot northeasterly had rolled the Gulf Stream into large, quick, dirty waves. Everyone on board was seasick. No one slept. A little rest was the best we could expect.

George clicked off the receiver, checked his plot and said it aloud. "Skipper, we're on a collision course with Hurricane Amy." With the understanding of a man himself used to being the skipper, he added, "It's your decision."

If we tacked, assuming that nothing went wrong in the tack (which is not to be lightly assumed in these conditions), we would be heading NNW, or back to Labrador. If we didn't, we had Amy to contend with: 75-knot winds in a violent Gulf Stream. I didn't much like either choice.

There was really no decision to make. We absolutely had to stay on the northeast quadrant of Amy. In the last hour, we had been headed 10 more degrees. I called for the tack, and hoped that Amy wouldn't follow. Again, we shortened sail, first to a storm jib and fully reefed main; later to just a storm trysail. *Robin* plunged into the night at better than five knots.

If the hurricane's course ran true to prediction (and we urgently hoped it would), the trick was to tack east again just in time to hook onto the back end of the depression and get towed across the Atlantic with it. Too short a northwesterly board and we'd meet Amy. Too long and we'd lose her. And one thing was for sure: you don't short-tack a hurricane under storm trysail.

George monitored the barometer. As we approached the hurricane area, the barometer had gently slid 1 1/2 inches. Now, as we headed away from it, it rose a little—just enough to tell us Amy wasn't following.

The crew was tired, but not exhausted. Morale was good, and we were all definitely still racing.

By eight in the morning we were able to bend on a jib. Each hour, we were headed a little more, and a final 10-degree knock told us we were solidly into the old weather system. Time to tack again, grab Amy's tail and go to England. And, as the storm mellowed, that's just about the way it happened. For the next 10 days the weather pattern behaved as though it had been studying the pilot chart—northwesterlies, westerlies and southwesterlies, mostly 10 knots or better, occasionally light and flukey. Every sail on the boat, drifter to storm spinnaker, had its day. And we had plenty of time to think about and work on the virtues that win ocean races.

Distance races are won by a set of conditions that are easy to understand, hard to practice. A good boat and good sails count for sure. But boats and sails are only as good as the crew that handle them; ours was damned good.

George Kiskaddon felt his way across the Atlantic with a sextant, a barometer, and a weather eye conditioned by years of skippering a series of good boats, the latest being 68-foot *New World* now under charter for oceanographic exploration. The wake of the depression left a mostly overcast sky, so George's sights and DR plot were carefully constructed and, ultimately, right on the nose.

Walter Greene had been part of the crew that built *Robin,* and knew her like a wife. He is a very strong sailor physically and emotionally and as fine a shipmate as I've sailed with.

Phil Steggal had sailed with Hood in the SORC and other series, and was as fastidious as his guru in the details of sail handling. The rigging was always organized, and the boat was ready for any maneuver, anytime. Every halyard was moved a little, eased or tightened, every 20 minutes all the way across the Atlantic.

The Hood boys are short on years, long on sea miles. And neither of them is what you'd call small. Rickie, who graduated to the age of eighteen during the race, is a particularly capable helmsman. Teddy, sixteen, in addition to his full deck watch, organized the food and made most of the meals including an artfully stage-managed party for his brother's birthday.

At fifty-six, I was literally the old man of the boat. My first transatlantic under sail was in 1939, as a merchant marine cadet aboard the three-masted bark *Nantucket.* It amused me that 40-foot *Robin* made about as good time in the passage as our tanker convoys had during the war.

Never once was there a harsh word among the crew. (Perhaps our daily tot of rum can take some credit for our good spirits.) And never once was a sail change left for the next watch. Good morale made an eager crew, racing by second nature to win.

Winning any race is a thrill. To bring *Robin* to the Admiral's Cup course already a transatlantic winner was among the finest moments of my life.*

---

*Quoted material reprinted with permission of *Sail Magazine.*

29 THE SOUTHERN OCEAN RACING CONFERENCE

The Southern Ocean Racing Conference is a six-race series held in February and March of each year. The scene is the sun-kissed Florida and Bahamas area. This event is an ideally situated winter offshore racing laboratory, a gigantic warm-weather test tank for trying out new ideas in designs, sails, equipment and methods. It doesn't take long to find out that some of these work and some don't. Those in the boat business consider it important for boats to do well here so that spring and summer sales can be influenced. Successful designers, sailmakers, builders and equipment manufacturers of top-finishing boats thus have a little more to offer their customers. Crews are the best in the business and include champions from the entire spectrum of the sport.

The SORC is very well organized and managed, considering what is involved. Each year improvements in the races have been made and contestants' suggestions have been well received. Scoring by computer (with print-outs available for each boat after each race showing that race and Series' results to date) is remarkably efficient.

Six yacht clubs are now involved in conducting the Series and the representatives from each form a loose coalition putting the whole thing together. Each club likes to preserve its territorial rights and relative importance in the overall scheme of things. Some of the races have long and illustrious histories and there is a table full of perpetual trophies assigned to a particular class or contest. The oldest race, the Lipton Cup, dates back to 1928 and has been changed in form many times. The next oldest, the Miami–Nassau, goes back to 1934 and was unchanged until 1977. The Circuit itself was born in 1940 when the Lipton Cup, the Miami–Nassau, St. Petersburg to Havana and Havana to Key West Races were put together to make a Series. The Havana races died in 1959 after the Castro revolution.

Change has always been a part of the SORC. The St. Petersburg–Ft. Lauderdale Race is relatively new, replacing a short-lived Miami to St. Petersburg Race. The Miami–Lucaya and St. Petersburg–Venice races were dropped in 1974 and replaced by the Ocean Triangle and Anclote Key Race. The Triangle Race as now constituted (Miami, Great Isaac, Palm Beach, Miami) stands out as the most sensible and most interesting race in the Series. Its course is long enough to make a boat race, the triangular shape minimizes the effects of wind changes, and sparring with the Gulf Stream on all three legs makes good navigation a premium factor. These all combine to equalize the fleet.

The Anclote Key Race was dropped in 1977. In its place, a revised version of the old Venice Race became the Boca Grande Race, 138 miles from Tampa Bay south to Boca Grande Buoy and return.

Another SORC improvement in 1977 was starting the west coast Florida races at Pinellas Point Light instead of St. Petersburg Pier, thus eliminating a tricky and inequitable five-mile leg in shoal-plagued, current-swept waters, always an aggravation for deep-draft yachts. The option of adding a Fort Lauderdale leg to the Miami–Nassau Race was also provided, to add to this SORC classic the potential for more windward work.

The statistics on SORC participation are indicative of offshore racing in general as shown in the chart. The peak was reached in 1973. A precipitous drop occurred thereafter. This was partly due to the feeling on the part of owners that their yachts were no longer competitive and partly due to the higher cost of participation, whether or not the yacht was competitive.

SORC PARTICIPATION BY RACE AND YEAR
1970–1976

RACE	1970	1971	1972	1973	1974	1975	1976
Venice (1) (2)	65	82	93	117	—	—	—
Anclote Key (3)	—	—	—	—	98	82	78
St. Pete–Lauderdale	87	90	89	112	94	79	76
Lucaya (1) (2)	91	82	95	112	—	—	—
Ocean Triangle (3)	—	—	—	—	101	86	75
Lipton Cup	118	90	113	135	117	95	79
Miami–Nassau	92	98	110	124	111	89	82
Nassau Cup	81	78	98	106	100	90	67
Total Starters	534	520	598	706	621	521	457

Notes
(1) Discontinued after 1973
(2) Optional until 1973
(3) Added in 1974

Equation crosses a northbound freighter in the Gulf Stream—Miami—Nassau Race, 1974.

Another interesting phenomenon in this bellwether series is the predominance of the smaller "Ton" boats in recent years.

The emergence of One-Ton boats began in 1972 and the Two-Ton influence appeared with *Robin* in 1975 and continued with a sweep of the Two-Tonners in 1976 with *Williwaw, Golden Dazy* and *Richochet,* all Two-Tonners, first, second and third in the "new boat division." This is partly explained by the appearance of new designs each year in these classes as well as this group's ability to attract the top sailors as crew members, all making for intense competition and high-level racing.

When Ted Turner won the Series in 1970 for the second time in four years, he was sailing the 67-foot sloop *American Eagle,* a converted America's Cup 12-meter. His performance was remarkable in that he won on corrected time four of the five races in which he participated. In those days one could drop either the Venice Race or the Lucaya Race. Ted, having won the Venice Race, chose to sit out the Lucaya by flying to Australia to skipper his 5.5-meter sloop *Nemesis* to a first in the Gold Cup and second in the World Championships. Coming back to the SORC scene to take the Lipton Cup and the Miami–Nassau Races, he needed a win in the Nassau Cup over the closest boat on points, the 73-foot *Windward Passage. Eagle* beat *Passage* boat-for-boat, taking this race and Series.

The following year the Committee began using the new International Off Shore Rule and boats such as *Eagle* and *Passage* were out of business. In 1971 Jacob Isbrandtsen's new 60-foot *Running Tide,* first boat launched that fit the IOR, took the Series in a seemingly effortless manner. It is now evident that this marked the end of the era of big boat dominance and the beginning of the concept that it takes a new small boat every year to stay in competition. In 1972, the 41-foot *Condor,* a four-year-old C & C Redline, began the small boat parade as overall winner and Turner, then sailing *Running Tide,* could only manage fourth behind *Aura,* Class B and *Elixir,* Class E.

In recent Series we have seen development in quantum jumps. Boats, sails and equipment became better and better. New crews, many recruited from top one-design ranks, skippers in their own right, brought new spirit and aggressiveness round-the-clock to what was formerly a now-and-then effort. This development was most evident in the smaller classes and most dramatic in the One-Ton class.

Dennis Connor, skipper of *Stinger,* a new One-Ton boat designed expressly to win the SORC, modestly credited his Series' victory in 1975 mainly to being ready. "Preparation is 60 percent of the reason. My boat was launched in mid-November. By the time the SORC started we had participated in 35 races. The boat was well shaken down and we could concentrate on sailing her fast," he remarked in Nassau at the end of the racing.

The diagrams that follow show the courses used in the six-race SORC Series as of 1977. The conditions run the gamut from light airs to gear-busting frontal winds with the moderate, balmy southeast trade winds in between.

SORC — TOP FIVE BOATS OVERALL 1970–1975

	PLACE	BOAT	CLASS	SPECIAL DESIGNATION
1970	1	*American Eagle*	A	
	2	*Windward Passage*	A	
	3	*Kialoa II*	A	
	4	*Ondine*	A	
	5	*Baccara*	A	
1971	1	*Running Tide*	A	
	2	*Yankee Girl*	A	
	3	*Dora*	A	
	4	*American Eagle*	A	
	5	*Nepenthe*	A	
1972	1	*Condor*	D	
	2	*Aura*	B	
	3	*Elixir*	E	One-Ton
	4	*Running Tide*	A	
	5	*Bay Bea*	B	
1973	1	*Munequita*	D	One-Ton
	2	*Lightnin'*	E	One-Ton
	3	*Robin*	E	One-Ton
	4	*No-Go V*	E	
	5	*Cascade*	E	
1974	1	*Robin Too, II*	E	One-Ton
	2	*Lightnin'*	E	One-Ton
	3	*America Jane II*	E	One-Ton
	4	*Country Woman*	E	One-Ton
	5	*Rabbit*	E	One-Ton
1975	1	*Stinger*	T	One-Ton
	2	*Inflation*	T	One-Ton
	3	*Bootlegger*	T	One-Ton
	4	*Fortune Hunter*	E	One-Ton
	5	*Robin*	C	Two-Ton

NOTE: Since the fleet was split into two divisions in 1976, there has since been no overall winner.

St. Petersburg – Boca Grande   138 Official Miles

Starting at Pinellas Point in Tampa Bay, this course leads out under the Sunshine Skyway Bridge, around the Sea Buoy and down the coast to Boca Grande entrance Buoy #2. Then it's northerly along the Venice "Gold Coast" to the finish just inside Egmont Key. Basic piloting skills are called upon, using the plentiful navigational aids and the depth finder.

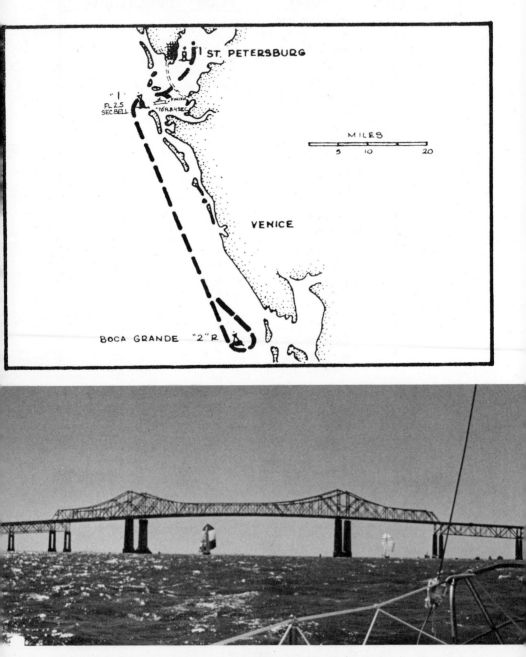

Baccara and *Equation* lead the fleet out under the Sunshine Skyway Bridge.

St. Petersburg – Ft. Lauderdale Yacht Race   366 Official Miles

A repeat trip out to the Gulf, then it's a 180-mile offshore rhumb line south to tiny Rebecca Shoal Light at the western end of the Florida Keys. Loran coverage is good on this leg and the 20-fathom line is useful as it roughly parallels the track.

After rounding the Keys into the Straits of Florida, the trick is to find and ride the maximum current in the northerly flowing Gulf Stream all the way to the finish. Excellent Loran coverage, high visibility shore lights and several well-placed Omni stations make navigation pleasurable.

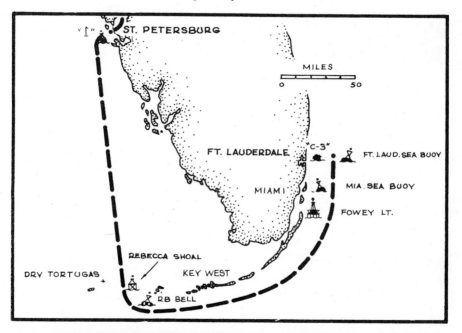

St. Pete–Lauderdale finish is marked by high-rise condominiums along the beach.

Ocean Triangle Race

Clockwise—198 Official Miles
Counterclockwise—176 Official Miles

Whether the course is regular (counterclockwise) or reverse, this race is a triple bout with the swift Gulf Stream as its main axis is running three to five knots and lies a few miles off the Florida coast. Westerly flowing currents north of Great Isaac Light emptying from New Providence Channel further complicate the task. But if all your gear is working, DF, Omni, Loran and Depth Sounder can provide all the navigational info.

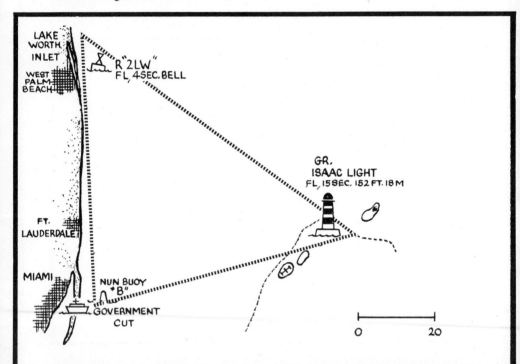

One leg of the Ocean Triangle Race runs along the Florida "Gold Coast."

Lipton Cup Race

Clockwise—110 Official Miles
Counterclockwise—130 Official Miles

A race similar to the Ocean Triangle but its different shape and location provide new challenges for the fleet, especially when finding the turning mark at Gun Cay.

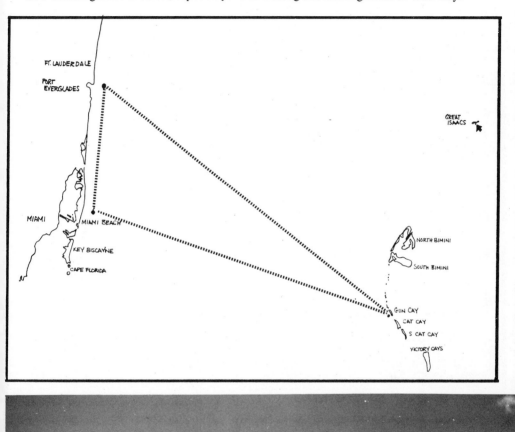

The fleet heads across the Gulf Stream twice in the Lipton Cup Race.

Miami – Nassau Race   Course A—Direct to Great Isaac Light: 176 Official Mile
Course Z—Great Isaac via Fort Lauderdale: 193 Official Mile

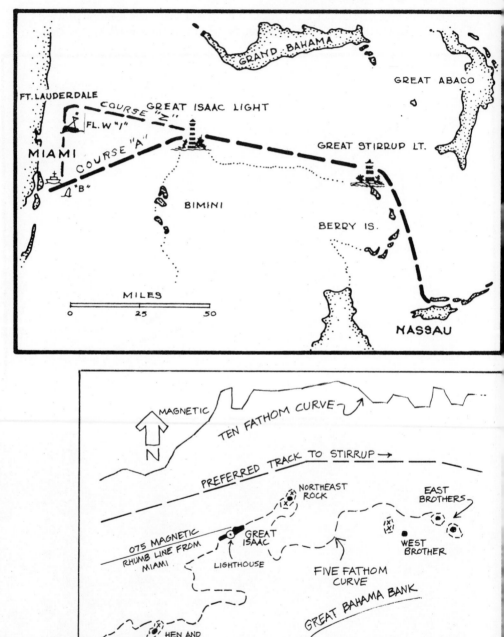

The wind direction at starting time determines whether Course A or Z will be used. In either case the fleet, through experience gained in the last two races, should now be familiar with either Gulf Stream crossing. Watch the low-lying rocks to the northeast of Great Isaac which claimed *Wimoweh* in 1974. (See chart for preferred track.) A night finish at Nassau is aided by long-range lights and New Providence Omni. The many cruise liners shuttling between Miami or Port Everglades and Nassau can be a guide in this race if you get lost.

Great Isaac Light

Gusto approaching the finish line, 1975—Miami—Nassau Race.

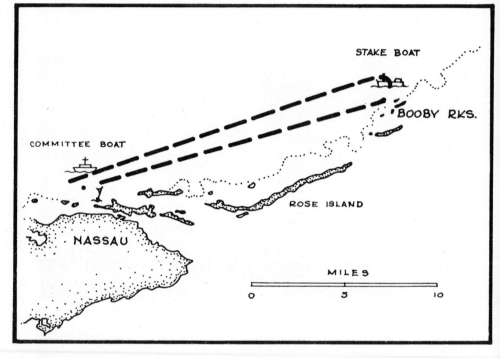

Nassau Cup Race

Regular—31 Official Miles
Short—21 Official Miles

Though this is the shortest and lowest weighted (for scoring) of the six-race series, it has sometimes decided the winner in a tight contest. Top competitors can't relax until it is over. Good visibility in the clear Nassau air and the many objects on which visual bearings may be taken make position-fixing rather easy. But it helps to sign on a Bahamian for this one, to provide the local knowledge of wind shifts and current data not found in the tables.

Class A yachts at rest in the Bahamas before the Nassau Cup Race.

Pride approaching the finish in the 1976 Bermuda Race *(Bermuda News Bureau Photo)*

30 THE BERMUDA RACE

If offshore racing is one of the ultimate games, then the Newport–Bermuda Race is the ultimate offshore race. This is not to downgrade the challenge inherent in other offshore contests, but the challenging course, the conditions applying to boats, equipment and crew as laid down by the sponsors and the quality and number of yachts involved, as well as the attractions of the destination combine to put this race in a class by itself.

It places great importance on navigation. Special limitations apply to electronic navigational equipment—only direction finders, depth sounders and Omni are allowed throughout. Loran, radar and Omega are barred except near the start and finish. This means that a navigator has to work hard with traditional equipment (sextant and timepiece) and weather radios to know what he is doing. It is a full-time job to do it right. The 635-mile course leads directly from Brenton Reef Tower off Newport, Rhode Island, to St. David's Head on the east side of the Onion Patch, as the Bermuda Islands are sometimes called.

These are a mere pinpoint on the chart, a collection of 300 islands, islets and rocks surrounded by coral reefs shaped like a fishhook, oriented northeast and southwest with an overall length of 22 miles. In the final 10 miles to the finish line at Bermuda's eastern extremity, Northeast Breaker Buoy, Kitchen Shoals Buoy and Mills Breaker Buoy must be left to starboard in turn as course marks when approaching from the north. There is also the option sometimes used of passing to the west and south of the islands en route to the finish, in which case these buoys will not be encountered.

In good weather aids to navigation in the islands can be seen some distance off. North Rock, a 60-foot tower guarding the northern coral bank, is readily distinguishable, as is the 354-foot Gibbs Hill Light in Southampton, the major navigational aid. The final approach is often where the race is won or lost. Even a two to three miles position error before landfall can be disastrous. To be sharp near the finish the trick is for the crew to get proper rest early in the race, and prepare as much as possible ahead of time.

But even before that, the Gulf Stream looms as a formidable obstacle. Finding the best spot to cross the Stream which snakes erratically across the Bermuda track in a more or less easterly direction can make or break you and your competitors. Satellite photos and Woods Hole Oceanographic Institute observations of the Gulf Stream are part of the modern scene, but as these have a built-in time lag, the only real way to know is by having frequent accurate positions when you are actually in the Stream to keep track of your speed and direction over-the-bottom vs. through the water. When approaching the Stream's edge, and while

Yachts moored at the Treadway Inn, Race Committee Headquarters in Newport

Brenton Reef Tower marks the starting

Clouds sometimes form along the north edge of
the Gulf Stream.

Northeast Breaker Buoy and Kitchen Shoals
Buoy are marks of the course near the finish.

Kitchen Shoals Buoy

The finish line extends seaward from St. David's Head.

in the flow, sea temperatures should be taken each half hour and recorded. This will give you a good indication of when you are in it and when you pass through. The temperature difference between continental slope water is about eight to 10 degrees F. The Stream itself averages from 78 to 81 degrees. Once through the Stream axis, temperatures of two to four degrees less than maximum can be expected.

Having successfully outmaneuvered the Gulf Stream and nearing Bermuda you may expect to pick up Gibbs Hill radio beacon on your direction finder at about 120 miles, and as you come in closer, Kindley International aircraft beacon should come into range at about 50 miles and its Omni at about 35 miles. Don't neglect your celestial work at this point. A quick line-of-position can augment the DF bearings.

Gibbs Hill has a visual range of 26 miles and North Rock 13 miles. Your approach will determine which one you will see first. A daytime landfall is helped by the clouds which often form above the islands.

The 1974 race was a good illustration of what is involved. *Ondine,* first boat to finish after a Friday A.M. start, arrived at 1123 Bermuda time on the following Monday morning and *Jubilee,* the last boat to finish, arrived Thursday evening. The wide disparity in the courses sailed accounts for some of the differences in the resulting elapsed times for the passage. But, barring casualties or unexpected flat spots, the scattering is still hard to understand when it is considered that all the contestants were supplied by the committee with the same weather and Gulf Stream facts on which to base their strategy. Some well-sailed small boats finished on Tuesday while larger craft, poorly sailed, came in 24 to 48 hours later.

The race started in a gray clammy fog at Newport and finished with a fine southwest breeze, brilliant sun and bright skies which turned the clear Bermuda waters to sparkling blue. In or near the Gulf Stream the yachts encountered sharp, confused 15-to-20-foot seas, thunder and lightning, up to 40-mile-an-hour winds and spotty areas of flat calm. Astride the rhumb line in the shape of a U was a gigantic 120-mile-long Gulf Stream meander, one of the most unusual configurations in recent memory of Bermuda Race veterans.

The new, radically designed, 79-foot ketch *Ondine* completed the passage first and in record time. The lean, more conventional 55-foot sloop *Scaramouche* was the overall corrected-time winner. *Ondine* was both skippered and navigated by owner Sumner "Huey" Long. *Scaramouche* was skippered by owner Charles "Chuck" Kirsch and navigated by Peter Bowker.

After the race I obtained the track lines of these yachts and have plotted them on the accompanying diagram along with the rhumb line to Bermuda and the predicted path of the Gulf Stream meander, as furnished by Marvel C. Stalcup of the Woods Hole Oceanographic Institute at the skippers' meeting. A glance at this diagram will show graphically why these two boats were equally successful. In fact, for a distance of nearly 50 miles in mid-route, the two tracks are identical, and for most of the rest of the race coincided very closely, both taking full advantage of the favorable current.

Key elements of this particular race were to get the maximum push from the

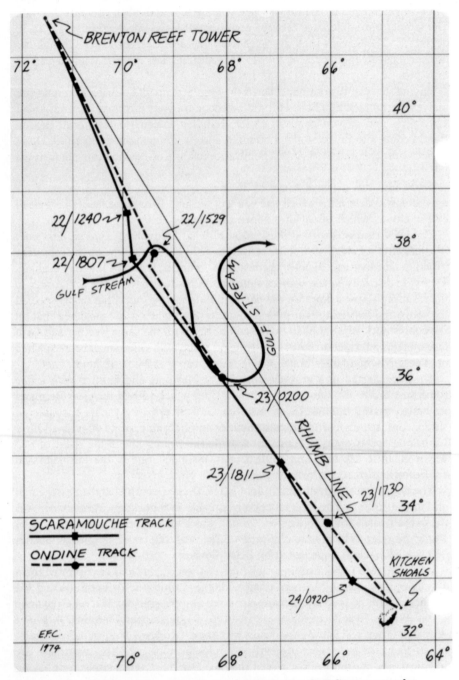

Astride the rhumb line was a 120-mile, southerly flowing Gulf Stream meander.

Vinnie Monte-Sano *(right)*, 1976 Bermuda Race Chairman

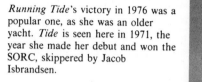

Running Tide's victory in 1976 was a popular one, as she was an older yacht. *Tide* is seen here in 1971, the year she made her debut and won the SORC, skippered by Jacob Isbrandsen.

Navigator Dick Stimson *(right)* with *Running Tide*'s co-skipper, Bo Van Metre

favorable west side of the meander and, because of the southwest wind near Bermuda, to remain well west of the rhumb line until the final approach so as to eliminate any on-the-wind sailing. Once the best point of intersection of the meander had been decided, it was not difficult to achieve that position as a southwest wind at the start veered to the west allowing the boats to sail a direct starboard tack course to the desired entry point and to maintain the proper heading in the Stream. It should also be evident from the diagram that those boats taking the rhumb line track derived no benefit from the Stream and with any easting were in danger of being captured by the unfavorable east side of the meander. One boat that sailed the rhumb line was becalmed shortly after entering the Stream, was set 40 miles to the northeast and then, when the wind finally did come up, sailed another 60 miles back through the unfavorable flow, accounting for her late finish on Thursday. Two years previously, the overall winner, *Noryema,* went over 70 miles to the east of the rhumb line. (A southeast wind prevailed at Bermuda.) In 1974 *Scaramouche* went over 45 miles to the west. Again in 1976 it paid to go east as noted below. This points up the fallacy of sailing this race on past practice and should be a lesson to rhumb line traditionalists who ignore the facts available for each race. It also emphasizes that in this world's best fleet of offshore boats, only heads-up, intelligent sailing can make a winner.

The 1976 race was completely different.

At 0930 on Friday, with 29 yachts still at sea after a week of agonizingly chasing after cat's-paws (eight had previously withdrawn), Vinnie Monte-Sano, Bermuda Race Chairman, assisted by members of the Start and Finish Committees, made an unprecedented but wise decision: All boats more than 20 miles from the finish off St. David's Head were instructed to abandon the race and motor to the Onion Patch. The finish line was closed at 1300 that day. Thus, a new record of sorts was established for the 70-year-old ocean racing classic, with 20 DNFs. By Sunday evening the last few had been accounted for.

The larger and faster yachts racing to Bermuda were able to make the finish line while there was still a fair amount of wind. The smaller yachts that were successful in finishing early had to obtain maximum effect from the Gulf Stream and skirt the edge of a stagnant and expanding high-pressure circle centered east of the rhumb line about midway to Bermuda, requiring good navigation, topnotch strategy and getting an extra tenth-of-a-knot boat speed whenever possible. As time went on, the light air dwindled into nothing, dashing the hopes of the majority still on the course.

First across the line was Eric Ridder's two-year-old *Tempest,* logging in at 0731 Bermuda time on Tuesday. In the 1974 race, this 79-foot ketch was second to finish, an hour and a half behind Huey Long's 83-foot ketch *Ondine.*

In 1976 no speed records were eclipsed and *Ondine* was 39th over the line, ignominiously behind, boat-for-boat, several yachts half her size.

Such is the capricious nature of offshore racing.

Once again the winning race strategy departed from past practice. This time it was east again, with Al Van Metre's *Running Tide,* the overall corrected time winner, sailing a long 98 miles east at latitude 36 degrees north. Navigator Dick Stimson's biggest worry was, "We were afraid of overstanding to the east and getting trapped in the high."

After the race I went over *Running Tide*'s track with Dick. Then I compared it with the track of Dick Jayson's *Pride,* winner of Class D, an updated Swan 44 in which I was navigator. The two tracks are remarkably similar, but in comparing the indicated positions, it was evident that *Tide,* a larger and closer-winded yacht, was gradually opening distance upwind through the light chop. Putting the tracks together and adding the path of the Gulf Stream meander (see chart) gives a graphic picture of which was the best way to go.

Winners of Classes B and C went along similar tracks. Winners of Classes E and F, sailing under different conditions, less wind and more current exposure, went farther east, some as much as 125 miles. Ted Hood, in the One-Ton sloop *Abino Robin,* top Class F yacht, drifted 24 miles in 24 hours, wound up over 100 miles northeast of the finish and had to tack downwind interminably with 140 degrees between tacks in a light northeasterly.

Pride's odometer recorded 706 miles for the 635-mile course, reflecting the longer distance sailed in spite of a 26-mile push from the Gulf Stream.

A few last-half-of-the-race excerpts from *Pride*'s deck log, faithfully kept by Watch Captains Bill Jayson and Dave Lindsay, tell the story:

2050/20	Variable winds and headings.
2230/20	Helmsman Dan Sullivan hit by flying fish!
2302/20 to 2203/21	Eleven tacks.
1030/21	*Syren* and *Christopher Dragon* in sight.
0205/22	Wind dying.
0615/22	Getting lifted, heading 195 degrees.
0835/22	Wind picking up some, heading 185 degrees.
1430/22	Plodding along under reacher and reaching staysail. Heading 180 degrees.
1957/22	Set starcut. It worked! Heading 165 degrees.
0100/23	Final approach. Heading 158 degrees.
0530/23	NE Breaker Buoy in sight. *Pinta* and *Carina* to leeward. Heading 145 degrees.

There was some doubt as to where to look for the Gulf Stream meander this time. The Woods Hole diagram dated June 14th, furnished at the Newport Skipper's Meeting, differed from the NOAA satellite photo also handed out at that meeting.

In Bermuda I obtained a copy of later satellite data which had been furnished to the Tall Ships before their start at Bermuda. (They were racing in the opposite direction to Newport.) This was dated 2319 GMT on June 17th. Finally, the NOAA satellite data of June 22nd arrived in the mail at home.

Comparing all these with the conditions we and other yachts actually encountered on June 19th and 20th, it seemed to me that the main body of the Stream had drifted northeast about 20–25 miles from where Woods Hole observers had seen it on the 14th. In addition, the satellite data were useful in revealing an incredibly wide band of current extending about 300 miles southeast from latitude 39 degrees north, 68 degrees west. This meant a favorable southeasterly set usable for a very long period of time, provided you were at least 50 to 60 miles east of the rhumb line when entering. Those who didn't go far enough east or tacked to the west went into the tank.

The Honorable E. Graham Gibbons, Mayor of Hamilton, Bermuda, speaking at the traditionally British prize-giving on the palatial grounds of Government House, borrowed a Biblical quote, when he opined that, "The wise men came from the East."

Normally, such a wide easterly divergence from the rhumb line course would have been a tremendous gamble, as the prevailing winds at Bermuda are southwest. But the easterly wind direction both predicted and experienced at Bermuda made it good strategy this year.

Those yachts equipped with the proper radio receiver capability could confirm weather reports from three separate regularly scheduled sources: The Coast Guard NW Atlantic Forecast from Station NMH in Washington, the NY to Bermuda weather from NY Aviation Radio and the local weather from Bermuda Harbor Radio. An extra bonus was the Tall Ships fleet area special weather from the S.S. *Bay State,* the Tall Ships' fleet escort. The Coast Guard broadcasts also gave helpful Gulf Stream information at regular intervals.

All of these proclaimed with monotonous regularity from race start that the winds at Bermuda were in fact and would continue to be east to southeast. The fleet started on starboard tack in a light southwest breeze which later backed to the southeast. The wind then shifted to southwest and back to east-southeast the closer one got to the islands.

We wound up setting a starcut about 75 miles out on the rhumb line course of 165 degrees and held it for several hours. Then we were able to harden up to as high as 140 degrees under jib to stem the strong westerly flowing current of two to three knots near Northeast Rock Buoy, generated by the persistent easterly winds.

In a nutshell, the trick was this: Going well east to catch the favorable meander, keeping boat speed through the Gulf Stream chop, then once through the main Gulf Stream current playing the headers while keeping the boat moving to get south fast and closer to the Bermuda wind, then lifting progressively on the port tack for the last 130–150 miles while skirting around the high; and finally, keeping a wary eye out for the local westerly set near the coral reefs surrounding the islands.

One reason for the continuing popularity of the Bermuda Race is the succession of elegant parties after the finish. These stretch for five days, ending in the very British windup at which multitudes of prizes are awarded. The warmth of sun-kissed beaches and Bermuda hospitality also provide a pleasant decompression from the trials and tribulations of the racecourse.

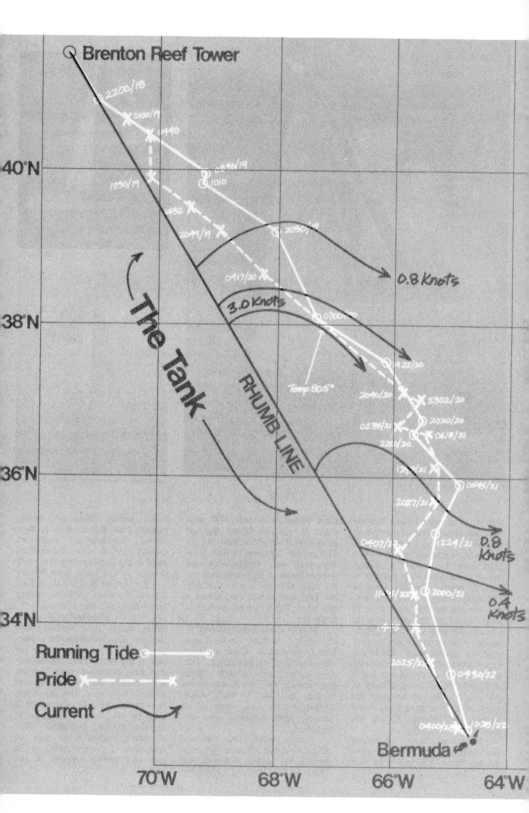

It paid to go east in 1976.

Al Van Metre claims the Bermuda Trophy in 1976.

Yachts decorated with signal flags at the Bermuda Dinghy Club in Hamilton Harbor

31 THE MACKINACS

When Norm Raben, the ubiquitous skipper of *La Forza del Destino,* a 51-foot sloop, invited me to be his navigator for the 259-nautical-mile Port Huron to Mackinac Island Race in Lake Huron, and the 293-nautical-mile Chicago to Mackinac Island Race in Lake Michigan on successive weekends in late July, my first reaction was lukewarm: A long way to go for summertime Long-Island-Sound-type racing. After I pointed out to Norm that I had never done these middle-American classics, he said, "Neither have I, we'll learn together." And learn we did!

While *La Forza* was being ferried from Long Island Sound to Lake Huron, I obtained Lake nautical charts and area aeronautical charts and spent a couple of evenings transferring the locations of Omni stations and aeronautical DF beacons. The Lake charts are not what coastal sailors are used to in terms of completeness. The Great Lakes Light List and the Great Lakes Pilot must be used in conjunction for full details. This, one gets used to quickly.

But what one doesn't get used to on the Great Lakes is the complete unpredictability of the weather and the low batting average of the professional weather forecasters. The breeze of the moment derives from a combination of highs and lows sweeping across the region and the cool Canadian air which occasionally intrudes between them. In the Lake Huron Race, this was graphically illustrated when, after a day of hearing that the northerly breeze would soon clock to the east, it died completely and then came up from the west, scrambling all the yachts' hard-earned positions.

The first impression a visitor gets is the long haul to the starting line for the Lake Huron Race. We deplaned in Detroit, Michigan, Friday night and found that this was only the beginning. It was a two-hour drive by rental car to Port Huron, Michigan, where the big racing fleet of 241 boats was moored. Port Huron is a typical Midwest community of 36,000 inhabitants nestled at the southern tip of Lake Huron near the mouth of the Black River. As we drove into the center of town we could hardly believe our eyes. Traffic was like the Long Island Expressway during the rush hour and literally thousands of people crowded the sidewalks. Our reaction was that the State Fair must be in progress, but we soon learned that the big attraction was the racing fleet. People had come from 50 to 60 miles around, and the crowds, according to one spectator, rivalled those of any other local event—a far cry from the blasé dockside denizens of such seafaring towns as Newport and Annapolis. By 3:00 A.M. the crowd had dwindled to a few diehards and the racing crews had settled down for a few hours of fitful sleep.

Saturday morning it was another two-hour trek under power out the Black

River, under the bridge between Port Huron and Sarnia, Ontario, and into Lake Huron where a gigantic spectator fleet, carefully shepherded into designated areas by the hardworking Bay View Yacht Club Committee, awaited the spectacle of eight class starts, celebrating the 50th Race Anniversary. Towering over all this was the massive Coast Guard icebreaker *Mackinaw,* now patrol headquarters for the races, but whose main job is to keep the passages from lake to lake open as long as possible before the thick winter ice closes in.

Class A started last, beating into a strong northerly and into the short, uncomfortable Lake chop. This combination caused several casualties in the fleet, notable among them the beautiful, natural-finish, wooden-hulled former 12-meter *Heritage* which lost her mast.

Next day the breeze deteriorated into a frustrating cat's-paw–ridden game for most of the day. We were beginning to feel that this race was going to be a bit slower than most. When we were invaded by a flight of aerodynamically unsound moths while 10 miles offshore, we were convinced.

The course is a dogleg with the turn at Cove Island at the northeastern part of the Lake, deep into sparsely settled Canadian territory. Calm weather floundering had made our DR plot rather suspect, and the lack of nearby visual aids or DF stations other than Cove Island made precise fixes difficult. Our Omni was not working. By combining a sun line with soundings of the bottom we were back in business.

The Lakes are not supposed to have significant currents, though they are connected, but when we rounded Cove Island Buoy we noticed a distinct easterly flow of about one knot rippling around the Buoy and into the channel to Georgian Bay. However, later on, when we were thinking of anchoring during the next big calm, we were glad we didn't, because visual fixes showed that, while our log reading for three hours indicated five miles through the water, our actual position showed six miles over the bottom, confirming now a westerly set.

Our experience in the first leg had taught us that we had better keep accurate hourly log entries for DR purposes. The plot was updated by visual fixes using the Duck Islands and sightings of Lake ore carriers running the north–south track out of False Detour Channel, the passage connecting with Lake Superior. DF bearings added to our inputs. By this time we had also learned that it was worth listening to the polka music from the commercial radio stations at Alpena and Cheboygan to catch the occasional unscheduled weather tidbits.

The tiny historic island of Mackinac (pronounced "Mackinaw" by the 500 permanent residents) measures three miles by one-and-three-quarter miles and was first settled in 1670 by the French missionary Father Doblon. It is accessible only by charter plane and passenger ferry, except in the sub-zero winter months when two-and-a-half feet of ice make snowmobile trips to the mainland possible. No cars are allowed, so the local transportation is by bicycle and horse-drawn vehicle. The finish line on the east side of the island is across a small harbor lined with well-preserved examples of the picturesque architecture of a bygone era. The main industries are tourism and fudge making.

We finally arrived at 12 minutes after midnight on Tuesday, fifth to finish, with

...ightseers view the racing fleet at Port Huron . . .

. and line the banks of the Black River under the Sarnia Bridge.

an elapsed time of just under 59 hours. Now came the next race—to get back to the office. Crews have to work for a living between races. With a 6:08 A.M. feeder flight departing from Pellston, Michigan, on the mainland, we first had to get off the island. Naturally, the last plane left at sunset and the last boat stopped running at midnight. A charter boat was available at 3:30 A.M. for the half-hour trip across the straits to Mackinaw City, then a waiting airport bus. We arrived at the rural airport in a 46-degree chill at 5:00 A.M. and waited for the doors to open. Three hours later, after being on and off the plane at Traverse City, a halfway stop, because we were in standby status, we arrived in Detroit to go our respective ways to the eastern cities.

Before leaving Mackinac where the race-finish-party was building, we chatted for a moment with Lynn Williams, skipper of *Dora,* the elapsed and corrected time victor, and Chuck Kirsch, skipper of *Scaramouche,* which finished second on elapsed as well as corrected time. Both of these experienced Lake skippers were properly modest about their fine performance, but we sensed that we still had something to learn. Lynn brought up a significant point. We had noticed in the two calm periods that there was wind at the masthead while there was none across the deck. He attributed his boat's ability to keep going to his new, taller rig which was able to capture these fragile breezes well above the water. While many of the boats stopped, his kept moving, albeit slowly. This also accounted for the fine elapsed time showing of the tall-rigged ex-12-meter, *Weatherly.* As for the small fry, their slow progress was highlighted by the last to finish, Edwin Boyer's 30-foot sloop *Breezing Through,* as she crossed the finish line in an elapsed time of just under 91 hours.

The following weekend we gathered at the venerable Chicago Yacht Club, founded in 1875 and located in the shadow of towering skyscrapers at the south end of Lake Michigan where 244 boats were being readied for the 67th Annual Chicago–Mackinac Race. This racing fleet caused hardly a ripple in the Windy City in marked contrast to Port Huron. The yachts, rating between IOR 21 and 70, were divided into four classes, each divided into two sections. In this race there is no overall winner. Instead, each class winner gets a prize and prizes are awarded to the section winners in each class. Additional prizes are given to the first boat to finish, to the Class I yacht over 20 years old with the lowest corrected time and to the first boat in the half-ton, three-quarter-ton, one-ton and Canada's Cup categories. Prizes were also provided for the second and third boat in each special class and section if nine or more boats competed. Something for everyone to shoot for.

We were off to a fine start in a light southeasterly. Our strategy in this race was to stick closely to *Scaramouche* and *Dora.* This worked fine for the first 24 hours but on Sunday afternoon as they disappeared over the horizon in a freshening SW breeze, we felt that a revision was in order. Banking on a wind shift around through west to the northwest under the influence of a deepening low, we gradually eased out into the center of the Lake away from the eastern shore. *Bay Bea* was about one-and-a-half miles to the west of us. When the westerly came in she got it first, and over the horizon she went also. To add injury to insult, we were

La Forza heads for Mackinac Island.

The fleet gathers again, this time at the Chicago Yacht Club.

Rounding Gray's Reef Light

set upon by a vicious horde of biting flies. Only by getting all hands on deck, buttoning up the boat and spraying the inside could we get rid of them.

Nearing the northern end of the Lake, we realized that following the leaders would not help us, so we took a flyer, going to the north of the Manitou Islands at dusk. This looked as though it was working as the rest of the fleet leaders went between the Islands and the mainland. But now we ran into a new weather system, and in a three-hour period of calm and wildly fluctuating wind directions, we went down the drain. By the time we reached Gray's Reef Light, a few hours from the finish, there were 13 boats ahead of us and the basic northwest wind was back in force. We managed to overtake *Tandem,* a well-sailed Tartan 46, but in the meantime the 69-foot ketch *Masker* and the 70-foot ex-12-meter *Northern Light* passed us, the latter, after a spirited downwind duel, only boat lengths from the finish.

As before, *Dora* had done it again, finishing seven hours ahead of us. Our conclusion was that this is a tough league—a different kind of sailing, but top competition, and one in which local knowledge, acquired over the years, pays off handsomely. We also understand better now why the best of these Lake sailors also do well when they compete in the Atlantic.

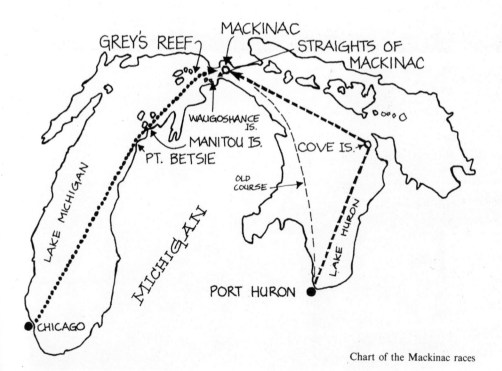

Chart of the Mackinac races

Masker, with race patrol plane overhead

Close finish with *Northern Light*

EPILOGUE

Nineteen seventy-six began on a hopeful note. The offshore hierarchy had finally accepted the fact that something was wrong. They began to listen to the complaints and to work on the evident problems. The overriding and most immediate problem was what to do with the older boats which were still useful but no longer competitive. The substantial side effect was that the entry lists were dwindling. Race committees were first to take note and the ever-innovative SORC Committee decided to divide their fleet into two parts with the dividing line being boats that were built before the first of January 1974. This meant that, still racing under the IOR Mark III, the "older" boats would not have to bang heads with the newest, most innovative and fastest designs. There would no longer be an overall fleet prize, but there would be a prize for the top boat in two fleets, old as well as new.

At about the same time, the Bermuda Race Committee for '76, tired of waiting for leadership from the IYRU or the USYRU, announced that they would not use the IOR Mark III, but would use a combination of that rule and the previously used Cruising Club of America Rule. The result of this was to *increase* the ratings of the newer designs while, at the same time, decreasing the ratings of older designs. The intricacies of this combination rule restructured the fleet's ratings automatically and there was no necessity for determining a precise boat age. This also allowed both older and new boats to race more equitably together, thus eliminating the problem of two sets of trophies.

These two separate but related actions induced the USYRU at its Annual Meeting in January in Jacksonville, Florida, belatedly, and as some knowledgeable observers said, reluctantly, to propose still another solution. This was the adoption of the IOR Mark IIIa which, by giving a greater credit for the heavier displacement and shorter rigs of older designs, resulted in a more favorable (lower) rating for older boats. Using the chop date of boats built prior to 1972 and with adjustments for boats not altered since that time, or only partially altered, this gave, in application to a particular yacht, a maximum of 7 1/2 percent reduction in rating. The USYRU left the use of this rule up to the decision of the sponsor of a particular event. That is, the rule was official, but the particular committee could use it or not as they saw fit. Automatically each boat that had been rated under the IOR Mark III would now receive two sets of numbers— one for the IOR Mark III and another for the IOR Mark IIIa. In the case of a brand-new boat, the two numbers would be the same. In the case of an older boat, the Mark IIIa number could be significantly less.

Two other groups were also approaching the basic problem of how to make their organizations more responsive to the needs and expressed desires of the members.

At about the same time the USYRU was meeting in Jacksonville, the Midget Ocean Racing Club (MORC) was having its Annual International Meeting 300 miles to the west on the Florida Gulf Coast at Fort Walton Beach. This group had organized 30-foot and under cruiser/racers into a very active group. In three and a half years it had grown to 54 fleets and over 2,000 members. It had departed from USYRU by establishing its own rating rule, its own time allowance tables, and set minimum standards for cabin space in MORC yachts. Since most of its members are racer/cruisers rather than all-out racers, its approach to rule-making is to keep competition within practical limits to minimize boat obsolescence. A close-knit, well-run organization with regular meetings and wide variety of racing events, local, national and international, it maintains interest and enthusiasm among its members.

The MORC rating rule was developed some years back as an outgrowth of the Cruising Club of America (CCA) Rule. It has been refined several times. The conclusions of a major rules study were accepted at the 1976 meeting in Fort Walton resulting in the latest revision called the MORC 3D Rule.

At present the MORC officers feel they have an excellent base on which to build. There are several features of this outfit that might be looked at by the older, glacially inactive organizations dedicated to preserving the status quo.

1) Rating certificates are returned within three days after receipt by the MORC international office, which now issues more rating certificates than USYRU.
2) Any MORC member in the world can call 216–333–0575 and get a prompt response to questions.
3) The MORC meetings actually decide issues and make progress rather than referring problems to another committee for further study.
4) MORC operates within the framework of a single rating system using measurements already established for each boat so that a rule change does not necessitate new measurements.

The Ocean Racing Club of America (ORCA), which had been in existence for a couple of years but was rather dormant, started to pick up and seek a role for itself. The only requirement for ORCA membership is actual offshore racing experience. Vice-Commodore Norm Raben, in speaking of what he felt the ORCA role should be, expressed these ideas:

"ORCA first and foremost should be a forum—a highly sensitive antenna listening to the membership and providing a sounding board. We are not a social club. If you don't wear the 'old school tie' you can still belong. The only requirement is a love of, and an active participation in offshore boats. We are the constituency that the national authority should minister to. As serious, involved participants, we must marshal our thoughts and then actively lobby to see that our reasonable desires are met. ORCA should be in the vanguard in conveying to USYRU what our members want."

So in February 1976 the officers of ORCA organized. After soliciting members' ideas and comments, they appointed regional fleet captains throughout the United States, hired Ted Jones to run the home office and increase membership, established an ORCA National Championship, appointed a delegate to the National Offshore Council (a body of the USYRU), formed a technical committee to look into ways to limit exotic materials, develop accommodation minimums and control the use of sophisticated electronics, and finally, scheduled a three-race fall series in Chesapeake Bay which would provide research data for Massachusetts Institute of Technology as part of its Ocean Racing Handicap Research Project. A large chunk of business for the new year.

A quote from an ORCA member expresses both the yearning that the typical offshore sailor has, as well as the hope that some organization will try to solve his problem someday: "Some of us can't afford a new custom offshore boat every year and many of us don't want to sail like a galley slave. However, we still want to have a chance to win a race now and then. If ORCA can develop an answer to this problem, it will indeed have filled an important place in sailing."

ORCA may be the gadfly that overcomes years of inertia by prodding the older, more influential organizations into action.

The first approach to be tested was that of the SORC in February. It was acknowledged that dividing the fleet was not successful. Neither did it attract more entries (the total fleet declined again), but it also failed to induce owners of older boats to race in the division designed exclusively for that category. No one really knew why this was so. All they knew was that skippers of boats with *no chance of winning* still elected to race against the newest and fastest designs rather than admit that their boats were no longer competitive by going into the "old boat" division. It made little sense, but half the boats in the "Hot Shot" division were there, not because they had to be, but by the owner's choice.

Ian McDonald Smith, a top British sailor who came over to race the Ocean Triangle (third race of the SORC) aboard *Williwaw,* had this to say: "Perhaps the owners of older boats wanted to race directly against the newer ones rather than with a separate group. In Europe we race all the boats together, but score older boats separately after the race is over."

Nevertheless, the SORC vowed to try it again in 1977 with a further incentive, a yacht "old-age allowance," and Ted Turner, so far without a brand-new boat, allowed as how he might give the old boat division a whirl this time. The fleet division date is still January 1, 1974, making the new boat division those three years old or less.

The 1976 Bermuda Race turned out to be quite pleasing to the owners of older boats. Four out of six class winners were, in fact, older boats, and the overall winner was none other than *Running Tide,* a six-year-old veteran of the offshore wars. The only new boats to break the trend were *Bumblebee 3,* winner of Class B and *Arieto,* winner of Class C. However, these results were really not representative of what might have been, as this race was primarily an upwind race which tended to minimize the downwind ability of newer designs. Still, the Bermuda Race Committee should receive full credit for not only doing something, but also for nudging the USYRU along in the right direction.

Now that race committees had a few more options than before, the IOR Mark IIIa was adopted by many of them for races in a wide variety of areas. Only by giving it a try could the worth or effectiveness of IOR Mark IIIa be evaluated.

In midsummer another development emerged from Paris, France, with the establishment of a new class called the "Mini-Ton." This class, with an IOR rating of under 16 feet was conceived to open up offshore racing to amateur designers and builders. The crews are limited to three persons, and the first World Championship for the Mini-Ton was raced at La Rochelle, France, with a fleet

---

SORC AGE ALLOWANCE

AGE ALLOWANCE
FORA Age Rating = IOR Rating X Age Allowance Multiplier. Age Allowance multiplier shall be:

$$[1 - (.022 \sqrt{} \text{ age of yacht}) \pm \text{adjustment}]$$

Age of yacht shall be year of season's beginning minus year of launching of first of one of a kind.

Adjustment shall be as follows:

Yachts launched 1973 and thereafter	+.030
Yachts launched 1972	+.015
Yachts launched 1971-1968	.000
Yachts launched 1967 and earlier	-.010

2/3 of rating reduction will be applied if hull shape has been modified below the shearline, including keel, but not rudder, propeller or centerboard.
Multiplier may not drop below .880.
Under the above formula, multiplier for yachts of the following age years are:

1974 = 1.0	1968 = .9378	1962 = .9077	1956 = .8917
1973 = .9919	1967 = .9240	1961 = .9048	1955 = .8892
1972 = .9710	1966 = .9205	1960 = .9020	1954 = .8869
1971 = .9509	1965 = .9171	1959 = .8993	1953 = .8845
1970 = .9462	1964 = .9138	1958 = .8967	1952 = .8823
1969 = .9418	1963 = .9107	1957 = .8942	1951 = .8800

Administration of the Age Allowance will require each owner to provide the FORA Secretary with: (1) a certification by the manufacturer of a stock boat as to the year of launching of the prototype boat, or, if a custom boat, a certification by the designer or builder; (2) a certification that the owner has not altered the hull since launching, or description of any changes made.

of 30 boats from five different countries. Will these catch on, for they can hardly be considered offshore boats in the 20- to 25-foot length overall range? Perhaps Jesse Phillips was right when he complained earlier in the year that, "Rapid obsolescence and rising costs are forcing us into smaller and smaller boats." The Mini-Ton would hardly be Jesse's cup of tea.

The Mini-Ton boat is expected to sell in the $10,000 range and its size will allow trailerability. A North American Mini-Ton Association has been established at 1045 Third Street South, St. Petersburg, Florida 33701. The IYRU took note by adding the Mini-Ton class to its study agenda.

And what about commercial sponsorship for race committees? It seems that day has arrived. The Cruising Yacht Club of Australia has announced that it has accepted a sponsor for the annual Sydney–Hobart Race. Hitachi Sales Company will provide 50,000 Australian dollars in funds for the next race. In return, the Committee will call that race the "Hitachi Sydney–Hobart Race." Will the next step be purse money for the winners instead of the traditional silver trophies?

Meanwhile, on the factory team front, the competition between Hood Sailmakers and North Sails, the two biggest guns among the 500 or so sailmakers in the industry, reached a climax. Ted Hood had for some time felt that the business of a sailmaker was in making good sails for owners to win with by themselves and not in supplying a "hot-shot" racing team to the purchaser, even though there were fine sailors on his staff.

As he said in a full-page ad in the September boating magazines: "We don't feel that a big ticket item like a suit of sails should be disposable—like Kleenex. And we can't in conscience build and sell sails that way.

"We feel the public should know the difference between sailmakers' products as products—in terms of win-ability and durability. Because that's all that really counts."

In fact, Hood had abandoned the factory team concept. The sailing world waited for Lowell North's response. However, it all may have been anticlimactic because many of the owners had abandoned the factory team concept also. That is, they don't want a factory team to take over and run their boat, but they are not averse to having their sailmaker's representative aboard as a crew member to take advantage of his specialized expertise. This approach allows the owner to retain control while profiting fron an expert's opinions.

Traditionally, the end of the year is the time when the highest levels of the sport's governing bodies meet to consider inputs from local and national bodies, usually in London, England, in concert with the IYRU Annual Meeting. As is customary, the "hot potatoes" were referred back to committee for further study, while simpler problems were dealt with and solutions proposed.

Here are the major decisions made in 1976, which would take effect on the dates indicated:

- The use of exotic materials in spars (such as carbon fiber which allows a reduced cross section giving less windage without decreasing structural strength) was not banned but would be subject to a penalty increasing a yacht's rating by 3%, March 1, 1977.

• Rules for the Mini-Ton class would be drafted looking toward an official world championship in 1978 with a class rating of 16.0 feet.

• Probably the most significant decision, to be effective on March 1, 1977, dealt with limitations on the number of jibs and spinnakers to be carried aboard an IOR rated yacht in a race. These are shown in tabular form below and are in addition to one mainsail and a spare, one storm trysail and one storm jib.

Mark III Rating (Ft.)	Jibs Shall Not Number More Than	Spinnakers Shall Not Number More Than
16.0–16.5	3	1
16.6–19.0	5	3
19.1–22.9	6	3
23.0–28.9	6	4
29.0–36.0	7	5
36.1–43.0	8	5
43.1–51.9	9	6
52.0–62.0	10	6
62.1 and above	11	6

• Of interest to owners of older boats was the liberalization of the Mark IIIa by increasing the maximum rating reduction under that rule from 7 1/2% to 10%, effective January 1, 1977.

All in all, the year 1976 was a time of significant change in the sport. Problems *were* being recognized rather than being swept under the rug. Ideas and solutions *were* being listened to from a wide variety of sailors and from many sailing areas.

Offshore racing would survive in spite of the tangle of regulations and rules, in spite of the lethargy of the rule makers, in spite of the rapid and confusing technological advances because these factors were really not what it was all about.

What still mattered was the thrill of competing at sea and the memories it evoked.

Those who had tried it and liked it would be back again. Happiness still was:

• Crossing the Gulf Stream at night during a thunderstorm with 200-foot-wide lightning bolts crashing into the sea all around your boat, but not on it.

• Leading the fleet into the tiny harbor entrance at Nassau with a 30-mile-an-hour tailwind and ten-foot following seas, while surging to 18 knots.

• After surviving the raging gale, celebrating the calmer seas and gentler sailing breezes with a quiet predinner cocktail at sunset.

• The satisfaction of a five-point star fix that plots perfectly.

• Inching out from the pack after the start and feeling that superior helming and sail trimming are what did it.

• Hearing the finish times of the larger boats on the radio when you, in a smaller one, are five miles from the finish and know you have your time saved.

• Or, after finishing first, watching the time allowances expire one by one for the boats lower than yours in rating.

• Breathing fresh, unpolluted sea air.

• Enjoying a dry bunk.

• Having foul weather gear that works.

• Using instruments that don't malfunction.

• Winning a fleet trophy.

• Winning a class trophy.

• Winning any trophy.

• Resailing the race in the club bar.

And, between races, telling and listening to the endless sea stories.

INDEX

A

Adams Cup, 146
Adams, Mrs. Charles F., 146
Admiral's Cup, ix, 32, 97, 99, 126, 215, 216, 217, 233, 237, 260
afterguard, 59, 242
Aiken, Max, 105
Aisher, Robin, 226
Allan, Robert M., 255
Allan, Scott, 20
altitude
  circle of equal, 179, 181
  computed, 180, 182
  observed, 182
Ambrose Light, 243
America Jane III, 32, 33
America's Cup, 23, 52, 94, 266
American Eagle, 53, 224, 237, 266
Amey, Ron, 116
Anclote Key Race, 263, 264
anemometer, 157
Annapolis–Newport Race, viii, 63, 127, 128, 207, 239
  race course, 240, 241
Apollo II, 228
Argyll, 94
Arieto, 299
Audacious, 126
Aura, 266
azimuth, 180

B

Baccara, 249, 268
Bahamas, 29, 275
  banks, 190, 212, 213
Baldwin, James French, 63, 101
Ballyhoo, 233, 234
Barbarian, 64
Barlovento, 39
Barney, John, 94
barometer, 157

Baruna, 93, 94
Bass Strait, 236, 237
Bavier, Bob, 65, 70, 94, 232
Bay Bea, 292
Bay View Yacht Club, 290
bearings, visual, 210
Beau Geste, 127, 242
Bechell, Ken, 69, 232
Bennett, James Gordon, Jr., 260
Berglund, Bob, 127
Bermuda
  Dinghy Club, 288
  Government House, 106, 107
  Hamilton, 105, 106, 107, 288
  Harbor Radio, 286
  Hotel Bermudiana, 109
  Islands, 162, 184
  Paget, 110
Bermuda Race, viii, 1, 12, 15, 61, 93, 94, 100, 101, 116, 123, 125–28, 141, 146, 167, 183, 191, 193, 194, 224, 233, 239, 253, 260, 277, 299
  Committee, 297, 300
  Trophy, 96, 288
Bickford, Daniel, 94
binoculars, 156, 157
Bishop Rock, 225, 227, 228
Blackfin, 49
Black Gold, 152
Block Island, 171, 172, 210, 239, 242, 243, 249, 250
  Light, 202, 244
  Race, 125, 245
  Radio Beacon, 202
  Sound, 244, 245, 249, 250
  Week, 15
Bolero, 126
Bonaventure, 214
Bowker, Peter, 61, 94, 126, 167, 281
Boyer, Edwin, 292
Brambles Buoy, 222
Breezing Through, 292
Brenton Reef Tower, 191, 244, 277, 278
Browning, Don, 242